B&T
$13.50

W9-AHP-774

Sociology
of the
Black Experience

CONTRIBUTIONS IN SOCIOLOGY

Series Editor: Don Martindale

Commitment to Deviance: The Nonprofessional Criminal in the Community
Robert A. Stebbins

Capitalists Without Capitalism: The Jains of India and the Quakers of the West
Balwant Nevaskar

Black Belonging: A Study of the Social Correlates of Work Relations Among Negroes
Jack C. Ross and Raymond H. Wheeler

The School Managers: Power and Conflict in American Public Education
Donald J. McCarty and Charles E. Ramsey

The Social Dimensions of Mental Illness, Alcoholism, and Drug Dependence
Don Martindale and Edith Martindale

Those People: The Subculture of a Housing Project
Colette Pétonnet. Rita Smidt, Translator

Sociology in Israel
Leonard Weller

The Revolutionary Party: Essays in the Sociology of Politics
Feliks Gross

Group Interaction as Therapy: The Use of the Small Group in Corrections
Richard M. Stephenson and Frank R. Scarpitti

Sociology
of the
Black Experience

Daniel C. Thompson

Contributions in Sociology, Number 14

Greenwood Press

Westport, Connecticut   •   London, England

Wingate College Library

Library of Congress Cataloging in Publication Data

Thompson, Daniel Calbert.
  Sociology of the Black experience.

  (Contributions in sociology, no. 14)
  Bibliography: p.
  1. Negroes—Social conditions. 2. Negro families.
3. Negroes—Civil rights. I. Title.
E185.86.T44   301.45'19'6073   73-20974
ISBN 0-8371-7336-1

Copyright © 1974 by Daniel C. Thompson

All rights reserved. No portion of this book may be reproduced,
by any process or technique, without the express written con-
sent of the author and publisher.

Library of Congress Catalog Card Number: 73-20974
ISBN: 0-8371-7336-1

First published in 1974

Second printing 1975

Greenwood Press, a division of Williamhouse-Regency Inc.
51 Riverside Avenue, Westport, Connecticut 06880

Manufactured in the United States of America

To My Wife

071478

Contents

Preface

No other racial or ethnic group in American society has had such a wide variety of sociocultural experiences as have Black Americans. First, they have participated to a significant extent in all of the experiences common to American citizens per se. Second, because of their race, they have been characteristically assigned a special substatus in every area of American life. Therefore, as *Blacks*, they have been subjected to a unique range of experiences endemic to the special substatuses they occupy within all major social categories. For instance, they are not usually allowed to be called simply farmers, blue-collar workers, professionals, businessmen, soldiers, or leaders; no matter what their level of competence or degree of dedication, they are instead regarded as *Black* farmers, workers, professionals, businessmen, soldiers, or leaders. This means that even when they are performing common social roles they usually have uncommon experiences. And third, from the very beginning of this nation until the present, Blacks have undergone a whole set of personal and sociocultural experiences entirely their own. Such experiences range all the way from slavery and total segregation in a biracial system, to the often subtle, yet very real, system of institutionalized racism that is so deeply rooted in every major aspect of American society.

This book describes and interprets several key experiences among Blacks according to the variables of time, age, sex, geographic location, vicissitudes in the local community and larger society, level of achievement, and social class status. Special attention is given to experiences related to selected aspects and conditions characteristic of the Black subculture. Among these are the changing nature and tactics of the civil rights movement, leadership, the ghetto, poverty, the distribution of power, religion, Black nationalism, family life, education, and the Black middle class.

While every attempt has been made to present all major points of view regarding "The Black Experience," basically the sociological interpretations presented are intended to reflect a Black perspective.

I am grateful to Dillard University and the Center for Advanced Study in the Behavioral Sciences for providing their excellent facilities and cooperative supporting staff during the research and writing phases of this study. I would also like to thank the expert editorial staff of Greenwood Press for several valuable suggestions for making this book more comprehensive and readable.

I extend special thanks to Mrs. Sonia M. Wilson who carefully and perceptively prepared the final drafts of the manuscript, and to Miss Barbara M. Guillory, associate professor of sociology at Dillard, who served as research associate in the New Orleans ghetto study included in this book.

Dillard University
November 1973

Sociology
of the
Black Experience

1

Introduction

The struggle of Black Americans to survive and attain first-class citizenship is one of the epic chapters in human history. Basically, it is the story of how a powerless, disesteemed racial minority invented, revised, adapted, and employed a wide variety of strategies and techniques in a constant, prolonged effort to achieve the security and rights inherent in American citizenship. Every significant move Blacks have made to improve their social, economic, and political status has been met with resistance—from simple dissuasion by powerful whites and the passage of disabling laws by state legislatures and Congress, to punitive extralegal measures and blatant mob violence.

The story of the Blacks' struggle for survival and equal citizenship began in 1619, when the first people of African descent were brought to Jamestown, Virginia, by a Dutch man-of-war. Since then they have had many unique experiences endemic to their changing status. At first they were indentured servants, but eventually were forced into legal slavery (1661); they were emancipated more than 200 years later (1863) and have lived ever since in a biracial society established on the doctrine of "white supremacy."

As slaves, Blacks were systematically deprived of all citizenship rights and privileges "and subjected not merely to prejudice and ethnic discrimination but to an atrocious racism that declared them virtually subhuman."[1] Their status, which had been characteristically regarded as chattel by state laws and general custom, was constitutionally affirmed by the U.S. Supreme Court in the 1857 Dred Scott Case, when it was decided that slaves were not citizens and had no legal rights which whites had to respect. Thus, it was from the depths as human chattel that Black Americans began the slow, frustrating, dangerous climb toward freedom and citizenship. The first decisive step in that direction was de jure freedom, which came as a result of the Emancipation Proclamation and the "Civil War Amendments" (the Thirteenth, Fourteenth and Fifteenth). Then came a century of Jim Crow laws and customs that supported all forms and degrees of racial segregation and discrimination. It was not until 1954 that the Supreme Court, in *Brown v. Board of Education*, declared the "separate-but-equal" principle of citizenship (established by the 1896 *Plessy v. Ferguson* decision).[2]

The de facto citizenship status of Blacks has been so tenuous and unstable that Black scholars and leaders differ widely in their opinions about the actual degree to which Blacks have made citizenship gains since the Supreme Court's 1954 decision. While some observers argue that Blacks have made truly significant gains, others insist that gains in some areas have been canceled out by losses in other areas. A growing number of reliable Black leaders have expressed concern about what they believe to be a powerful move on the part of the federal government, state governments, and certain segments in the private sector to "turn back the clock," so to speak, in the whole area of civil rights during these first years of the 1970s. They point out that while a few Blacks have, in fact, experienced large individual gains, Blacks, as a racial group, are still subject to the same relative deprivation now as prior to 1954. They still do not have *equal* protection of the law, *equal* economic opportunity, *equal* political participation, *equal* educational opportunity, *equal* access to health facilities and housing. They remain, on the whole, a disesteemed, disadvantaged, relatively power-less racial minority outside the mainstream of American life. Throughout this book, this viewpoint and other interpretations of the Black experience will be analyzed and interpreted in the light of substantive sociological theory.

The New Civil Rights Movement

During the 1960s the dominant domestic issue in the United States was the civil rights of Black Americans. The perennially disesteemed, second-class citizenship status accorded Blacks had always been a challenging, embarrassing ideological issue because it underscored a serious, fundamental contradiction inherent in this nation's avowed commitment to equal citizenship and the democratic process.[3] Nevertheless, until the 1960s most social institutions, agencies, communities, states, and the nation at large managed to keep their particular race problems more or less subrosa. As a rule, they attempted either to discount the true magnitude of their ''Negro problem'' or to deny its existence altogether. At most, the complex pattern of disadvantage experienced by Blacks was regarded as primarily a moral issue to be decided by individuals and was seldom acknowledged to be a significant social issue meriting open and honest debate and consideration as a major social problem. The fact is, that for almost 100 years, between the Emancipation Proclamation (1863) and the latter part of the 1950s, practically all of the most influential white leaders in religion, economics, politics, and the mass media tended to ignore the ''Negro problem.'' When they were forced to acknowledge its existence, it was generally interpreted as an inevitable consequence of the Blacks' alleged inferiority. Until the mid-1950s, when community welfare was threatened by the urgency of racial problems that had to be solved, whites in positions of authority made quite certain that the solution employed would not disturb the deeply ingrained patterns of segregation and discrimination characteristic of the institution or community in question.

The turning point in race relations in the nation came on December 1, 1955, with an episode involving a Black woman, Rose Parks, who refused to obey a Jim Crow law regulating the segregated seating of races on public busses in Montgomery, Alabama. Beginning with the arrest of Mrs. Parks, there developed a dramatic escalation of racial confrontations which led to a year of complete boycotting of public busses by Blacks (the boycott lasted until December 21, 1956); the emergence of the heroic, charismatic leadership of the Reverend Dr. Martin Luther King, Jr.; and a radical change in the philosophy, strategies, and direction of the civil rights movement.[4]

From about the mid-1940s to mid-1950s, civil rights organizations attempted to advance the status of Black Americans through self-improvement, skilled race relations diplomacy, social pressure within the law, and persistent use of the courts. Black leaders were usually overcautious in their tactics so as not to antagonize white men of power and influence, because a more aggressive policy might stimulate and solidify a national white backlash or embarrass white friends of the traditional civil rights movement. As a result, Black leaders and institutions pressed for equal citizenship opportunities strictly within the biracial system—not for the abolition of the system itself. Whatever limited success their efforts brought, then, was always slow, indirect, costly, and almost imperceptible insofar as the lot of the Black masses was concerned. In all instances Black progress was carefully controlled by white decision-makers, so that the biracial system, based upon a tradition of white supremacy and racial discrimination, was left intact. Some applied the concept "caste" as an accurate assessment of race relations in the United States, especially the South, because there were few if any noticeable relative changes in Black-white relations from one generation to another.

Under the daring leadership of Dr. King, the civil rights movement adopted a radical philosophy of civil disobedience as the most direct and effective means of achieving true equality of citizenship. *Inherent in this philosophy was the assumption that equal citizenship for Blacks was only possible in an integrated society*. Thus, the new civil rights movement was committed to the annullment of all restrictive Jim Crow laws because they were deemed unjust and unconstitutional.

This bold, new direct-action approach involved the adoption of a wide variety of extremely dangerous strategies and techniques in dealing with socially tense race relations. Most of them had been rejected or even condemned by civil rights leaders and organizations in the past. These social action devices were usually designed to defy or thwart a local or state law supporting the biracial system. Specific tactics ranged from sit-ins at segregated lunch counters in otherwise public places (department stores were the first targets) to unauthorized, legally forbidden street demonstrations and public protest meetings, which were calculated to disturb the established social order. Consequently, while the traditional civil rights leaders and their followers constantly boasted about their respect for law and order, the new leaders openly expressed scorn for all laws they regarded as unjust. They carefully planned various types of public demonstrations calculated to violate such laws, disrupt social order, and create crises so intense that even the police would become frustrated in their efforts to uphold the law and restore order.

At first these dangerous tactics shocked whites because generally they had been led to believe that Blacks were basically lethargic and would not openly resist constituted authority or participate in actions aimed at incurring the wrath of the southern police. The police in the South, after all, already had a reputation of brutality in handling Black suspects. Later, when there was no doubt about the tremendous courage and determination of Dr. King and his followers, many white leaders and spokesmen representing every walk of life mounted a systematic campaign to discredit him and condemn his strategy of civil disobedience.

Because Dr. King with his direct-action programs provided more exciting news items than any other Black leader, he was constantly given opportunities by the mass media to answer his critics and defend his nonviolent, civil disobedience philosophy. According to Lerone Bennett, Jr., Dr. King "was particularly concerned about a widely-publicized letter circulated by eight leading white ministers of Birmingham—Roman Catholic, Jewish, Protestant—who denounced King as an interloper and extremist. The churchmen had urged 'our Negro community to withdraw support' from these 'unwise and untimely demonstrations.' "[5]

In the now famous "Letter from a Birmingham Jail," Dr. King formally answered his critics in an apologia directed at his fellow ministers who had circulated the castigating letter. He wrote, in part: "I am here, along with members of my staff . . . because injustice is here . . . Nonviolent direct action seeks to create such crisis and establish such creative tension that a community that has consistently refused to negotiate is forced to confront the issue."[6] Dr. King then defined what he regarded as unjust laws and explained why they should be disobeyed:

> Any law that uplifts human personality is just. Any law that degrades human personality is unjust. All segregation statutes are unjust because segregation distorts the soul and damages personality. . . . I submit that an individual who breaks a law that conscience tells him is unjust, and willingly accepts the penalty by staying in jail to arouse the conscience of the community over its injustices, is in reality expressing the very highest respect for law.[7]

The crucial difference, therefore, between the new civil rights movement, as it clearly unfolded during the 1960s, and the old civil rights movement was that its key leaders no longer acknowledged the validity or moral constraint of laws "inflicted upon a minority which that minority had no part in enacting or creating because they did not have the unhampered right to vote."[8] Therefore, dedicated participants in the new phase of the movement regarded arrest for civil disobedience as a badge of honor and a mark of truly creative citizenship.

Not only did the basic philosophy of the civil rights movement change, but its general mood or ethos was transformed and became infinitely more dynamic. Nearly all influential Black leaders and organizations eventually manifested a determined impatience with the slow, grudging, red-tape-ridden process of change meted out by the courts.[9] They carefully planned direct action designed to force the courts and other powerful social structures to move quickly and steadily toward eliminating all vestiges of slavery: Black codes, unequal justice, disfranchisement, and countless techniques employed to preserve racial discrimination in every aspect of American society.

The radical civil disobedience strategy of the new civil rights thrust met with unprecedented success, even in communities with notorious reputations for racial prejudice and hostility toward Blacks who engaged in civil rights activities. Underlying the specific reasons for this success is the important fact that, despite Dr. King's avowed admiration for the nonviolent Indian leader Mohandas K. Gandhi and his civil disobedience tactics, the new civil rights movement was essentially American in all of its official beliefs, goals, and methods, as expressed by its leaders and the constitutions of its organizations. Basically, its grand strategy was to achieve goals and effectuate values that have always been acknowledged to be inherent in the national culture. In a real sense Black leaders became the most articulate champions of the "American Creed."[10] Those who manifested a determined willingness to suffer for the long-cherished values undergirding this nation's commitment to democracy were therefore bound to affect the national conscience, in the abstract, and national policy, in a concrete way. As a result, during the 1960s, the hitherto closed and rigid biracial system, which some social scientists had described as a caste system, began to respond positively to the persistent, unyielding efforts of Blacks to remove all barriers to equal citizenship. So noteworthy were the gains made that some skilled social observers began to declare that a social revolution was taking place, especially in the South. Dr. King summarized it in this way:

> This Great Nation of ours is in the midst of a social revolution. Few of us realize the gravity of the change which is taking place, because it proceeds so steadily. Only the burning of a church by Alabama Klansmen, or the rioting of students at Ole Miss, and the protest marching of over a thousand Negro citizens in Albany, Georgia, punctuate the tremendous transformation which is underway.
>
> It is a testimony to our democratic institutions that we can accommodate such changes without chaos, and a testimony to the minorities in our midst that we do so without wholesale violence.[11]

By the mid-1960s, then, the success of the new civil rights movement was becoming evident to all concerned. This fact lent renewed hope and determination to Blacks in all walks of life, most of whom had been described by Dr. King as being "complacent. . . . [and] as a result of long years of oppression, have been so completely drained of self-respect and a sense of 'somebodiness' that they have adjusted to segregation."[12]

For the nation as a whole, by the end of the decade the social revolution had become dismaying. A national study of race relations reported that:

> By the late 1960s, the Negro revolution was getting under the skin of millions of white people in America. Whites were beginning to realize that the surge of Negroes for freedom and equality was not a passing phase that could be appeased by a single generous or moral act and then would not be heard from again. By now . . . 85 percent of all white people feel that the pace of civil-rights progress was too fast.[13]

Appeal to the Masses

As the civil rights movement neared the zenith of its social and political influence, it came to rely increasingly upon direct-action, civil disobedience tactics in its relentless assault upon very deeply entrenched, formidable bastions of racial segregation and discrimination throughout the United States, especially in rural southern communities. Since public demonstrations in which large numbers of people participated had proven to be the most effective strategy employed, it became necessary to find a means to mobilize the active, dedicated support of the complacent Black masses. This, of course, was difficult because many Blacks, in order to survive, had worked out patterns of adjustments within the biracial system. Stimulating and motivating the generally inarticulate masses to make the heroic sacrifices anticipated to bring about real changes in the rigid, zealously protected biracial system—in which they had always been more or less powerless victims—was indeed a challenge of the first magnitude. The first logical step had to be the establishment of sustained, meaningful communication that would bridge the social gap between the Black masses and the Black middle class. The economically deprived, poorly educated masses of Blacks were alienated to an important degree from the Black middle class as well as from the mainstream of American life.

Black leaders attempted to facilitate interclass consensus and unity in the Black community by articulating the basic needs, frustrations, and aspirations of this most oppressed element in the Black community. Direct appeals were made to indigenous Black preachers and their congregations. Efforts to communicate to them the essential nature of the civil rights struggle—its rightness, promises, and the sacrifices demanded—inevitably led to the development of what amounted to a new, colorful, ethnocentric rhetoric. There emerged, in fact, an ingeniously structured discourse patterned after the old-fashioned, traditional gospel preaching and singing motif familiar to the Black masses. Dr. King's was the most eloquent representative of this style of communication. His keynote speech, "I Have a Dream," delivered before a throng of more than 300,000 followers in the "March on Washington" demonstration on August 28, 1963, is a classic example.

This new Black rhetoric, therefore, was consciously or unconsciously developed to achieve two main goals essential to the success of the ambitious and daring direct-action civil rights strategy: to create a viable interclass unity within the Black community, and to inspire and convince the hitherto powerless Black masses to participate in extremely dangerous civil disobedience tactics. Accordingly, mass meetings were held in which prominent, articulate Black leaders and spokesmen utilized local Black churches, their ministers, and choirs in appeals for total community support. They delivered stimulating addresses that included emotion-packed, catchy, ethnocentric phrases and slogans designed to condemn the existing biracial status quo and to inspire Blacks to struggle against it. Among the most widely publicized and enduring of these were "Freedom Now," "Black is Beautiful," "Soul," "Black Ghetto," "Black Power," "Black Control," "Black Separatism," and the "Black Experience." "Street" leaders and spokesmen, of course, elaborated on these basic concepts and gave them their own, peculiar esoteric meaning and interpretation. Thus it was that the animated, provocative new Black rhetoric proliferated and eventually came to enjoy wide currency in the mass media and even in some sophisticated academic quarters. Despite much popular debating and some deliberate attempts at systematic analyses of these concepts, there are still no generally accepted definitions of what they really mean.[14]

One of the most misunderstood of the concepts in the Black rhetoric is "Black Experience." This concept, if formally defined, could be a very valuable academic tool. As it stands now, it is too loosely defined and is therefore quite limited as an analytical tool in empirical social research and sociological communication. Dr. Joyce Ladner has noted that the concept Black Experience is often used synonymously with such concepts as "Black Culture," "Black history," "subculture," "subsociety," and "soul."[15]

When the concept Black Experience is systematically defined, it promises to open up new vistas of research, analysis, interpretation, and understanding in the sociology of race relations. It will suggest dimensions of racial adjustments, dynamics, and changes that have been generally overlooked or underemphasized by sociologists, particularly influential white sociologists.

The potential fruitfulness of this concept is indicated by the fact that unlike most of the other concepts in the new Black rhetoric—which usually express some persistent hope or valuation on the part of Black Americans—the concept Black Experience says some very concrete and verifiable things about inherent social and psychological realities characteristic of the Blacks' perennial struggle to survive and advance in a rather hostile, biracial American society. Therefore, the concept does speak to certain fundamental aspects and themes in the national culture as well as to basic realities and experiences peculiar to the Black condition. One thing is certain: *the Black Experience is a dynamic concept that can be understood only within the broad context of American history and culture*. To define it in terms of the narrow, and quite fuzzy, concept "Black Separatism," as is so often done, is misleading, and thus academically unsound and unrewarding.

Social Context of the Black Experience

Since its inception, the civil rights movement and the influential Black leaders identified with it have placed major emphasis on the attainment of two interdependent and logically inseparable goals: the elimination of legal and traditional barriers to the full and equal citizenship of Blacks, and Black self-improvement.

Wingate College Library

Before the Emancipation Proclamation and the Civil War, Black leaders among the 400,000 or so free Black population tended to give greater emphasis to self-improvement than to protest against legal and traditional barriers to equal citizenship for Blacks. Self-improvement was the major theme presented in their writings, sermons, lectures, convention proceedings, and in informal contacts with fellow Blacks. The very influential newspaper, *Freedom's Journal*, which was published from 1827 to 1829, took a functional reform stance, under the editorship of Samuel Cornish and John Russwurn. This journal was commonly referred to as the "organ" of the Black abolitionists,[16] and an early crusader for the civil rights of free Blacks. Its central goal was Black self-improvement.

The great emphasis free Black leaders placed upon self-improvement through education and the development of useful occupational skills has been summarized as follows:

> They [Blacks] must make themselves hard-working and practical, abstemious and God-fearing, obedient to law and self-respecting, frugal and upright. . . . Black leaders paid scant attention to what government could do to facilitate reform; they urged black communities to develop their own organizations to help those in need, spread literacy and promulgate the moral values in which they believe.[17]

Most free Black leaders during the antebellum period, when 90 percent of their race was in slavery, naively assumed that if they improved themselves individually by getting an education on the level with whites of their time, by developing a salable occupational skill, and by adhering to strict moral codes, white prejudice against them would disappear. They did not fully understand that Blacks were rejected by whites primarily because of their racial identity, not because they did not measure up to certain social and economic standards. "They did not realize that whites might hate an educated black as well as an ignorant one."[18] Even the eminent Black leader, Frederick

Wingate College Library

Douglass, while protesting legal and traditional handicaps experienced by members of his race, also emphasized the need for self-improvement. In a published article, he asserted that a sure way to full citizenship would be for Blacks to develop "industry, sobriety, honesty, and intelligence."[19]

Black leaders constantly called upon fellow Blacks to facilitate their own progress through various forms of mutual aid, by reading, temperance, and in other ways which would make them more alike and thus, they assumed, more acceptable to whites. They organized literary clubs, developed libraries, attended lectures, and engaged in all available forms of cultural activities. Perhaps the most significant self-improvement efforts were related to the Black church, which began as a separate institution in 1787 and soon became the center of the free Black community, especially in the North.

Throughout the decades since emancipation, all bona fide civil rights organizations and spokesmen have continued to advocate and employ many different strategies to attain these two goals. For example, in order to remove racial barriers to their progress Blacks have engaged in such activities as protest, negotiation, bloc voting, mass demonstrations, and the persistent use of the courts—particularly the U. S. Supreme Court. Likewise, efforts at self-improvement have included the encouraging of Blacks to buy land, establish businesses, patronize Black businessmen and professionals, work hard, strengthen family life, live according to the highest moral and ethical principles, and—most of all—get a good education.

During the turbulent years of the 1960s Black militants gained unprecedented influence in the civil rights struggle. They were primarily concerned with achieving equal employment, open housing, and full political participation, especially for the Black masses in large cities. Thus, the Black militants did not emphasize white middle-class values nearly as much as traditional Black leaders had. They tended to play down the white middle-class view of success as essentially the reward for superior performance in an allegedly open, competitive society.

Instead, some articulate Black militants demanded the dispensation of established rules for success. They strongly argued for special, compensatory treatment of Blacks because they have been historically subjected to patterns of discrimination that made it difficult or impossible for them to compete as equals in American society.

The Black militants' contention for special consideration received wide attention from all forms of the mass media and was especially appealing to the disadvantaged Black masses. Eventually, the most established Black leaders began to echo the militants' demand. Those few who didn't were labeled "Super Toms" (Black leaders who supported the biracial status quo) and were severely criticized by young Black leaders who sought to oust them from their positions as heads of influential organizations in the civil rights movement. Therefore, by the mid-1960s nearly all Black leaders and organizations had adopted some version of the compensatory approach to Black advancement. This approach was most logically systematized and enunciated by Whitney M. Young, Jr., the late executive director of the National Urban League. In essence, he contended that Blacks cannot achieve equal participation in American life without special assistance such as this country extended to certain underdeveloped and war-torn nations after World War II, through the "Marshall Plan." He insisted that—

> For at this moment in history, if the United States honestly drops legal, practical, and subtle barriers to employment, housing, education, public accommodations, health facilities and services, the American Negro still will not achieve equality in our lifetime. That is why the National Urban League and I, together, have called for an unprecedented domestic "Marshall Plan" approach to these problems. . . . In today's complex, technological society a sound mind, a strong back, and a will to succeed are no longer sufficient to break the bonds of deprivation as was the case with minority groups in the past. . . . Unless this is

done, the results of the current heroic efforts in the civil rights movement will be only an illusion, and the struggle will continue, with perhaps tragic consequences. . . . In our plea for such a domestic Marshall Plan, we are asking for special effort, not for special privileges. . . . The program has a simple, practical aim: to provide the Negro citizen with the leadership, education, jobs, motivation and opportunities which will permit him to help himself.[20]

The compensatory approach as spelled out by Young was carefully worded in order to allay the expressed fear of some Black leaders, and the main contention of many white opponents, that Blacks were asking for special privileges and had abandoned the self-improvement goal of the civil rights movement. Certain prominent Black leaders continued to insist that the self-improvement strategy through education was still a central goal. Again, this was emphasized by Young, who was certainly one of the two or three most influential Black leaders throughout the 1960s. He said:

For people desperately seeking answers to civil rights and other problems that face us today—whether in employment, race relations, or automation—the panacea seems to be education. Both the expert and the man on the street seize on this as the remedy for the difficulties that besiege us. . . . Education has performed magnificently in helping individuals vault barriers such as race.[21]

In 1970, six years or more after the National Urban League had become recognized by some powerful white policy-makers as the most reliable advocate of sound Black progress, Whitney Young was interviewed by a reporter of *Time* to get his assessment of strategies employed in the new civil rights movement. Young elaborated upon the following summary: ''There are three or four viable techniques. . . . Economic power, . . . political power, [and] there is brain power, where one can, through sheer competency, move into strategic places in the Establishment and from that vantage point have an influence on policy.''[22] Consequently, despite constant racial turmoil and bloody confrontations throughout the 1960s, Blacks continued to rely upon education as the most efficacious technique for achieving true dignity and equality in American society. This point was underscored by a Louis Harris poll which found that 97 percent of all Black youth interviewed still believed that ''getting more Blacks better educated'' was the best way for the race to ''make real progress.''[23]

The most convincing evidence that the new civil rights movement functioned to sustain and renew Blacks' faith in education has been the tremendous upsurge in school enrollment and retention on all academic levels, particularly on the college level. For example, the number of Blacks enrolled in college almost tripled during the 1960s. The actual increase, as most reliably reported, was from 192,344 in 1960 (1960 U. S. Census) to 522,000 in 1970. The rate of increase in the college enrollment of Blacks was considerably higher than that for whites. While in 1965 just 10 percent of college-age Blacks (18-24) were enrolled in college, by 1970 Black enrollment had increased to 16 percent, or by 6 percent. By comparison, in 1965, 26 percent of white college-age youth were enrolled in college; by 1970 the enrollment had increased by only 1 percent, or to 27 percent.[24] Again, between 1964 and 1968, Black enrollment in all colleges increased from 234,000 to 434,000, or by 85 percent. During that same period the increase in enrollment in colleges in the nation on the whole was from 4,643,000 to 6,801,000, or by only 46 percent.[25]

Even more significant from a sociological point of view is the fact that the proportion of Black students enrolling in white colleges has been increasing at a much faster rate than it has in Black colleges. For example, in 1964, less than half, 48.7 percent, of Black college students were in white colleges. By 1970, this proportion had increased to 74.4 percent.[26] There are, of course, many complex reasons why an increasing proportion of Black youth are choosing white colleges over Black colleges. Perhaps the most crucial factor is that they obviously accept the white upper middle class as their cultural reference group. Essentially they feel that, for the most part, white colleges will better equip them for equal competition with upper middle-class whites who are in the mainstream of American life. However, their increasing choice of white colleges underscores a major paradox and reveals an inherent dilemma in the Blacks' struggle for equality and full participation in American life. They feel compelled to hold onto their racial roots and identity, but they also want to be accorded all of the rights and privileges their qualifications merit, regardless of their racial identity.

The dramatic emergence of Black pride and a strong sense of community among Black youth during the 1960s should have resulted in an unprecedented increase in enrollment in Black colleges. Instead, Black college students chose to go to white colleges where they made an even more convincing and dramatic display of Black pride. They employed and elaborated various civil disobedience tactics of the new civil rights movement to coerce the white colleges they attended to institute Black studies courses, and even departments, as legitimate, officially recognized innovations in their traditional curricula. Furthermore, they insisted that these colleges officially sanction a wide range of Black activities and Black cultural events.

A "militant" Black professor gave a widely accepted rationale for the establishment of Black studies programs. He insisted that

a thorough and well-planned Black curriculum is indispensable to the liberation efforts of Black people in America . . . Black studies programs are designed to investigate and examine the sources of problems faced by Blacks in this nation and to aid in the solution of those problems . . . These programs are relevant, for they seek, in addition, to acquaint Blacks with their rich cultural heritage and thus to augment their sense of identity and assurance as a people. . . . Being a student is transient; being a Black is eternal and immutable. It is not enough to think Black or even to look Black. One must act Black. . . . If revolution is to be the lot of America, . . . among the ashes that were the educational institutions of the United States, surviving peoples shall find that several frustrated, often confused, but always determined and inspired generations of American Black students once passed this way. . . .[27]

Another rationale for Black studies courses argued that

There is considerable evidence that the primary source of the damaging, dangerous racism so prevalent in the United States is the general ignorance of the true place of Black people in the building of this nation and in the enrichment of American culture. This widespread ignorance of the facts and essence of the Negroes' contributions, successes, and sacrifices has been the fountainhead of all manner of misconceptions, distortions, stereotypes and indignities they have always encountered.

In pointing out why white students particularly should take Black studies courses, the writer concluded:

Generation after generation of students have completed their formal education and have taken their places in every walk of American life—including the very top places of leadership, responsibility, and power—who have had little or no knowledge and appreciation of the extent to which Black Americans have participated in and contributed to the greatness of American society and culture. Therefore it is not surprising that some otherwise democratic-minded, powerful white leaders have helped to create and maintain the vicious pattern of racism which has tarnished the image of this nation and kept it divided and in conflict.[28]

There has been much debate and wide disagreement among educators, Black and white, about "the significance of the Black experience to intellectual pursuits and scholarly studies," as phrased by a very important Yale conference called to discuss the question of Black studies.[29] Whatever may be the proper valuation of it, one thing seems certain: the Black studies movement has made its mark on higher education, especially on the sociology of race relations. An important dimension of that impact was researched and reported by a distinguished white professor, Wilson Record, who specializes in the sociology of race relations. He has written that "The Black studies challenge cuts two ways: first, it denies the validity of standard sociological treatment of race and ethnic relations, the concepts, findings, and theories through which it has been articulated. Second, it demands that whatever courses are offered in the field be taught from 'a black perspective' and that only 'qualified black professors' teach them."[30]

The peculiar "Black perspective," which is central to authentic Black studies courses—both in content and method —tends to be infused throughout the curricula in colleges with substantial Black enrollments. Some college administrators and professors are apparently making honest attempts to integrate certain relevant information about the Black Experience into established courses in literature, the fine arts, and in all courses in the behavioral sciences.[31]

Simultaneously with the Blacks' determined bid in the 1960s for racial dignity and full citizenship, the development and acceptance of Black studies courses, and the acknowledgment of the intellectual validity of the Black perspective, the concept "Black Experience" has come into vogue. Today sociologists wishing to describe the unique experiences of Blacks in white-dominated, biracial, American society regularly employ this concept. Yet most of the research and concepts used to understand the Black community have been severely limited because they have focused on race relations—on how Blacks get along with whites and how they differ from whites—rather than on the Black Experience in the broader, more comprehensive sense.

This point of view was expressed at the Yale conference on Black studies in 1969. Gerald A. McWorter, one of the conference participants, contended that:

> The traditional approach is to define a community of Black people on the basis of standards of the white community—and not only the white community in general, but specific white people in particular. Rather than an intelligent approach, that black people are different so one must understand the way in which *they* live and try to determine *their* values and standards. . . . White values and standards have been imposed on black people.

McWorter then gave a narrow, esoteric, separatist view of the Black Experience: "There was no inkling in their minds (white researchers) that over a period of time black people could create a community, a culture, that would be functionally autonomous from the white oppressors who raped them from Africa."[32]

Apparently, the concept Black Experience is rather loosely used by all sociologists, whether they are white racists, liberals, or Black militants. As stated earlier, if this concept is to become a more useful sociological vehicle, it must be more rigidly defined and sharpened. A paradigm on the Black Experience is badly needed because at present the state of sociological inquiry and interpretations in this area of knowledge is far from adequate. This deficiency was emphasized in all of the several thoughtful papers and subsequent discussions presented at the 1972 conference on "The Black Sociologists: Historical and Contemporary Perspectives," co-sponsored by the University of Chicago, Center for Policy Study and the Department of Sociology, in connection with the Caucus of Black Sociologists.[33] The central theme energing from that conference was that *sociologists, especially white sociologists, are too apt to accept traditional middle-class values and established moral norms as a basis for their analyses, insights, and interpretations of the Black Experience.* Of course, as a result otherwise objective sociologists are prone to judge the social actions and cultural patterns of Black Americans by empirical, and even conceptual, models or norms characteristic of middle-class whites. This means that they tend to study and interpret the Black Experience outside of its proper, interactional context in the larger society, as if it were a self-contained, self-explanatory unit.

The tendency of white sociologists to approach the study of the Black Experience from a position of judgment rather than from unbiased objectivity was expressed in a paper presented at the 1972 Chicago University Conference by Professor Stanley H. Smith of Fisk University. His paper was entitled: "The Institutional Setting of the Sociological Contributions of Black Sociologists: A Case Study." He emphasized a position taken to some extent by the other authors of papers presented at the conference. Smith said that sociologists too often misinterpret the Black Experience because they attempt to study it outside of its proper social and cultural context:

> Sociologists who hold membership in the majority group tend to be concerned with adjustment to conditions as they exist in our present society. . . . The *status quo* oriented emphasis could conceivably be explained in terms of what seems to be a consistent pre-disposition on the part of majority groups sociologists to view the existence and life of minority groups. . . . in terms of the pathological.[34]

Then he made a pointed criticism:

> Many white sociologists, with their methodological approaches, basic assumptions, frames of references,

analyses and interpretations in sociology, are collectively conspirators with basic values of the society in reinforcing and perpetuating the "mark of oppression" with their pathological definitions of the situation. Their findings reflect the negative and ethnocentric values and traditions of society.[35]

Most of the papers presented at this conference, and the subsequent discussions of them, tended to elaborate on Smith's theme. They generally agreed that the sociology of the Black Experience has been essentially moralistic, value-laden, and often patronizing. In the main the conference participants were critical of the basic theories, assumptions, and interpretations underlying most well-known studies of Black social stratification, institutions, socialization, achievements, life styles, movements, and leadership. One of the several provocative papers called attention to influential sociological works which reflected certain biases of both conservative and liberal sociologists.[36] Some of these biases are inherent in what is generally regarded as the most fruitful scientific methodology and sound reasoning and interpretation in the sociology of race relations.[37]

Most of the procedural booby traps in the study of the Black Experience are snugly concealed in traditional middle-class norms which sociologists, like other social scientists, usually accept as the basis for their research orientation—from the initial selection of the research problem, the methodology employed, interpretation or explanation of findings, to the summary of conclusions and recommendations. This persistent bias inevitably leads some researchers to a manifest or latent ethnocentrism that traps them into functioning as critics or judges rather than as objective scientists. This is the main theme of a book, dramatically entitled *The Death of White Sociology*, edited by Joyce A. Ladner. In the introduction, Professor Ladner insists that

Blacks have always been considered to be a deviation from the ambiguous white middle-class model, which itself has not always been clearly defined. This inability or refusal to deal with Blacks as a part and parcel of the varying historical and cultural contributions to the American scene has, perhaps, been the reason sociology has excluded the Black perspective from its widely accepted mainstream theories.[38]

The acceptance of classical middle-class norms as a valid basis for research orientation has, indeed, led some otherwise objective sociologists to view the whole range of the Black Experience as a deviation from such norms and, by definition, to be pathological in nature. This tendency was again emphasized by a Black sociologist, Robert Staples, in his interpretation of the dilemma of Black scholars in the "environs of the white ivory towers." He charges that—

If one checks the indices of sociology texts printed prior to 1970, blacks are usually discussed in the sections on crime, delinquency, illegitimacy, etc. Most of the theories in this field constitute some sort of justification for the existing social order. And any discipline that sanctifies the status quo automatically counts black people out.[39]

While conservative white sociologists tend to label the Black Experience as pathological, liberal sociologists, Black and white, generally sanction established white middle-class valuations by becoming apologists for the Blacks' adjudged deviation from middle-class standards. Both persuasions function to deny the legitimacy of the Black Experience.

NOTES

[1]Eugene D. Genovese, *In Red and Black* (New York: Vintage Books, 1971), p. 58.

[2]*Brown v. Board of Education*, etc., 347 U. S. 494.

[3]For a systematic discussion of this issue, see Gunnar Myrdal, *An American Dilemma* (New York: Harper and Brothers, Publishers, 1944), Chapter 2, especially pp. 30-44.

[4]For a careful documentation of these events, see L. D. Reddick, *Crusader Without Violence: A Biography of Martin Luther King, Jr.* (New York: Harper and Brothers, Publishers, 1959), pp. 108-234.

[5]Lerone Bennett, Jr., *What Manner of Man: A Biography of Martin Luther King, Jr.* (Chicago: Johnson Publishing Co., Inc., 1968), p. 140.

[6]The full text of this "Letter" is quoted in ibid., pp. 140-155. (For the original text, see Martin Luther King, Jr., "Letter from a Birmingham Jail," in *Christian Century* 80: 767-773.)

[7]Ibid., pp. 146-147.

[8]Ibid., p. 147.

[9]Lerone Bennett, Jr., *Confrontation: Black and White* (Baltimore: Penguin Books, Inc., 1965), pp. 217-260.

[10]Gunnar Myrdal, in *An American Dilemma*, pp. XLVI-XLVII, defined the American Creed as a moral and rational conviction on the part of most Americans that every citizen should be guaranteed liberty, equality, justice, and fair opportunity.

[11]Daniel C. Thompson, *The Negro Leadership Class* (Englewood Cliffs, N. J.: Prentice-Hall, Inc., 1963), "Foreword."

[12]"Letter from a Birmingham Jail," p. 150.

[13]William Brink and Louis Harris, *Black and White: A Study of U.S. Racial Attitudes Today* (New York: Simon and Schuster, Publishers, 1967), p. 120.

[14]See, for instance, the discussion in Sethard Fisher, ed., *Power and the Black Community* (New York: Random House, Inc., 1970), pp. 248-253.

[15]Joyce A. Ladner, *Tomorrow's Tomorrow* (Garden City, N. Y.: Doubleday and Co., Inc., 1971), p. 276.

[16]See an insightful, full discussion of this by Benjamin A. Quarles, *Black Abolitionists* (New York: Oxford University Press, 1969), passim.

[17]Frederick Cooper, "Elevating the Race: The Social Thought of Black Leaders," *American Quarterly* 24, No. 5 (December 1972): 605.

[18]Ibid., p. 624.

[19]Cited by Cooper in ibid., p. 612, from the *North Star*, July 14, 1884.

[20]Whitney M. Young, Jr., *To Be Equal* (New York: McGraw-Hill Book Co., 1964), pp. 22, 23-33.

[21]Ibid., pp. 102-136.

[22]*Time*, April 6, 1970, p. 23.

[23]Ibid., p. 29.

[24]U. S. Department of Commerce, Bureau of the Census, *The Social and Economic Status of Negroes in the United States, 1970*, pp. 82-83.

[25]The Carnegie Commission on Higher Education, *From Isolation to Mainstream* (New York: McGraw-Hill Book Co., 1971), p. 14. See also *The 1972 World Almanac* (New York: Newspaper Enterprise Association, Inc., 1972), p. 457.

[26]U. S. Department of Commerce, *The Social and Economic Status of Negroes*, p. 83.

[27]Harry Edwards, *Black Students* (New York: The Free Press, 1970), pp. 204-205.

[28]Daniel C. Thompson, "The History of Black Americans," *Faculty Forum*, No. 46 (October 1968): 1.

[29]For an extended, detailed discussion of whether the Black Experience is one of worthy intellectual inquiry, and the whole issue of Black studies departments in universities, see Armstead L. Robinson, Craig C. Foster, and Donald H. Ogiluie, eds., *Black Studies in the University* (New York: Bantam Books, 1969).

[30]Wilson Record, "White Sociologists and Black Studies," 1972, presented at the American Sociological Association meeting in New Orleans, August 1972.

[31]James A. Foley and Robert K. Foley, *The College Scene* (New York: McGraw-Hill Book Co., 1969), pp. 16-17.

[32]Robinson, Foster, and Ogiluie, *Black Studies in the University*, pp. 62-63.

[33]The conference was held on May 5-6, 1972, at the University of Chicago. The papers presented are still unpublished.

[34]Ibid., p. 1.

[35]Ibid., p. 4.

[36]Walter L. Wallace, "Sociological Theories and Studies of Black Americans," Paper presented at the University of Chicago Conference 1972.

[37]For a perceptive statement on this, see Barbara A. Sizemore, "Social Science and Education for a Black Identity," in James A. Banks and Jean D. Grambs, *Black Self-Concept* (New York: McGraw-Hill, Inc., 1972), pp. 141-156. A comprehensive study of the major sources of misinformation and lack of information about Blacks in American history textbooks was done by historians at the University of California at Berkeley, Kenneth M. Stampp, etc., "The Negro in American History Textbooks, 1968," in David D. Anderson and Robert L. Wright, eds., *The Dark and Tangled Path: Race in America* (New York: Houghton Mifflin Co., 1971), pp. 325-331.

[38]Joyce A. Ladner, ed., *The Death of White Sociology* (New York: Vintage Books, 1973), p. xxiii.

[39]Robert E. Staples, "The Black Scholar in Academe," *Change Magazine* 4, No. 9 (November 1972): 43.

2

The Black
Experience

A promising clue to an understanding of the uniqueness of the
Black Experience may have been suggested by an American
social scientist, W. I. Thomas, who states that all basic human
wishes can be subsumed under four general categories: the
desire for new experience, security, recognition, and response.[1] To the extent that this is so, the unique component that
distinguishes the Black Experience from the American Experience is the historical fact that insofar as these basic wishes are
concerned, Black Americans have experienced unusually frustrating, prolonged socioeconomic deprivations that have been
greatly exacerbated by informal and institutionalized racism.

New experiences. Though many basic human desires may be
classified under the general heading "new experiences," in one
way or another all of them presuppose freedom of the individual, which is at the very core of the urge to explore and to
create.

Certainly no other racial or ethnic group in American history
has had freedom withheld from it for so long and so completely
as have Blacks. Soon after its founding, each American colony

began systematically to force Blacks into slavery. Virginia made the practice legal in 1661, after which the number of slaves increased rapidly. The treatment of slaves was so inhumane that Black resentment mounted to the point where slave masters lived in constant fear of slave uprisings. "The Colonial Assembly therefore adopted a rigid slave code, restricting the freedom of movement of the slaves, inflicted severe penalties for even minor offenses and denying slaves civil and criminal rights."[2]

This succinct summary of the status of slaves indicates the extent to which Blacks were denied all of the elementary rights that the founders of this nation insisted were the birthright of every human being. They held that the ultimate *raison d'être* of any legitimate government is to guarantee every person the right of "life, liberty and the pursuit of happiness." The categorical denial of these rights to Blacks is the primary source of the uniqueness of the Black Experience.

Not only was the Blacks' freedom denied by legal restrictions imposed upon them, but extralegal sanctions were often even more severe. Blacks were completely at the whim of their masters and enjoyed no degree of personal or social freedom their masters elected to deny them. This complete denial of what the U. S. Constitution holds to be an inalienable right was validated by the U. S. Supreme Court in 1857 when it held that a slave, Dred Scott, was not an American citizen and had no rights that his master needed to respect.[3]

Any valid interpretation of the Black Experience must take into account the frustrating denial to Blacks of even the elementary rights of humanity and citizenship for more than 200 of their 300 or so years in this country. Even after the Civil War, the collapse of the Confederacy, and the emancipation of slaves, Blacks continued to be denied the freedom inherent in full citizenship. The South quickly set about to create a biracial system based upon white supremacy, undergirded by a new set of Black codes or "Jim Crow" laws.[4] At first this system was informal and contrary to the spirit of Reconstruction. Nevertheless, bitterness on the part of the defeated South, the almost complete economic destitution of the vast majority of the South's population, the awkwardness of Blacks as new citizens, as well as the ideological confusion of northern liberals and "carpetbaggers" and the ready willingness of the federal government to compromise the citizenship status of Blacks for the sake of "National Unity," proved to be a potent combination of political and social ingredients. These factors nurtured the speedy growth of a durable, punitive biracial system in which Blacks were left almost as powerless and unfree as they had been during slavery.[5]

The very eloquent and influential spokesman for the "New South" concept after the Civil War, Henry W. Grady of Georgia, made the perpetuation of Black suppression the primary goal of the South. His definition of the "Solid South" was predicated upon the prevalent fear that Blacks might control the balance of political power if they were enfranchised. He said: "This fear has kept and will keep, the whites solid! It would keep the intelligent and responsible of any community, North or South, solid. . . . The supremacy of the white race must be maintained forever."[6]

When Grady issued his formal call for a Solid South, the status gains made by Blacks immediately following the Civil War had already been erased. For all practical purposes, southern whites were solidly allied against the advancement of Blacks in all areas of life. Severe informal restrictions placed upon Blacks had been sanctioned by state legislatures without a single dissenting voice. Without compunction regarding the question of constitutionality, Jim Crow laws had been passed restricting the freedom of Blacks in all phases of racial contacts—from place of residence to marriage.

Black codes passed by state legislatures were vigorously enforced by "lily-white" police and courts. These two agencies became the very strong right arm of anti-Black sentiment, notwithstanding the guarantee of full citizenship accorded Blacks by the federal government.[7] The South was indeed solidly mobilized to oppose the full citizenship and freedom of Black Americans.

In 1883, in support of the South's anti-Black movement, the U. S. Supreme Court declared unconstitutional the Civil Rights Act of 1875 which had guaranteed Blacks equal rights to the full and equal enjoyment of public accommodations. This decision gave federal sanction to the large body of Jim Crow laws that had already been passed and enforced by southern states, and solidly paved the way for many other Black codes which followed. Finally, in 1896 the Supreme Court gave its approval of southern apartheid in its far-reaching support of the doctrine of "separate but equal" in regards to all areas of race relations.[8] This decision functioned to make the biracial system, with its inherent assumption of white supremacy and the discrimination it presupposed, a legitimate, constitutional policy.

The "separate but equal" decision did, in fact, "stamp the colored race with a badge of inferiority," as Mr. Justice Brown predicted in his famous dissent, and condemned them to an inferior, limited citizenship with the firm approval of the highest court. This meant that all levels of government in the United States countenanced the practice of limiting the freedom of Black Americans. It determined the sociocultural setting of the Black Experience: outside the mainstream of American life.[9]

For more than fifty years following the "separate but equal" decision, the Supreme Court repeatedly refused to grant Blacks freedom to participate in the wider society as equal citizens. Finally, in 1954, the Court reversed itself and declared, unanimously, that the 1896 decision was null and void.[10] This decision laid the foundation for the new civil rights movement of the late 1950s and 1960s and for a multitude of new Black experiences designed to implement this newly found legal freedom.

Security. Again, understanding the essential uniqueness of the Black Experience presupposes that one must take into account the fact that no other racial or ethnic group in the United States has been subjected to the degree and variety of complex insecurities as have Blacks. As mentioned above, they were regarded as chattel for over 200 years, during which time they had no more formal security of person than domestic animals. There was no legal or established extralegal machinery through which they could receive redress of wrongs committed against them.

The Emancipation Proclamation and the Reconstruction Amendments—the Thirteenth, Fourteenth, and Fifteenth —were intended to accord Blacks full citizenship status, including, of course, equal protection of the law. The extent to which they have actually received protection of the law varies considerably from one state to another and from one community to another. It may also vary from one time to another in the same community. Some have even observed that the degree and kind of violence that whites have meted out to Blacks in the South varied according to the price of cotton: violence increased as the price of cotton decreased.[11] Anyway, even now, Blacks still complain that very often they do not receive equal personal security. A national report on urban riots during the 1960s underscores this complaint. It concludes:

> We have cited deep hostility between the police and ghetto communities as a primary cause of the disorders surveyed by the Commission. . . . in practically every city that experienced racial disruption since the summer of 1964 —abrasive relationships between police and Negroes and other minority groups have been a major source of grievance, tension and, ultimately, disorder.[12]

Ironically, then, a primary source of insecurity constantly experienced by Blacks is the police. According to recent reports, in most sections of the United States the police still tend to use excessive force in dealing with Black people—whether they are college students, Black militants, or hardened criminals.

As uncertain and threatening as the racial practices of constituted legal authority have been, the greatest threat to the Blacks' security has been mob violence. In 1892 the very famous Black leader and ex-slave, Frederick Douglass, noted that

> The frequent and increasing resort to lynch law in our southern states, in dealing with alleged offenses by Negroes, marked as it is by features of cruelty which might well shock the sensibility of the most benighted savage, will not fail to attract the attention and animadversion of visitors to the World's Columbian Exposition.
>
> . . . Lynch law violates all of those merciful maxims of law and order which experience has shown to be wise and necessary for the protection of liberty, the security of the citizen, and the maintenance of justice for the whole people.

Then he commented about the South:

> . . . today it is the bold defender of the usurpations of the mob, and its territory, in many parts, has become the theater of lawless violence against defenceless people.

Douglass concluded that

> The distressing circumstance in this revival of lynch law in different parts of the South is that it shows that prejudice and hatred have increased in bitterness with the increasing interval between the time of slavery and now. . . . The Negro meets no resistance when on a downward course. It is only when he rises in wealth, intelligence, and manly character that he brings upon himself the heavy hand of persecution.
>
> . . . when he shakes off his rags and wretchedness and presumes to be a man among men, he contradicts this popular standard and becomes an offense to his surroundings.[13]

A generation later Myrdal regarded lynchings as still a very serious threat to the security of Blacks. He said: "It is the custom in the South to permit whites to resort to violence against the life, personal security, property and freedom of movement of Negroes. There is a wide variety of behavior, ranging from a wild admonition to murder, which the white man may exercise to control Negroes."[14]

The climate of opinion throughout the South between the Civil War and the 1950s was such that open violence against Blacks could proceed with little serious legal or moral censure from the general public or from the state or federal government. Therefore, mob violence designed to stifle any significant move by Blacks to achieve ordinary independence and security proceeded unchecked. "In the last sixteen years of the nineteenth century there had been more than 2,500 lynchings. . . . In the very first year of the new century (1900) more than 100 Negroes were lynched, and before the outbreak of World War I (14 years later) the number for the century had soared to more than 1,100."[15]

As Ralph Ginzberg has reported, "between 1882, when Tuskegee Institute first began keeping a record, and 1901 an average of about 150 lynchings a year took place in the South."[16] Actually, there are no official records on exactly how many Blacks have been lynched. Some were never recorded as such, and for about two decades after the Civil War no official effort was made to determine the number and kinds of lynchings which took place regularly. However, it has been estimated that approximately 5,000 Blacks have been lynched since emancipation.[17]

Although lynching has been diminishing since World War II, it still occurs in certain southern communities when Black protest and advancement begin to threaten the deeply entrenched biracial status quo. For instance, during the 1960s when some solid gains were being made by Blacks throughout the social system, there was a revival of the Ku Klux Klan in several states where Black progress was beginning to be obvious. The wave of violence against Blacks included several extremely sadistic lynchings in which Klan members were suspected of having participated.

Until recent years no white person was ever legally punished for participating in a lynch mob. Since 1965 a few have been convicted by federal courts for "violating the civil rights" of Blacks. But none has yet been sentenced for murder by state courts; at most, they have received relatively light sentences and have been soon paroled or pardoned.

Though incidents of mob violence is no longer a serious, widespread threat to Black security, Blacks continue to experience citizenship insecurity as a result of their relatively powerless minority status in American society. Despite significant political gains during the last decade, only a small number of Blacks are in top-level political decision-making positions anywhere in the United States. Those who, as individuals, hold such positions on a local, state, or federal level are so few that they can only expect to contribute little more than an effective protest group. This is the main role played by the Black Congressional Caucus. Therefore, when vital political decisions are being made that might affect the welfare of Blacks, they are considerably uneasy because they are most vulnerable.

There are those who insist that the most debilitating insecurity chronically experienced by Blacks is an economic one. It is true, of course, that the economic status of Blacks has gradually continued to improve since their emancipation from slavery, and has gained significantly for about a fourth of the Black population since World War II. Yet the fact remains (as will be presented in subsequent chapters) that they still lag far behind whites in this regard. By and large, they are still one of the most deprived racial groups in the United States.

Recognition. A third basic human desire cited by W. I. Thomas, and one which tends to be a fountainhead of deep frustration for Black citizens, is the desire for recognition. This fact was emphasized in a 1970 study of Black teenagers in New Orleans.[18] Either in response to direct questions or spontaneously, every one of the subjects said in effect: "I want to become somebody. I want to be a success" in some professional field and/or as a person. Just about all of them expressed the belief that as Blacks they would have much greater difficulty achieving recognition than they would if they were white. They frequently volunteered such statements as this: "All things being equal. . . . if I were white I would have a much better chance" of. . . . enrolling in a given college, becoming an architect, getting an opportunity to win an award in music, getting a particular job, being elected to some political office, or being recognized. A group of twenty-five of these teenagers, participating in a forum, unanimously agreed with the proposition that "it is twice as hard for a Black person to succeed in American society as it is for a white person."

The fundamental *raison d'être* of the biracial system in the United States is precisely that of denying Blacks equality of opportunity to become recognized. Thus, while some Blacks have undoubtedly gained higher social status in the Black ghetto than they could have achieved in the society at large, where their competitors are more numerous and the rules for competition are more rigid, the fact remains that in every area of American life there is a ceiling on the estimable aspirations of Blacks, or at least on the number of Blacks who may aspire.

No one knows, or perhaps could ever know, exactly what proportion of Blacks are underemployed in terms of their qualifications or abilities, the extent to which the talents and potentialities of Black youth have been allowed to remain fallow or unused, and the degree to which ambitious Blacks are frustrated because of their blackness. Yet, every systematic study of this problem agrees that in practically every area of American life the vast potential and talents among Blacks are greatly underdeveloped and unrecognized.[19]

Not only does the biracial system limit opportunities of Blacks to achieve recognition in most areas of community and national life—to fulfill normal aspirations of American citizens—but, as a rule, Blacks who actually succeed according to the highest standards in certain areas of American life are not extended the recognition they deserve.[20] For example, outstanding accomplishments of Blacks are generally omitted from public school texts. The most salient reason for this is racial prejudice whereby some school systems would not adopt a book if Black heroes or Black accomplishments were given deserved recognition. Likewise, until the 1970s most of the mass media either systematically omitted Black accomplishments or tended to deemphasize them by labeling them "Black" and limiting their significance to the Black community. Thus, no matter how noteworthy or important Blacks' accomplishments might have been, the individual would receive little or no recognition outside the Black community.

A valid interpretation of the Black Experience must necessarily include basic knowledge of the ways Blacks have responded to little or no recognition, and how the lack of recognition by the larger society has functioned to undermine aspirations and dilute the satisfaction of success accomplished.

Response. The fourth basic human desire cited by Thomas is much more subtle (yet nonetheless potent) than the other desires just discussed. As used in this context, it is the desire to be respected, and accepted, and loved. It is entirely obvious that throughout American history Blacks have experienced many unusual frustrations in satisfying this very human desire. The truth is that some Blacks who have had notable success in terms of personal freedom, security, and recognition have a deep sense of frustration because they have not received the deserved respect and acceptance from the larger American society. They are denied the ordinary rewards that motivate white Americans.

The many and various Black professional groups, business organizations, and caucuses usually begin and continue to function because those involved do not get the respect and acceptance their accomplishments merit from their white counterparts. As a general rule, Black organizations are concrete manifestations of the degree to which Blacks feel alienated from the mainstream of American life. "Black separatism," as advocated by a large number of Blacks, is too often a counter-response to white rejection. It indicates, among other things, that Blacks have lost faith in the theory that they will be respected and accepted as they measure up to white upper-middle-class standards. Some cite this as the central fallacy in the theory of racial integration.

The particular pattern or technique of rejection whites employ in dealing with Blacks varies from place to place, situation to situation, and from time to time. Upon analysis, however, all forms of rejection share certain basic characteristics: some degree of corporal threat or punishment either by the police, zealous individuals, or the mob; personal insults, though often subtle and veiled; anti-Black propaganda, theories, and stereotypes; epithets; suggestions of racial inferiority; refusal to extend simple courtesies, such as addressing Blacks as "Mr.," "Mrs.," or "Miss"; and well-calculated gestures which indicate rejection.

The Black Experience must, then, include not only white rejection but the responses and adjustments Blacks have made and continue to make to ubiquitous patterns and techniques of disesteem on the part of white Americans.

Survival as the Basic Fact of the Black Experience

Any productive approach to the study of the Black Experience must necessarily take into account a fundamental fact: *Historically, Black Americans have constituted a disesteemed, despised, relatively powerless racial minority. As such, they have had a unique, constant struggle to survive personally and as a socially conscious, viable group.* It is very important to realize that in order to facilitate their own survival under various conditions and degrees of servitude, discrimination, and individual and institutionalized hostility, they have invented, refined, and borrowed intact a variety of survival techniques and strategies to be used in their constant confrontations with powerful, often legitimate, untoward social forces.

The most important fact the sociologist should remember about the Blacks' struggle to survive in American society is that they have succeeded. Their survival has been dramatic. Within the first century after emancipation from slavery (1863), the Black population increased from about 4,440,000 (1860 census) to 22,727,000 (1970 census) and is now approaching 25,000,000.[21] This growth in population has been more or less constant despite the fact that Blacks have always been assigned the most difficult, unhealthy, unrewarding jobs; denied normal medical facilities and care; customarily refused ordinary police protection; judged by avowedly anti-Black courts; generally provided the lowest quality of education; kept politically weak and economically powerless by deeply entrenched Jim Crow laws and traditions; long subject to widespread lynchings; and regularly singled out for unusual physical, psychological, and social abuse.

All of these forces militated against survival, yet not only have Black Americans survived demographically, but, under the most difficult circumstances, they have managed to advance as a distinct, viable social entity. Despite legal and social restrictions and frequent organized opposition from reactionary white groups, Blacks have succeeded in developing their own social groups, agencies, and institutions. These are peculiarly designed to facilitate their survival in the face of the many vicissitudes Blacks have had to encounter from slavery toward true freedom and full citizenship.

Two of the most provocative pieces on the survival techniques employed by Black Americans were written by W. W. Phillips, sociologist with the Center for Urban Social Science Research of Rutgers, and Samuel Proctor, professor of education at Rutgers, and a widely acknowledged authority on the Black middle class. Phillips tends to emphasize adjustive survival techniques, while Proctor stresses positive or creative techniques.[22] For instance, Phillips holds that:

One feature appears to distinguish most of the techniques

of survival black folk have developed in American society. This is their involuntary character. These survival techniques all seem to have the distinguishing character of being responses to force, coersion, oppression, and bestiality. I am saying simply that the survival techniques of black folk appear to have the mark of devices created by people who have to deal with an enemy.[23]

Phillips discusses several survival techniques that he believes to be involuntary in character: "Collective solidarity," which he regards as "a primeval form of survival," where Blacks have been "forced into the position of a self-conscious out group" which results in social isolation, imposed, artificial, and powerless pseudosolidarity, and group injury, insult, and humiliation; the development of a "counterculture," where the "ethos has as a key axiom the belief by black folk that dealings with white folk entail grave risk and that they can be deadly"; mobility, or "the freedom to move, roam, and migrate" in a never-ending search for better jobs and less hostile social environments; religion, "in which black folk could give expression to their deepest anguish, agony, and desperation and at the same time achieve status and perform satisfying roles to give meaning to their existence."[24]

Phillips, then, focuses on the psychological price Blacks have had to pay for "socialization to an oppressive system." Among the survival mechanisms he cites are:

Self-hatred, shame, negative self-esteem, suppressed aggression and rage, dependency, and subserviency. . . . These survival mechanisms manifest themselves in such conduct as refusal to have aspirations or shying away from competition; denial of the possession of ability, intelligence, and talent; the tendency to react submissively or to avoid the display of aggressiveness; an overwhelming feeling of insecurity, helplessness, and powerlessness; the adoption of protest or liberation movements founded upon philosophies of passive resistance and nonviolence; . . . and a vulnerability to such deviations as alcoholism, drug addiction, and compulsive gambling.[25]

Proctor emphasizes the positive, even creative, techniques Blacks have used to facilitate their precarious survival in American society. He strongly insists that the Black middle class has made the most expeditious use of available survival techniques: "As is the case for the middle classes everywhere, the habits of life that brought these people success may be described as low-risk. These people are prudent. And their habits of life are incompatible with the spirit of revolution. They have made it on safe bets, hard work, self-confidence, skillful manipulation, and brutal competitiveness."[26]

Proctor expresses disappointment in this "massive manpower pool comprising hundreds of thousands of blacks who have discovered survival techniques for themselves but who have not found a way to articulate these techniques in the revolutionary causes that engage many younger and more vocal black protagonists."[27] He then answers the criticism of Black militants who charge hat the Black middle class "is shot through with apathy, cowardice, or both." He argues that:

The black middle class is not quite that naive. It does not purport to have a program. It has only a survival strategy. Middle-class blacks looked up a long time ago and found injustice and racism rampant and due process of law applicable only to whites; the state police and the county sheriff were aligned against them and they concluded that open confrontation with the system was futile. Peaceful protests like sit-ins and the marches they could take, and did support, . . . But the idea of a blood bath looked like genocide. They rejected it. . . . This rejection is, and was, no program. It was a survival strategy.[28]

The main theme throughout Proctor's essay is that the most

dependable survival techniques available to Black Americans are inherent in classical middle-class virtues, particularly formal education. "Higher education must assume a major responsibility for correcting this unfair distribution of advantages. . . . In a technological society, formal education turns out to be the most effective lever for lifting one out of the bottom. . . . As far as the black community is concerned, education has to be far more the (effective) agent of change."[29]

A balanced study of the Black Experience must take careful note of both the negative and positive techniques Blacks have used during the more than 350 years they have survived as a distinct, disesteemed, oppressed racial minority in American society.

Paradigm on the Black Experience

In order that the concept Black Experience might be better employed in empirical research and sociological communication, I suggest the development of the following paradigm consisting of four distinct levels of experience:[30]

Level 1. *The extent to which the Black presence has influenced the ideology, structure and function of specific social organizations, movements, and, ultimately, the overall nature of the American social system.*[31] Here we are concerned with the complex ways in which powerful white spokesmen and leaders, social agencies and institutions, and government on all levels have responded directly and indirectly to Blacks as a viable, racially distinct segment of the population.

Too often, socially significant responses to the Black presence by individuals, local communities, and even the nation at large, are difficult to ferret out of the larger social contexts in which they are embedded. For example, a slogan like "states' rights" reflects the individualism and independence inherent in our national culture. However, as employed by southern white power figures, it really means that southern states should be left alone to develop and perpetuate any political structure, judicial procedure, or tradition deemed necessary to preserve a biracial system in which white supremacy would prevail in every walk of life.

Again, anti-Black attitudes on the part of a majority of whites may become embedded in certain established ''standards'' adopted by various private and public groups, and may be eventually reflected in the constitutions and bylaws of basic institutions. These standards may apply to membership in particular groups, entrance requirements to certain schools and colleges, qualifications for political participation, qualifications for jobs, merit systems influencing promotion, eligibility for welfare, and any number of other apparently ''objective'' standards adopted by public and private groups, and government on all levels.

The white majority adopting these standards may intend them to apply only to Blacks. Frequently, however, they have some far-reaching unanticipated consequences. A very important case in point is the South's deliberate efforts to disfranchise Blacks. All southern state legislatures passed laws—''Black codes''—intended to prevent Blacks from registering and voting. Some of these codes had unforeseen consequences in that they were eventually used to perpetuate the power of some individuals and political factions by excluding the great masses of whites from participating in the political process.[32] Therefore, in a very direct way the fundamental rationale for Black codes resulted in the one-party system in the South because it emphatically held voting to be a privilege to be extended or withheld by state governments, rather than an inalienable right. As expected, this conception of voting disfranchised all but a mere handful of Blacks. In 1940 only about 5 percent of voting-age Blacks were qualified to vote, and most of these were in metropolitan areas. In rural counties there was a definite correlation between the proportion of Blacks registered to vote and their percentage in the total population: ''As the proportion Negro increases beyond 30 percent . . . Negro registration rates begin to decline very sharply until they approach zero at about 60 percent Negro and above. There would seem to be a critical point, at about 30 percent Negro, where white hostility to Negro political participation becomes severe."[33]

One of the most efficient devices to keep Blacks from voting in the South was the poll tax. It was a direct form of voluntary taxation, justified as a means for raising revenue but actually intended to restrict the size of the electorate. The amount levied was from $1 to $2 annually, and this was usually cumulative. This tax would begin at 21 years of age. If a citizen did not attempt to register until he was 30, he would have to pay from $10 to $20 before he qualified. As stated earlier, this tax, originally designed as a Black code, had important, complex consequences: it disfranchised the great masses of poor whites, along with Blacks, and nurtured the development of one-party state governments. V. O. Key, Jr., points out that between 1920 and 1946 (when the poll tax was levied in most southern states), "usually less than 30 percent of all citizens 21 years of age and over vote[d] for governor in Democratic primaries in most southern states. . . . In Ohio and New York about five times as large a proportion of the electorate vote[d] for governor in the general election."[34] He found that this same differential voting pattern prevailed in voting in presidential elections, where less than 25 percent of those of voting age in poll tax states in 1948 actually voted, in contrast with a national percentage of 52, with ten nonsouthern (nonpoll tax) states having an average of 65 percent of the potential voters voting.

A small, rather highly selected electorate was well-suited for the machine type, one-party state governments dominating the South. These governments increased their power by establishing a shrewd complex of legal and extralegal procedures and practices (ranging all the way from poll tax and unusual residential requirements to complicated literacy tests and "moral" qualifications) designed to control the size and the nature of the electorate. Ultimately, then, a few key power figures were able to stifle freedom of speech, limit the scope of issues to be debated in political campaigns, and guarantee the perpetual economic and political powerlessness of Blacks.

From the beginning, anti-Black, ultraconservative ideologies and antidemocratic political devices and strategies, invented by white southern politicians in direct response to the size and dynamics of the Black presence, have pervaded and influenced almost every facet of our national life. They have also colored decisions regarding a variety of basic issues and policies that far transcend the Black condition. Nevertheless, these unanticipated consequences are in reality legitimate aspects or dimensions of the Black Experience since they were originally intended to apply only to Blacks and cannot be properly understood outside of that context. As such, they should be identified, analyzed, and interpreted according to scientific research methods and substantive social theory rather than current moralistic valuations.

Level 2. *The concept Black Experience should be defined so that it would include experiences resulting from conditions imposed upon Blacks by the direct and indirect actions of white (or non-Black) individuals, groups, institutions, and special social power arrangements*. Such conditions may be functional for Black survival as well as dysfunctional. They may facilitate adjustment, self-esteem, and progress, or they may control the behavior, aspirations, and achievements of Blacks. What distinguishes these conditions as inherently *imposed* is that in both instances Blacks serve as the object of social action by whites and do not possess the structured authority necessary to resist or alter decisions made for them, or the ultimate consequences of these decisions. They are relatively powerless, then, and may be regarded as pawns or victims in a dominance-submission pattern of race relations.

A promising approach to the study of this dimension of the Black Experience would raise a set of fundamental questions ordinarily neglected by sociologists. Two examples may illustrate the potential value of this approach if pursued according to rigorous social research methods and theory:

1. Most viable Black institutions, civil rights organizations, and efforts made by individual leaders to uplift the race or

improve the Black condition depend upon the support, or at least the legitimation, of the white community. Such support may be extended by government on all levels, foundations, or individual philanthropy, all of which are ultimately influenced by white public opinion. The nature of this support may indeed facilitate or hinder the Black Americans' bid for equal citizenship and economic and social progress. It is precisely at this point that some crucial empirical questions should be raised about the function of support whites give to Black institutions, leaders, and programs. Some of these questions are: To what extent are the curricula, programs, and faculties in Black colleges influenced by the sources of their support? In what ways do white trustees of Black colleges and other Black institutions influence the role these institutions play in the Black community specifically and in the American social system at large? Is there a distinct process of "routinization" or legitimation imposed upon Black charismatic leaders? Is this same process operative where Black institutions and organizations are concerned? In this same vein, to what extent is the image of Black leaders, entertainers, and professionals molded by those who would have them conform to the white image of what Blacks *should be*? What have been the nature and consequences of efforts by white philanthropy and legitimizing agencies in regard to the development and contributions of Black scholars, leaders, and executives—or the Black middle class generally? To what extent do the white-controlled mass media influence the nature and direction of Black progress?

These are only a few questions to illustrate a relatively neglected orientation of research on the Black Experience. Systematic research designed to answer such questions would lead to a much more definitive understanding and interpretation of the strengths and weaknesses characteristic of Black institutions, programs, and movements. For example, this approach could provide two very different, opposite, answers to this often debated question: "Why isn't a given Black institution (a school, a family pattern, or business enterprise) stronger or

more effective than it is in facilitating Black advancement?''
The answer could be: ''Blacks do not have the ability or resources needed to make it more effective,'' or, what is likely to
be a more definitive answer, ''whites don't want it to be too
much stronger or effective, thus they withhold the kind and
amount of support required to make it so.'' In any case, seldom
indeed can we expect to find the true answer to questions about
the strengths or weaknesses of Black organizations or institutions by studying them as if they were isolated from the larger
American social system and developed independently of white
public opinion and pressure from the white community.

2. Even now, as noted above, most sociological treatises
dealing with the Black community tend to place central emphasis on pathological elements of the Black Experience and
attempt to explain them in terms of failings within the Black
community itself. Among the numerous examples is a basic one
on the problem of poverty. Since this is such a widely debated,
persistent condition among Blacks, all prominent sociologists
have chosen to deal with it to some extent. Several traditional
intraracial explanations or theories are emphasized: lack of
adequate formal education or training, weak or disorganized
family life, defective socialization patterns, emasculation of the
male image, inadequate or dishonest leadership, a superficial or
disinterested bourgeoisie, and so forth. Even when interracial
interpretations are offered, intraracial characteristics usually
remain the key interpretative variables.

Intraracial explanations of poverty (by far the most frequently used among white men of power, especially politicians)
assume two fundamental conditions. (1) All Americans who
want a job can, in fact, secure one, and the job will provide a
salary sufficient to living above the poverty level. (2) If Blacks
measure up to white middle-class standards and internalize
certain basic middle-class values, their differential poverty
would disappear. These highly questionable assumptions discourage the raising of other promising sets of legitimate ques-

tions regarding Black poverty which could lead to new insights into the Black Experience.

Among the many researchable sets of questions regarding Black poverty are the following:

(a) Is full employment feasible in a capitalistic system? To what extent are unemployment and the culture of poverty due to the personal or group failings of Blacks in the labor force, and to what extent are they due to inequities inherent in the economic system?

(b) What is the nature of the forces operating in specific industries and the social system at large which determine *who* shall be employed on available jobs? In what ways do these forces militate against the equal employment of Blacks? To what extent do our schools and colleges actually prepare students for economic participation? At what points are some schools more relevant to the facts of economic competition than others? How do Black schools measure up in this regard? To what extent are Blacks prepared or could measure up in this regard? To what extent are Blacks prepared or could be easily prepared to hold jobs not now available to them? What is the real nature of racial discrimination by labor unions? In what verifiable ways do informal, interpersonal relationships influence or shape employment opportunities in different industries, communities, and the nation at large?

(c) To what extent does the rate of unemployment generally, and Black unemployment specifically, reflect a lag between advanced technology and traditional economic policies and practices? Under what definite set of circumstances have Blacks, as individuals, succeeded in achieving equal economic opportunities in American society? Is there a valid profile of economically successful Blacks? If so, does this profile differ significantly from that of economically successful whites? Are certain rules or expectations for economic success incumbent upon Blacks a contradiction to the race pride and dignity for which Blacks strive?

These questions are posed here only to suggest lines of sociological inquiry that might yield useful data, not only about the Black Experience in a narrow sense, but about the essential nature of the economic system in which poverty must be interpreted. Such an approach would minimize the temptation to moralize about the Black condition and would form a more valid basis for truly objective research and analysis of the Black condition throughout the social system.

Level 3. *The Black Experience includes the nature and consequences of responses Blacks have made, and continue to make, to their unique condition in American society.* As discussed earlier, perhaps the most valuable orientation of empirical research on this subject is the assumption that most of the social responses made by Blacks have been consciously or unconsciously conditioned by their constant struggle to survive in a racist, hostile white society.

Sociologists are generally prone to emphasize such Black responses as accommodation, withdrawal, identification with white middle-class values, protest, bloc voting, legal action, antisocial behavior, urban riots, escapism (religion, music, the creation of an elaborate "world of make-believe,"), and means of self-improvement.[35] These are, of course, techniques of survival which merit continual study; research into these areas should yield significant information and fresh insights regarding the nature of the Black Experience. However, sociologists tend to emphasize these adjustment or accommodation responses exclusively. They usually focus upon Blacks as *objects* of action by whites rather than as *actors*. Indeed, very little research has focused on the unanticipated ways in which the Blacks' responses have inspired, initiated, and directed changes in the larger social system that extends far beyond the peculiar, esoteric interests of the Black community. There are numerous examples of this. Consider Black ideology and tactics supporting, even celebrating, the concept of equal citizenship and participation in American society. Their responses have been a major factor in keeping the issue of civil rights constantly before the American people—so much so that most prominent leaders, political representatives, public and private agencies, and all institutions have been pressured to take a definite stand. Even when a given organization has taken little or no action to effectuate equal rights, it has usually sanctioned them in principle, as reflected in its constitution or bylaws. Thus, in one way or another, the egalitarian ideology so central to the civil rights movement, and primarily propagandized by Blacks, has infused non-Black movements here and abroad, seeking to advance the citizenship and social status of other relatively powerless groups.

The ideology and tactics originally employed by Blacks to effectuate changes in their own condition are, even now, utilized by such groups as women liberationists, the aged, labor, "white parents for segregated or 'community-controlled schools,' " several ethnic groups, and especially students. Seymour Martin Lipset points out that a powerful and far-reaching student movement was inspired by the civil rights struggle of Blacks during the 1960s. He maintains that during the early stages of the student rebellion, "The bulk of those who were directly involved in actual demonstrations had been active in earlier political or civil rights protest." Thus, he insists that:

> To understand the reasons why the relatively passive postwar generation was replaced by one which contains an activist minority of the "enraged," it is important to note the extent to which some of the conditions that dampened ideological controversy among intellectuals during the forties and fifties changed in the sixties. . . . The shift in ideological climate, as well as the rather rapid escalation of protest from word to action, was facilitated by the struggle for Negro rights which emerged in the years following the Supreme Court's school desegregation decision of 1954. This was the perfect issue around which to create a new activist movement, since it engaged the principal aspect of American society, in which the system engaged in actions

which were at sharp variance with its manifest creed of equality and democracy. Most Americans, and the university system in toto, recognized that Negro inequality is evil, and in principle approved all action designed to reduce or eliminate it. . . . the (civil rights) struggle contributed greatly to radicalizing sections of the young. . . .

The confrontation tactics of civil disobedience which first emerged in the South, were then diffused by the American student movement to other parts of the country and the world, and to other issues both inside and outside of the University.[36]

The ideological and tactical responses of the Blacks to their own peculiar, circumscribed, powerless condition in American society have thus resulted in much more than the advancement of narrow Black interests. They have served as an effective social catalyst triggering basic changes throughout the society, and affecting the outlook and circumstances of various segments of the total population.

In order to arrive at meaningful analyses and interpretations of the Blacks' responses to their life conditions, it is necessary to study them in the total context of the American social system. This approach was emphasized by Andrew Billingsley in his study of the Black family. He insists that the Black family is "imbedded in a network of mutually inter-dependent relationships with the Negro community and the wider society."[37]

What is true of the Black family is also basic to an understanding of all Black institutions and the complex network of responses channeled through them. All are imbedded in the larger white community and must necessarily interact with other institutions. Therefore, to an important extent the structures, programs, and achievements of Black institutions are influenced by the expectations and conditions imposed by the larger society of which they are a part.

Level 4. *The Black Experience includes contributions Blacks have made, and continue to make, to their own survival and progress, and to the enrichment of the culture of the wider society of which they are an integral part.* Of particular interest here are the contributions made by Black institutions, voluntary organizations, leadership, professionals, businessmen, artists, and the generally overlooked Black masses.

While sociologists, among others, have given considerable attention to this dimension of the Black Experience, their interpretations are too often biased toward one of two extremes. At one end of the spectrum is a persistent tendency, especially among scholars who are socially isolated from the Black community, to measure and evaluate contributions of Blacks in terms of the rather narrow, ethnocentric norms and values established by and for the affluent, intellectual, tradition-oriented segment of the white middle class. A few (mostly radical) Black scholars and leaders gravitate toward the other extreme. That is, they reject the validity of white middle-class norms and values when employed in evaluating the Blacks' abilities and contributions. The most obvious example is the fact that Blacks generally deny the validity of all forms of standardized tests when applied to other than the white middle class. Thus, Robert E. Staples complained that

> among the first barriers the Black student encounters are the white-oriented qualifications for getting into graduate school, the most significant being the graduate entrance examinations. Like other qualifying exams, this one has been standardized for white middle-class students. In fact, they have been shown to have almost no validity in predicting the future success of black students in graduate school. But their pervasive use has effectively maintained the low number of black students in white graduate schools.[38]

Further, Staples contends that even after the Black student qualifies for graduate school on the basis of having passed inappropriate, invalid standardized tests, he encounters another set of subjective valuations designed for white middle-class students. An example of this is the required term papers:

His termpapers must be written in standard Anglo-Saxon English. . . . These termpapers (must) reinforce prevailing racist beliefs, attitudes and practices of white people. Papers that challenge those beliefs are usually required to provide an arsenal of supporting evidence, a request that is rarely made of those who accept the normative description of wisdom.[39]

Two strong advocates of "Black power," commenting on racist biases inherent in white middle-class valuations per se, concluded that—

The values of this society support a racist system; we find it incongruous to ask black people to adopt and support most of those values. . . . The goal of black people must *not* be to assimilate into middle-class, for that class—as a whole—is without a viable conscience as regards humanity. The values of the middle class permit the perpetuation of the ravages of the black community. The values of that class are based on material aggrandizement, not the expansion of humanity. . . . The values of that class do not lead to the creation of an open society. . . . *This class is the backbone of institutional racism in this country*. . . . Thus we reject the goal of assimilation into middle-class America because the values of that class are in themselves anti-humanist and because that class as a force perpetuates racism.[40]

Following this line of reasoning, Black separatists or nationalists would argue that Blacks must develop and establish their own ethical and moral systems and adopt standards and values compatible with their own unique life conditions and goals. This, they believe, is necessary because in this biracial society, based on white supremacy and special privileges, what is "good" for Blacks is not necessarily "good" for whites. Thus, what may be regarded as a noteworthy contribution by Blacks may be regarded as pathological, antisocial, or vulgar according to white middle-class standards. A Black scholar put it this way: "So, our agenda, our definitions, our perceptions are all different from the forms which others wish—as usual —to impose on us."[41] This same point of view was expressed by a much-celebrated Black militant leader and author who insisted that the whites' evaluation of Black contributions is intrinsically biased because whites are motivated to maintain and perpetuate the illusion that they are superior and Blacks inferior:

One device evolved by the whites was to tab whatever the blacks did with the prefix "Negro." We have *Negro* literature, *Negro* music, *Negro* doctors, *Negro* politicians, *Negro* workers. The malignant ingeniousness of this device is that it concealed the paramount psychological fact: that to the white mind, prefixing anything with "Negro" automatically consigned it to an inferior category.[42]

Again, in contradistinction to white middle-class valuations, another Black scholar interprets the Black ghetto confrontations with representative forces in white society (particularly the police) during the mid-1960s as *revolts* rather than riots. He argues that they were revolts because they were means by which Blacks

deny the very legitimacy of the system itself. The entire value structure which supports property rights over against human rights, which *sanctions* the intolerable conditions in which the black people have been *forced* to live is questioned. . . . Therefore, the *revolts* are the overt denials of legitimacy. . . . (they) say to the larger society, that a wholly new norm of "law and order" must be established.[43]

Finally, Julius Lester, a former leader in the once-militant Student Nonviolent Coordination Committee (SNCC), calls dramatic attention to anti-Black valuations implicit in certain white cultural standards. He says that when Blacks

adopted the cultural standards of the white majority . . . straight hair became "good" hair; a light complexion became the standard for beauty; western literature, music and art became representative of "culture"; and kinky hair, dark skin, black speech and jazz were to be avoided and eschewed as attributes which would prevent the race from being accepted by the white majority. . . . The acceptance of the cultural standards of the white majority meant a denial of selfhood for the black minority.[44]

It is methodologically unlikely that any valid or productive assessment of Black Americans' contributions can be arrived at by research employing either of the extreme approaches outlined above. Ultraconservative, middle-class-oriented research is too apt to overlook or demean Black contributions that seem not to measure up to the ideal standards established by and for the much more affluent, culturally rich segment of the population—no matter how significant such contributions may be in terms of Black survival and progress. Likewise, research oriented to the ideas of Black nihilists would have to be superficial and inconclusive because it would attempt to evaluate Black contributions outside the context of the wider society and culture of which they are an integral part. Their approach is anomic in that it would judge and condemn certain white individuals, programs, institutions, and attitudes according to norms and values in the wider culture that they emphatically reject as legitimate standards when applied to ideologies, social action, and institutions designed by and for Black Americans.

These two extremely opposite orientations articulate a common misleading fallacy: both are based on the assumption that American society is in fact two societies—one Black and the other white; that each is the enemy of the other; that the interests of one must be opposed to the interests of the other; and that what may be legitimately regarded as a contribution to the survival and welfare of one is likely to be of no importance, or even detrimental, to the other.

Empirical research designed to understand the nature and meaning of Black contributions must be based on a realistic understanding of subcultures in American society. The main principle to be relied upon in a study of indigenous subcultures in this society, whether articulated by different racial, ethnic, or social class groups, is that they tend to vary from that of the dominant group (in this instance, upper middle-class whites) to about the same degree as that group experiences social isolation from the dominant group. All viable subcultures in the United States represent different degrees of innovations on basic or universal traits in the general or dominant culture. Some innovations begin by accident while others are more or less calculated, expedient adaptations. They become elaborated in different directions and are given varying degrees of emphasis and *value*, depending largely upon the nature and extent of isolation experienced by the minority group in question.[45] Essentially, however, the particular pattern of culture adopted is likely to be a bona fide version of traits, themes, and norms characteristic of the "parent" or dominant culture.

In the sense just sketched, all distinct subcultures in American society may be best understood as more or less authentic variations on a major, common cultural continuum or arc.[46] Accordingly, all subgroups are given a number of different ways of satisfying individual needs and wants and solving basic social problems. Thus, a wide variety of culturally legitimate foods, types of shelter, dress, patterns of worship, styles of music, dialects, patterns of voluntary organization, family structures, forms of mutual aid, economic pursuits, belief systems, and so forth are presented to each subgroup in the society. It is not possible for any given group to know, appreciate, or adopt all of the great variety of traits available in any one of the many cultural categories presented. Selections in each fundamental category are made mandatory by the ultimate urgency to survive. The particular, discreet cultural choices made by a given subgroup will be greatly influenced by a complex of interwoven internal and external conditions and forces. Among the most persistent of these are its geographic location and climate, available natural resources, size of the population, level of education and skills, level of wealth, historical background and experiences, attitudes and actions of the majority group, quality of leadership, general conditions and issues existing in the society at large, and historical accidents. Within this broad, complex spectrum of dynamic forces each subgroup must select from among those traits and ideas available to it, those that seem to have the greater functional value for solving its own unique sets of imperative problems. Those that prove useful for the survival and progress of the subgroup are likely to be adopted and elaborated; those that seem to have little or no functional value, or appear to be dysfunctional, are likely to be ignored, picked over, or deliberately rejected.

Blacks, like other indigenous subgroups in the United States, have tended to adopt and elaborate only those traits and values that are deemed legitimate choices in the general culture and that seem to be best suited to their peculiar needs and circumstances. Consequently, a meaningful, scientifically valid assessment of the Blacks' contributions may be done best in terms of three distinct levels or categories:

1. The extent to which Blacks have selected and elaborated otherwise neglected traits, themes, and ideas in American culture. In this category belong the unique styles and themes in music, worship, socialization, speech, social tactics, and so forth. These unique cultural contributions in fact enrich the general culture in that they color and influence the direction in

which non-Blacks will elaborate other cultural items or traits. Perhaps the most commonly recognized example is the way Black music has influenced all forms of American music. What has been true of music is also true in almost all areas of American culture.

2. The extent to which Blacks have selected common traits from the general culture and have transformed, reshaped, and adapted them to serve the peculiar needs and goals of their community. Of special concern here are most Black organizations, all major social institutions, ideologies, and styles of leadership. While these social forms were invented by whites, for the most part, Blacks have developed, refined, and refashioned them to achieve ends established by Blacks and thus to facilitate their survival and progress vis-à-vis hostilities from the white majority. An excellent illustration is the Black church. While all of the major Black denominations grew out of white Protestantism and still articulate the same general beliefs and maintain the same organizational structures as their spiritual white "parents," their historical role in the Black community has been much more diversified than that of white churches. In many instances, these social forms are used effectively to counter patterns of racial discrimination inherent in the white parent structure.

The various creative institutional innovations introduced and developed by Blacks have not only contributed significantly to their own survival and progress, but in a much larger sense they have multiplied cultural choice for all Americans and, through the process of diffusion, have enriched the culture of contemporary civilization.

3. The extent to which Blacks have contributed to the development of common aspects of American culture. Interest here is focused on activities designed to advance the knowledge, welfare, and enrichment of all segments of the population—not for the Black community specifically. Such contributions are made by Black professionals, public officials, executives, artists, workers, and soldiers who serve the larger

society primarily and are only incidentally participants in the Black subculture.

Methodologically, objective studies of the Black Experience must take into account two fundamental historical facts. One, American society has always been biracial. The more or less powerless, disadvantaged Black community has had special, unique needs and more threatening survival problems. Two, though divided along many different lines, Blacks and whites have maintained constant, meaningful interaction. It is necessary, then, to analyze and interpret the Black Experience in the dynamic context of the total American society in which Blacks constitute an integral segment.

These two assumptions will be the central orientation for the analysis and interpretation of several key aspects of the Black Experience which will be presented subsequently.

NOTES

[1]W. I. Thomas, "The Four Wishes and the Definition of the Situation," Talcot Parsons, et al., eds., *Theories of Society* (Glencoe, Ill.: The Free Press, 1961), Vol. II, pp. 741-744. See also Daniel C. Thompson, "The Rise of the Negro Protest," *The Annals of the American Academy of Political and Social Science*, Philadelphia, Pa., Vol. 357, January 1965, pp. 18-25.

[2]Rayford W. Logan, *The Negro in the United States* (New York: D. Van Nostrand, 1957), p. 9.

[3]In 1866 Congress adopted the Fourteenth Amendment and "recalled" this implication in the Dred Scott Decision, and clearly defined citizenship in terms of birth in the United States.

[4]For a brief but insightful discussion of Jim Crow laws, see C. Vann Woodward, *The Strange Career of Jim Crow* (New York: Oxford University Press, 1961), passim.

[5]For an excellent presentation of this subject, see Rayford W. Logan, *The Betrayal of the Negro* (New York: Collier Books, 1968), pp. 15-61, passim.

[6]Henry W. Grady, *The New South* (Robert Bonner's Sons, Inc.,

1890), pp. 239-243. See also Thomas N. Page, *The Negro: The Southerner's Problem* (New York: Charles Scribner's Sons, 1904), pp. 104-108.

[7]Gunnar Myrdal, *An American Dilemma* (New York: Harper and Brothers, Publishers, 1944), pp. 550-555.

[8]*Plessy v. Ferguson*, 163, U. S. 537.

[9]Logan, *The Betrayal of the Negro*, pp. 105-124.

[10]*Brown v. Board of Education of Topeka*, 347, U. S. 483 (1954).

[11]John Dollard, et al., *Frustration and Aggression* (New Haven: Yale University Press, 1939), p. 31.

[12]*U. S. Riot Commission Report* (New York: The New York Times Co., 1968), p. 299.

[13]Frederick Douglass, "Lynch Law in the South," first published in *The North American Review* 45, No. 428 (1892): 17-24. Quoted in Harvey Wish, ed., *The Negro Since Emancipation* (New York: Farrar, Strauss and Co., 1964), pp. 22, 23, 24, and 26.

[14]Myrdal, *An American Dilemma*, p. 558.

[15]John Hope Franklin, *From Slavery To Freedom* (New York: Vintage Books, 1969), p. 439.

[16]Ralph Ginzberg, *100 Years of Lynchings* (New York: Lancer Books, 1962), p. 244.

[17]Ibid., p. 244.

[18]Daniel C. Thompson and Barbara M. Guillory, "Socialization of Black Teenagers in an Upward Bound Program, Dillard University," an unpublished study, 1970.

[19]Several empirical studies documenting this phenomenon are included in Harold G. Vatter and Thomas Palm, eds., *The Economics of Black America* (New York: Harcourt Brace Jovanovich, Inc., 1972). See especially pp. 71-84, 101-113, 112-135, and 139-143.

[20]This is the main reason why Black students have been pressuring for Black studies in white colleges and universities. See Armstead L. Robinson and others, eds. *Black Studies in the University* (New York: Bantam Books, 1969), preface, p. IX, and passim.

[21]Extrapolated from figures presented by Reynolds Farley, *Growth of the Black Population* (Chicago: Markham Publishing Co., 1970), p. 22.

[22]W. W. Phillips, Jr., "Survival Techniques of Black Americans," and Samuel D. Proctor, "Survival Techniques and the Black Middle Class," in Rhoda L. Goldstein, *Black Life and Culture in the*

United States (New York: Thomas Y. Crowell Co., 1971), pp. 153-164, and 280-294, respectively. Copyright © 1971 by Thomas Y. Crowell Company, Inc. All quotations therefrom are with permission of the publisher.

[23]Ibid., p. 154.

[24]Ibid., p. 161.

[25]Ibid., p. 163.

[26]Ibid., p. 282.

[27]Ibid., pp. 280-281.

[28]Ibid., p. 285.

[29]Ibid., p. 291.

[30]In this connection I wish to express my indebtedness and appreciation to Professor Robert K. Merton. See his discussion of paradigms in his *Social Theory and Social Structure* (New York: The Free Press, 1968), pp. 69-72.

[31]For a comprehensive analysis, see Eli Ginzberg and Alfred S. Eichner, *The Troublesome Presence* (New York: A Mentor Book, 1966), passim.

[32]For a full discussion of this, see Myrdal, *An American Dilemma*, pp. 474-504.

[33]Donald R. Matthews and James W. Prothro, "Social and Economic Factors and Negro Voter Registration in the South," in Harry A. Bailey, Jr., *Negro Politics in America* (Columbus, Ohio: Charles E. Merrill Publishing Co., 1967), pp. 186-187.

[34]V. O. Key, Jr., *Southern Politics* (New York: Vintage Books, 1949), pp. 491, 502-508.

[35]See Myrdal, *An American Dilemma*, pp. 727-747; Thomas E. Pettigres, *A Profile of the Negro American* (Princeton, N. J.: D. Van Nostrand Co., Inc., 1964), Chapter 2, "Reactions to Oppression," pp. 27-55; E. Franklin Frazier, *Black Bourgeoisie* (New York: The Free Press, 1957), pp. 153-209; Lewis M. Killian, *The Impossible Revolution?* (New York: Random House, 1968), pp. 125-145; and Allison Davis and John Dollard, *Children of Bondage* (Washington, D. C.: American Council on Education, 1940), pp. 3-20, passim.

[36]Seymour Martin Lipset, *Rebellion in the University* (Boston: Little Brown and Co., 1971), pp. 7, 9, 64.

[37]Andrew Billingsley, *Black Families in White America* (Englewood Cliffs, N. J.: Prentice-Hall, Inc., 1968), p. 5.

[38]Robert E. Staples, "The Black Scholar in Academe," *Change Magazine*, 4, No. 9 (November 1972): 42-43.

[39]Ibid.

[40]Stokely Carmichael and Charles V. Hamilton, *Black Power: The Politics of Liberation in America* (New York: Vintage Books, 1967), pp. 40-41.

[41]Vincent Harding, "Toward The Black University," *Ebony Magazine* 25, No. 10: 156.

[42]Eldridge Cleaver, "The White Race and Its Heroes," in Arthur C. Littleton and Mary W. Burger, eds., *Black Viewpoint* (New York: A Mentor Book, 1971), pp. 254-255.

[43]Charles V. Hamilton, "Riots, Revolts and Relevant Response," in Floyd B. Barbour, ed., *The Black Power Revolt* (Boston: Porter Sargent Publishers, 1968), pp. 174-175.

[44]Julius Lester, "The Necessity For Separation," *Ebony Magazine* 25, No. 10 (August 1970): 167.

[45]For a comprehensive discussion, see Daniel C. Thompson, "Teaching the Culturally Disadvantaged," *Speaking About Teaching* (New York: College Entrance Examination Board, 1967), pp. 51-56.

[46]For a comprehensive discussion of the concept "cultural arc," see Ruth Benedict, *Patterns of Culture* (New York: Houghton Mifflin Co., 1934), p. 25, passim.

3

The Black Ghetto:
The Family

The primary data to be presented here were gathered in an extensive study which a research team conducted in New Orleans in 1968-1969. Supporting primary data will be selected from several other empirical studies of community life done in New Orleans over a period of fifteen years.[1]

The main purpose of the study was to gather data according to which an assessment could be made of the nature and extent to which the family and the school cooperated in the process of socializing the child. Two elementary public schools in the Black ghetto were chosen as the target area. All families with children enrolled in these two schools were included in the study. These families were studied in the context of the larger community as well as that of the particular neighborhood in which they were a part.

Three interrelated research procedures were employed: the questionnaire, the interview schedule, and participant observation.

The questionnaire. There were about 2,000 pupils enrolled in the two schools in the target area. These children represented about 1,100 family units. (No definite count was made because of confusion over extended families, etc.) We were able to ascertain the names and addresses of 920 heads of families who had children enrolled in these schools. After several meetings with the teachers and administrators of these schools, in which they provided extensive information about the culture of the target area and the children enrolled in the schools, we developed a pertinent questionnaire consisting of forty-six carefully worded, simple, but basic questions. Most questions could be answered by a check mark opposite the most correct or appropriate of several suggested answers.

Of the 920 family heads given questionnaires, 789, or 86 percent, responded by giving complete answers to all questions. Their answers provided valuable census-type data and made it possible to select 309 "representative" families to be studied in depth.

The interview schedule. The 309 families selected for intensive study represented all of the apparently significant variables characteristic of the total sample of 789. They represented various family structures, levels of education, incomes, number of children, religious affiliations, ages of parents, occupational background, styles of life, residential mobility, and so forth.

The interview schedule designed for the study included approximately 100 questions, some of which were open-ended. It took about two hours to administer the schedule. In several instances, particularly informative families were visited two or three times. At least forty families served as the "core sample" in that all adult members were interviewed, the children were studied individually, and members of the research team participated in their community activities over a period of twelve months.

In order to get a wide range of interpretations of the Black Experience observed by the interviewers, regular meetings or "de-briefing" sessions were scheduled. In these sessions, each interviewer, and occasionally some leader, social worker, or businessman from the community provided insights into the nature and meaning of a particular aspect of life in the Black ghetto generally and the target area specifically.

Participant observation. One very valuable dimension of information was that received from actual participation in activities and interests in which members of the sample families engaged. This included attendance at meetings of the Parents-Teachers Association (PTA), church services, mass meetings, weddings, private parties, and recreational activities. On such occasions we were able to observe a dimension of social interaction and aspects of community life and culture that could not be seen in any other context. The subjects' responses in these situations provided important insights into various areas of information which the research team accumulated about them.

Ghetto Subculture

In order to understand the way of life in the Black ghetto, it is necessary to take into account some basic facts about its origin and expansion. To begin with, from all available reports, *the Black ghetto of central focus in this study is essentially like Black ghettos in other large cities throughout the United States*. All represent collective responses by recently urbanized, poor, relatively powerless, disesteemed Black people to basic survival demands in a highly organized, competitive, impersonal, racist urban society. Thus, while particular patterns of responses do vary somewhat from one Black ghetto to another and among different groups and families within a given neighborhood, common types of responses seem to be prevalent in all Black ghettos which set them apart as subcultural areas. The more or less cultural unity that exists among Black ghettos stems from the fact that the lives of the urban Black masses everywhere in the United States are fraught with similar problems and frustrations and the range of survival tactics and strategies available to them are always severely limited and tenuous. Therefore, the special empirical study that constitutes the primary source of data in the subsequent discussion was designed in the narrow sense to get full, primary information about the way of life in one particular ghetto, and in a much larger sense to utilize the New Orleans ghetto as a sort of social laboratory in which to test some general hypotheses on Black ghetto life in the United States.

Black urbanization. In 1940 there were 12,900,000 Black citizens in the United States. Of these, 9,905,000, or 77 percent, resided in the Deep South (the eleven Old Confederate states), with about a third (33 percent) living on farms. During World War II the Black population began a new, dramatic shift away from farms and out of the South. (The first "great migration" which began during World War I had slowed down by 1940.) By 1970, when the total Black population had increased to 22,727,000, only 3 percent remained on farms and the overwhelming majority, 16,800,000, or 74 percent, resided in cities. In addition, almost half—10,600,000, or 47 percent—of the Black population lived outside the South.

The most pertinent statistic for this discussion is that in 1970, 13,100,000, or 58 percent, of the Black population was concentrated in just thirty large cities. Furthermore, over 75 percent of those in the North, 66 percent of those in the West, and 41 percent of those in the South lived in the most congested transitional areas of central cities.[2]

Ecologically, the central or inner city areas of large metropolitan centers, where the great majority of Blacks are concentrated, are referred to as Black ghettos. Theoretically, a ghetto is an area in which a racial or ethnic group is segregated. It may include individuals and families representing all degrees of wealth. For example, "the expression *gilded ghetto* recognizes that even well-to-do members of a minority group may live in relative isolation from the larger society, whether this is the result of voluntary or of involuntary segregation."[3] However, more realistically, Senator Jacob Javits of New York concludes that "today's ghetto is no voluntary affair. It is a racial concentration from which the only escape is often into another racial concentration. Its residents are generally American in background, language, and custom. They include the wealthy and the poor, the uneducated and the intellectuals. . . . 95 percent of them are Negro Americans."[4]

There are many persistent, interrelated causes for the origin and continuing expansion of segregated Black neighborhoods or enclaves in large central cities. These causes have ranged from legal codes or "restrictive covenants" forbidding the sale or rental of houses in white neighborhoods to Blacks (prevalent throughout the United States until declared unconstitutional by the U. S. Supreme Court in 1948), and the still prevalent "gentlemen's agreements" involving homeowners, real estate agents, and lending agencies who *agree* not to sell or rent homes to Blacks in white neighborhoods, to formidable informal barriers such as openly expressed anti-Black attitudes, systematic attempts by those who represent white interests to dissuade Blacks from moving into white neighborhoods, and physical violence initiated by white neighbors.

Basically, then, the two most pervasive causes for the segregated Black ghetto are white racism and Black poverty. Thus, some Blacks who could well afford to purchase or rent homes outside the ghetto, even in some of the wealthy lily-white suburbs, find it necessary to remain in the Black ghetto because white homeowners still find many effective ways of preventing them from becoming their neighbors. The great masses of Blacks, however, live in ghettos because they are too poor to pay for more expensive housing. They are victims of institutionalized racism, which functions to limit their economic potentials, renders them unable to move out of Black ghettos, or to improve conditions in them.

Racism and poverty interact in such a dynamic way that directly or indirectly they distort every aspect of life in the Black ghetto and tarnish our national image. On the one hand, they are the primary source of many of the complex, debilitating, unique survival problems characteristic of the Black ghetto. On the other hand, they limit the range and effectiveness of social strategies and techniques available to Blacks for the solution of these problems.

Physical characteristics of the ghetto. Compared to other areas of the city occupied by the more affluent segments of the population, the Black ghetto is physically ugly. Only 6.3 percent of Blacks in the central city own the dwellings they occupy, compared to 41.9 percent of whites who live in central cities.[5] The rented houses they live in are usually old and dilapidated. A very large proportion of them are located in unzoned, transitional neighborhoods where businesses and industries are progressively invading. It is not at all uncommon to find unsightly commercial enterprises, such as junkyards, smelly markets, noisy eating places, and freight yards located in the same block as, and often adjacent to, dwelling units. Landlords are usually reluctant to make needed repairs on houses in unzoned areas because they plan eventually to sell or use the land for more profitable commercial ventures, and the tenants are seldom successful in forcing them to comply with even minimum housing standards. Therefore, the Kerner Commission in 1968 found that "decent housing remains a chronic problem for the disadvantaged urban household. . . . Nearly two-thirds live in neighborhoods marked by substandard housing and general urban blight."[6] This was found to be especially true in cities with large Black populations.

Since the demand for any sort of housing is so great in Black ghettos, landlords usually receive exorbitant rents for quite substandard dwellings. Again, the Kerner Commission concluded: "Negroes in large cities are often forced to pay the same rents as whites and receive less for their money, or pay higher rents for the same accommodations."[7]

Most of the families in the sample were hard pressed to pay rent on their substandard houses. Some lived in constant fear that their landlords would increase their rent—in which case they would have to find cheaper housing or move in with some other family. Some parents interviewed were afraid to ask their landlord to make badly needed repairs because they were afraid that he might retaliate by raising the rent.

Ironically, when asked "Are you satisfied with the house (or apartment) in which you live?" 63 percent of the family heads in the ghetto studied answered "yes." Interviews revealed that most who gave a positive answer actually meant that they could not afford to pay for better housing. Thus, 53 percent of those who first expressed satisfaction later said that they needed additional rooms or that their houses needed extensive repairing, new plumbing, and so forth. Also, some families had no clear conception of "adequate" or "good" housing according to generally established standards. The heads of such families had often grown up in rural areas or in some other slum where housing was even worse than it was when they were interviewed. Therefore, from a relative point of view they expressed satisfaction with present housing because it was at least better than what they had before—despite the fact that in some instances male and female teenage siblings had to sleep in the same room; children had no place set aside for study; young adults had no room set aside to entertain their friends; parents often had to share their bedroom with the children; and several family members (often 6 to 10) shared one bathroom.

There is seldom anything physically beautiful about the Black ghetto. Even the so called "modern apartments" in the target area were dilapidated and ugly, primarily because they were not well-kept. Housing officials acknowledged that the apartments needed extensive repairs but tended to blame tenants for either deliberately damaging or defacing their houses and fixtures or for not knowing how to use them properly. Tenants, of course, claimed that housing officials simply neglected to keep up the dwellings. They pointed to broken steps, unworkable doors, window panes not replaced, no paint jobs for years, inoperative toilets, and various other evidences of neglect by housing authorities or landlords.

When asked why they did not try to grow flowers and make

their yards more beautiful, some parents pointed out that the large number of children in the neighborhood had no supervised playgrounds or recreational facilities and had to use available yards in which to play. They simply trampled down anything growing, and it was difficult to prevent them from defacing property. This particular ghetto situation is obviously quite typical of Black ghettos generally. It is certainly well-described in the following vivid description by St. Clair Drake:

Black Ghettos in America are, on the whole "run down" in appearance and overcrowded, and their inhabitants bear the physical and psychological scars of those whose "life chances" are not equal to those of other Americans. . . . They inherit the worst housing in the city. . . . white "flight to the suburbs" has released relatively new and well-kept property on the margins of some of the old Black Belts. Here "gilded ghettos" have grown up . . . But the character of the Black ghetto is not set by the newer "gilded" . . . but by the older sections.[8]

Then Drake gives an insightful glimpse into the way of life in these racially segregated neighborhoods:

The "ghettorization" of the Negro has resulted in the emergence of a ghetto subculture with a distinct ethos. . . . For the average Negro who walks the streets of any American Black ghetto, the smell of barbecued ribs, fried shrimps and chicken emanating from numerous restaurants gives olfactory reinforcement to a feeling of "at-homeness." The beat of "gut music" . . . and the sound of tambourines and rich harmony [from] storefront churches gives auditory confirmation to the universal belief that "We Negroes have soul." The bedlam of an occasional brawl. . . . the whine of police sirens. . . . the spontaneous vigor of the children. . . . and the cheerful rushing about of adults, free from the occupational pressures of the "white world" in which they work, create an atmosphere of warmth and superficial intimacy which obscures the unpleasant facts of life in the overcrowded rooms behind doors, the lack of adequate maintenance standards, and the too prevalent vermin and rats.[9]

There are, then, two fundamental facts common to Black ghettos: they are geographically distinct, segregated areas ("on the other side of the railroad tracks") within central cities, and they are characterized by a more or less well developed, unique subculture that articulates a desperate survival motif. Their geographical and cultural distinctiveness, which is an ultimate result of institutionalized racism, in turn exacerbates that same racism because it tends to reinforce old traditional, anti-Black stereotypes and attitudes. Therefore, ghettorized Blacks have come to symbolize precisely those traits regarded as evil, ugly, discordant, and undesirable in our national life and culture. They are intentionally or unintentionally treated as outsiders, foreigners, or even enemies by established institutions and socially powerful individuals in both the public and private sectors of American life.

Since Blacks are associated with the evils (poverty, powerlessness, crime, etc.) that "good" citizens would reject or purge, they, like some other disadvantaged minorities in history, often suffer most at the hands of otherwise good, "solid," hardworking, fair-minded citizens and groups who are sincerely concerned about their progress. In their desire to build a good society, they are likely to develop a consuming intolerance of ideas, values, and people that differ from their often narrow conception of good. This means that some of the most intelligent, circumspect, influential leaders in this country, representing all basic social institutions and walks of life, have always constituted the greatest survival threat for the Black poor who live among them. As a rule, their main indignation is directed against the unfortunate people who suffer from the "evils" they despise rather than against the evils per se. Thus, as noted earlier, some powerful white leaders in our national life are constantly criticizing and persecuting the Black unemployed and underemployed without ever coming to grips with inherent injustices in an economic system that presupposes a backlog of unemployed indigent workers, unequal distribution of opportunity, and blatant racial discrimination—all of which are the ultimate causes of the Black ghetto.

This phenomenon, whereby unfortunate minority groups come to symbolize the evils in the larger society, has been analyzed by Nevitt Sanford and Craig Comstock:

> From the beginning of our history American society has been based on exclusion and repression—First, the intrapsychic repression of rejected impulses. . . . Originally this distinction was put in religious terms: the elect against the reprobate. Later, the distinction was between moral upstanding members of the community and the lazy and recalcitrant. Finally, it was a distinction between the successful and the failures.
>
> At every stage there has been a tendency to equate these distinctions with that between good and bad. . . . Any action taken against groups seen to be evil is justified. . . . Thus, in America the enslavement of Blacks, the mass murder of Indians, the lynching of Negroes, the atom bombing of Japanese, and the massacring of Vietnamese have all had their defenders.
>
> In America we have not been able to establish effective controls over aggression against a variety of powerless outgroups. . . . The American Negro has received more brutality and aggression from the majority population over a longer period of time than have all other groups combined. . . . The Negro is punished, restricted and reviled in order symbolically to help the white man to keep his self-control.[10]

Thus, inhabitants of Black ghettos are not just physically isolated as much as possible from the mainstream of life in the cities in which they are located, but they also tend to be psychologically alienated as well. Most are simply too poor to participate in the cultural, recreational, and organizational activities of the more affluent middle class. When they attempt to do so, they usually display certain mannerisms that automatically identify them with the despised ghetto subculture, and they are then subjected to various forms of rebuff and frustrating embarrassment. They know that they are stereotyped by many middle-class persons as "underprivileged," "culturally deprived," and "socially disadvantaged," and resent being treated as inferior outsiders or tolerated as strangers or "foreigners" in their own country, even their own neighborhoods. Consequently, just about all residents of the Black ghetto, even those who occupy the "gilded" sections, tend to withdraw from contacts with white people unless it is necessary or at least expected. Few, indeed, are fully participating members of white churches, recreational groups, forums, political factions, citizens committees, neighborhood organizations, or local chapters of professional groups. Those who do participate usually limit their contacts with whites to a secondary level. Seldom do Black members of predominantly white groups belong to the inner circle that determines the direction and ultimate goals of these groups. When they are invited to participate in the inner circle, they are generally expected to concern themselves primarily with issues and concerns that directly impinge upon the Black community, not with those of the wider community.

Though there are many dimensions and ramifications of the Black Experience, they all come to focus in the Black ghetto family. Let us, then, examine some basic aspects of the Black Experience from the point of view of the ghetto studied in New Orleans.

The Ghettorized Black Family

The research reported here validates a basic hypothesis: At the core of the Black ghetto subculture is the Black family. It is not only the primary source of the Black Experience, but it is, itself, the cardinal Black Experience. No significant aspect of life in the Black community can be adequately understood apart from the varying structure and flexible role of the Black family. Today, complex historical forces, contemporary social problems emanating from the lag between fantastic technological advancements and relatively slow, erratic, positive social changes, together with the rapid urbanization of Blacks during and after World War II, have conspired to make the Black ghetto family a major focus of extensive political, economic, and scholarly concern. This is so because it is now generally understood that the influence of the Black ghetto family far transcends the more or less segregated Black community. It is now quite clear to trained observers that the quality of life in American society at large will continue to be significantly affected by the quality of life in the Black ghetto, which is inextricably enmeshed in the larger society.

An excellent example of how the Black ghetto family interacts with other basic institutions and agencies in the larger society, and thereby influences national policy which transcends Black interests, is the welfare system in the United States. The welfare system is, of course, designed to extend aid to indigent individuals and families. Blacks are greatly overrepresented among the nation's poor. According to the very conservative definition of poverty established by the U. S. Social Security Administration, in 1970 there were 7.7 million Blacks and 17.5 million whites whose income placed them below the poverty level. This means that 9 percent of the white population and 34 percent of the Black population were eligible for public welfare.[11] Therefore, Blacks who constitute about 11 percent of the population account for a third of the poor. The poverty rate among Blacks is three times as high as would normally be expected.

Since Blacks are so greatly overrepresented among the poor, as would be expected they are overrepresented among welfare recipients because *poor Blacks are poorer than poor whites*. In 1969, only 8 percent of white families had incomes under $3,000, compared with 20 percent of all Black families in that income bracket. Therefore, about 17 percent of the Black population were receiving public assistance in 1969.

The majority of Black and white families and unrelated individuals *eligible* for welfare do not in fact receive public assistance: only 35 percent of eligible Blacks and 14 percent of eligible whites receive welfare. Moreover, only 10.8 million of the 25.2 million—just 43 percent—of those who were officially eligible for public assistance in 1969 had ever received it.

> Less than two-fifths of the poor receive aid from any of these [fifty different assistance programs]. Because programs are restricted to specific categories, many poor persons are excluded entirely. . . . Eligibility is determined by an income which falls below a minimum standard set by the state of residence, membership in an aid category, and a variety of nonfinancial tests. . . . States have been free to apply these criteria despite the fact that most of the programs' costs are paid by the Federal Government. . . . Many regulations have operated to treat welfare recipients as a class apart; they have imposed restrictions on recipients that would not be enforceable if applied to the general public under civil law.[12]

The Kerner Report held that a major cause for the urban riots during the latter part of the 1960s was the unjust, poorly administered welfare system. Everywhere welfare recipients gave concrete evidence of arbitrary, punitive eligibility requirements, ranging from unrealistic residency requirements (some states require up to five years) and the taking into account of the income of relatives (e.g., grandparents), to the so-called man-in-the-house rule, according to which a woman and her dependent children will be denied eligibility or be dropped from the welfare roll if a man, not necessarily her husband, is found, even temporarily, residing in the house with her. Furthermore, according to certain regulations, welfare applicants as well as recipients may be required to answer, for public records, embarrassing, even incriminating, personal questions. In some states, visiting social workers and special welfare investigators are expected to subject welfare recipients to invasion of privacy or illegal search.[13] Every year some new, punitive measures are established by state legislatures.

According to all available evidence, the vast majority of Americans, including some powerful decision-makers, erroneously regard the welfare program in this country as essentially a "Black relief program." *This is so despite the fact that over 60 percent of all welfare recipients are white*. This fallacious assumption is widely publicized by politicians who desire to unite a "white backlash" composed of anti-civil rights, anti-federal taxes, and anti-Black individuals and groups. They have had considerable success in perpetuating the myth that "Black" equals "welfare." A Black face or some pathetic Black situation is very likely to appear on the covers of books, magazines, pamphlets, and official reports in which the welfare system is a main topic of discussion.

Labeling the welfare program "Black" has created nationwide consternation among white citizens who react by supporting political candidates who advocate the kinds of undemocratic, punitive welfare rules and procedures just mentioned. This, then, is only another example of how the white response to the Black presence tends to influence patterns of national behavior that have consequences far beyond the Black community per se. Thus, nearly all national polls in which the welfare issue is raised, "on the spot" interviews in formal and informal settings, numerous political speeches, and the 1972 landslide presidential election, where the welfare philosophy and system was a major domestic issue—all attest to the Black stereotyping of public welfare programs in this country. Generally, voters who were avowedly anti-Black or anti-civil rights were also antiwelfare. They obviously accepted the projected image of the welfare recipients as "cheater," "loafer," "deadbeat," "immoral," "criminal," "parasitic," and "Black."

Bitter criticism of the welfare system, particularly welfare recipients, during the last decade has resulted in numerous official investigations by independent individuals, private groups, welfare agencies, and the government on all levels. Any number of "white papers" have been issued from these investigations. Generally, these investigations were originally intended to expose allegedly extensive, flagrant cheating and dishonesty on the part of public welfare recipients. However, the most authoritative of these investigations discovered that even when all local and national eligibility technicalities are rigidly applied, only 2 to 5 percent of welfare recipients fail to qualify for the kind and amount of benefits received.

After an extensive examination of the welfare system in the United States and a careful assessment of arguments supporting charges that welfare rolls are swollen by "deadbeats" and "chiselers," Whitney Young, the late director of the National Urban League, concluded:

> Often citizens have curious misconceptions about typical relief recipients and resent paying money to "all those able-bodied men." It should be noted that approximately nine out of ten persons who receive assistance is either too young or too old to work, is disabled or busy caring for youngsters who are receiving ADC—aid to dependent

children. Of the remaining 10 percent, most want real jobs rather than work relief or welfare subsistence.[14]

In another connection, he added: "Most of these charges turn out to be unfounded because, contrary to ill-informed public thinking, the honesty of welfare recipients is significantly higher than that of the general population."[15]

There are at least two primary reasons why so many whites bitterly oppose not only the present welfare system in this country, but the necessity of welfare as well. (1) They have a strong tendency to deny the existence of the evil of poverty which public assistance programs emphasize, and (2) welfare programs aid a larger proportion of Blacks than whites. Therefore, they are eager to find a plausible basis for open opposition to any existing or proposed welfare program. The general public, as well as some scholars, concur with the recklessly sweeping, distorted generalization made by Daniel P. Moynihan that "at the heart of the deterioration of the fabric of Negro society is the deterioration of the Negro family."[16] According to his assessment the Black family is the ultimate cause of all the problems besetting the Black ghetto. This point of view would logically exempt the white community of any responsibility for Black poverty or obligation to pay for Black welfare.

There is mounting evidence that neither the "fabric of Negro society" nor the "Negro family" is as deteriorated as Moynihan and his ilk of intemperate evaluators of the Black Experience would lead us to believe. The fact is, during the 1960s, when Blacks were accorded somewhat greater freedom than in previous decades, Black progress in most crucial areas of American life—education, income, community and political participation, and homeownership—was greater than the progress made by whites.[17] Instead of indicating a deteriorating Black family, the impressive progress made by some Blacks during the last decade strongly supports the main findings of the study of the Black ghetto in New Orleans, namely, that the

Black family—because of its long history in dealing with social crises stemming from racism and its unique flexibility—is the most effective instrument Blacks have had in their precarious struggle to survive in American society.

The role of the ghettorized black family. In an attempt to evaluate the role of the family in the Black ghetto in New Orleans, we were guided by four basic propositions:

1. Certain traits and behavior patterns characteristic of the ghetto subculture may, on the one hand, facilitate the survival and progress of Blacks, while, on the other hand, alienate Blacks from the ultimate source of their primary security—the larger white society. In other words, in a biracial society based upon dominant-submissive ethics, what is "good" for the subject race is not necessarily "good" for the dominant race.

2. Some traits and patterns of behavior which the dominant race would impose upon certain members of the subject race may be functional for their individual survival and advancement, but may be dysfunctional for racial welfare and progress on the whole. While this principle may apply to many different Black-white situations, it is especially apropos when applied to the ways whereby Black leadership is manipulated by white men of influence or wielders of social power.

3. Fundamentally, the Black ghetto is a result and a manifestation of a complex of negative social forces emanating from American society at large. Individuals and families in the ghetto are ipso facto severely limited, insofar as personal and social resources are concerned, in dealing with the many threatening problems inherent in ghetto living. All too many are apt to surrender and become hopeless victims of prevailing untoward circumstances.

4. In order to better cope with the wide variety of problems common to all poor people in the United States, as well as numerous unique problems stemming from their blackness, Black families have had to be unusually inventive and flexible regarding their hierarchy of values, family structure, and the content of family roles.

Family size. The average Black family is large. This was especially true of the sample families in the New Orleans ghetto. While the average white family in the United States is composed of 3.6 persons, the average Black family has 4.8 persons.[18] The average family in the Black ghetto in question was composed of 5 or 6 persons. Hence, it was about 40 percent larger than the average white family in the United States.

The large number of children in Black ghetto families is regarded as a very serious problem by government representatives and agencies on all levels, demographers, and many economists. It is viewed as a special evil by antiwelfare leaders and a majority of the white electorate. Some powerful politicians repeatedly accuse Black women of deliberately having a large number of children in order to qualify for larger welfare benefits. This is, of course, a very dubious, shallow explanation of the relatively high birth rate among poor, Black women.

According to information we obtained from the mothers themselves and from intensive observations in the New Orleans ghetto, there are at least five interrelated reasons why Black ghetto families are large:

1. About two-thirds of the mothers in the sample obviously loved children. Researchers for this study witnessed deep and varied dimensions of parental love evinced by these women. There were touching, sentimental manifestations, and numerous examples of love that were revealed through the amazing psychological strength of the mothers. We saw this in relationships between women and small children—with mischievous children, with children who had experienced failure and disappointment, with ill children, with delinquent children under arrest or before the courts, with adult children who were parents themselves, and with children who lived antisocial, criminal lives.

The love most mothers had for their children was obvious, even when some ambivalence was expressed. Some mothers who complained most about the behavior of their children and about how they had to sacrifice for their children were those who had spoiled their children through indulgent, pampered love.

2. Motherhood is an honorable status in the Black ghetto. Children born into an already impoverished home do tend to complicate strenuous living conditions. Nevertheless, only 43 percent of the mothers had ever practiced any form of birth control at the time of the interviews, despite the fact that most had been advised, often pressured, to do so by representatives of welfare agencies.

To many women in the Black ghetto, motherhood is about the only truly honorable, creative role in which they can reasonably hope to participate. All other roles normally open to them are either socially unrecognized, unsung, or disesteemed. Therefore, when asked why she refused to limit the number of children she had, a welfare mother of six reasoned: "Having babies is a natural god-given thing to do. A normal woman wants children. That's how you know you are a real woman. How would you like it if your mother had stopped you from being born?"

The honorable status of motherhood in the ghetto subculture was noted by David Schulz in his study of a northern Black ghetto—Pruitt-Igoe:

> Common themes in the conversation of the women of the project concern the problems and pleasures of raising children. . . . the woman in the ghetto is closely identified with the home, with kin and the continuity of her family, and with more respectable institutions such as the church and school, all of which tend to substantiate an almost unchallengeable respectability about motherhood.[19]

In the Black ghetto, which is generally characterized by anonymity, alienation, disorganization, and powerlessness, motherhood is the only reliable symbol of belongingness, strength, and stability.

3. Despite the fact that they expressed some serious fears

and ambivalence, most of the men interviewed apparently wanted their wives or mistresses to have babies. Some obviously wanted children as a means of validating their manhood. They often boasted about the number of children women had had for them. This is to be expected because the ghetto subculture places great value upon sexual prowess and virility. The phrase "I am a man," so often repeated by Black men, is not simply ghetto rhetoric—it is a concept with deep historical and psychological roots. It is a sort of reassuring proclamation that somehow they have preserved their manhood in spite of centuries of strong, constant, prevailing emasculatory social forces endemic in the role of the Black male in American society. Therefore, even when they are unable to support their children, some men insist that their wives should not practice birth control.

A full discussion of this subject was presented in a three-generational study in 1960. The authors held that:

> While the matriarchy and the gang (loosely organized Black males in the ghetto) agree that sex is the most important of all social categories, it is clear that sex is seen in quite different terms by the two groups. What is for the woman a matter of preserving family solidarity becomes for the man a question of individual assertive virility.[20]

Of course, the best evidence of this virility is to be the father of several children.

4. There is a reluctance to practice birth control. In many cases even the mothers (43 percent) who had practiced birth control tended to express some ambivalence. Some felt that it was ethically wrong; others feared that the "pill" and other methods were dangerous. A few concurred with a position succinctly expressed by an unmarried mother of three:

> All of this talk we hear today about the pill is just another plot by white folks to get rid of Negroes. Ever since I got

on welfare white doctors and social workers have been trying hard to get me to take things so I won't have babies. They have been talking to other women I know about the same thing. White people will do anything to get rid of us. They won't do it to me. I won't let them.

It is difficult to conclude how many Black women, despite pressures from professional and political sources, refuse to practice birth control because of this genocidal fear. Anyway they tend to reject the theory that the best way to improve their own economic status is to drastically reduce the size of their families. Instead they see children as a long-range investment.

5. Although no definite count was made—because it was a "serendipity finding" revealed after most of the interviews were completed—all interviewers observed that most of the mothers regarded children as valuable insurance against unemployment, illness, and old age. Some made outright statements to that effect, and others implied it in numerous indirect statements. For example, one mother who cared for her unmarried daughter's children and insisted upon listening to the interview sessions volunteered this information: "God has blessed me. I raised my children to look after me when I got old. Now I don't have to want for things." Another mother implied the same thing when she expresssed sympathy for a lonely aged woman who lived next door to her:

I feel sorry for her. When she was young she lived a fast life (a prostitute) and didn't take time to have children. Now she sits there alone day after day. When she is sick there is no one to give her a glass of water or a mouthful to eat. I don't know what she would do without me and my mother. We do what we can for her.

It may well be that the instinct for personal survival and the fear of helplessness and loneliness are the most fundamental, primitive reasons for the family. For those in this sample, they are certainly basic, realistic reasons for having children. They are quite knowledgeable about the horrible reputation of "old folks homes," or "convalescent homes" for Black people. Some young mothers or daughters who cared for their own mothers (or grandmothers or other aged female relatives) said that they did so because "I couldn't stand to see my mother locked up in one of those terrible places"; "I just couldn't face myself if I put her [an aunt] away like she is dirt. She's been too good to me"; "What sort of tramp could just stand by and see her mother rot in one of those places. I've been told that they slap those old people around whenever they want to"; "I know a girl who took some food to her mother. Those other old people were so hungry that they snatched it away from her before she could even open it. I hear that those poor people go days at a time without getting one good, hot meal."

As allegedly dismal and frustrating as the homes for the aged are, apparently it is very difficult to have old people committed to them because of a long waiting list. Consequently, children assure their parents, especially the mother, that she will not be cast aside and forgotten when she is too old or infirm to care for herself. This is doubly significant to women such as those in the sample, who do not qualify for federal social security because, as domestic workers, their occupation is not covered and who will not receive retirement benefits.

We may conclude that, by and large, Black parents in the ghetto, more than is true of affluent parents, need children to validate their sexual identities; to give them a feeling of possession; to afford them a sense of responsibility, power, and usefulness; to project their frustrated egos; to provide a means of security otherwise denied them; and to give them a grasp upon immortality.

The personal and social need for children expressed particularly by Black ghetto mothers is much more characteristic of agrarian societies than of modern, urban, industrial societies. This is because poor Blacks have not had ample opportunity to participate in or enjoy the sophisticated technological advancements of American society. The vast majority of the Black masses still occupy the tenuous bottom rung of our industrial ladder and encounter, by far, the most difficult survival problems. They are usually shut off from the ordinary securities inherent in a highly developed industrial society, such as labor union protection, unemployment benefits, insurance against illness, and retirement benefits. Their need for children is similar to what the average American family's was in a preindustrial economy. Therefore, like the *proletarians* of the Industrial Revolution, the propertyless Black masses have no "wealth" or reasonable security except their offsprings. As long as this is so, we may continue to expect the Black ghetto family to be about 30 to 40 percent larger than the average American family.[21]

NOTES

[1]The research project was under the direction of Daniel C. Thompson. Barbara M. Guillory coordinated the field work, and Dillard University students did most of the interviewing. Also of special importance is the study by John H. Rohrer, Munro S. Edmonson, Daniel C. Thompson, et al., *The Eighth Generation* (New York: Harper and Brothers, Publishers, 1960). Other studies will be cited in their proper context.

[2]U. S. Department of Commerce and Bureau of the Census, *The Social and Economic Status of Negroes in the United States*, Bureau of Labor Statistics, Report No. 394 (1970), pp. 9-19.

[3]Robert E. Forman, *Black Ghettos, White Ghettos, and Slums* (Englewood Cliffs, N. J.: Prentice-Hall, Inc., 1971), p. 3.

[4]Jacob K. Javits, *Discrimination U. S. A.* (New York: Washington Square Press, Inc., 1962), p. 118.

[5]U. S. Department of Commerce, *Statistical Abstract of the United States*, 1972, Bureau of the Census. Table 1158, p. 689.

[6]*U. S. Riot Commission Report* (New York: The New York Times Co., 1968), pp. 467-472.

[7]Ibid., p. 472.

[8]St. Clair Drake, "Social and Economic Status of the Negro in the United States," in *Daedalus* 94, No. 4 (Fall, 1965): 777-778.

[9]Ibid., p. 778.

[10]Nevitt Sanford and Craig Comstock, *Sanctions for Evil* (San Francisco: Jossey-Bass, Inc., Publishers, 1971), pp. 184-185.

[11]Data in this connection were taken from U. S. Department of Commerce, Bureau of the Census, *The Social and Economic Status of Negroes in the United States, 1970*, pp. 23-43.

[12]The President's Commission on Income Maintenance Programs, *Poverty Amid Plenty: The American Paradox* (Washington, D. C.: U.S. Government Printing Office, 1969), p. 116.

[13]National Advisory Commission on Civil Disorders, *U. S. Riot Commission Report*, pp. 459-461. See also Daniel C. Thompson, "New Orleans and the Riot Report," *New Orleans Magazine* (Official Publication of the New Orleans Chamber of Commerce), June 1968, pp. 11, 24.

[14]Whitney M. Young, Jr., *To Be Equal* (New York: McGraw-Hill Book Co., 1964), p. 165.

[15]Whitney M. Young, Jr., *Beyond Racism: Building an Open Society* (New York: McGraw-Hill Book Co., 1969), p. 38.

[16]*The Negro: A Case for National Action* (Washington, D. C.: U.S. Department of Labor, Office of Planning and Research, March 1965), p. 5.

[17]Data validating this conclusion can be found in the U. S. Department of Commerce, Bureau of the Census, *The Social and Economic Status of Negroes in the United States*, passim.

[18] *The Social and Economic Status of Negroes in the United States*, p. 40, Table 31.

[19]David A. Schulz, *Coming Up Black* (Englewood Cliffs, N. J.: Prentice-Hall, Inc., 1969), pp. 21, 180.

[20]John H. Rohrer, Munro S. Edmonson, Daniel C. Thompson, et al., *The Eighth Generation*, p. 160, passim.

[21]*The Social and Economic Status of Negroes in the United States*, p. 40, Table 31. Black Families classified as poor have 4.8 members. White families so classified have just 3.6 members.

4

The Black Ghetto: Socialization

Socialization is a process of teaching and learning whereby the child becomes an integral part of a well-defined social world that centers around the family. A systematic three-generational study of personality development of Black youth in New Orleans revealed that they were socialized in such ways that they tended to identify with one of at least five different "social worlds" within the Black community: the middle class, matriarchy, gang, nuclear family, and marginality. Insofar as the personality development of the subjects used in that study was concerned, their particular social world was a far more significant social and psychological reality than race, the ghetto subculture, or the geographic area in which they were reared.[1] Therefore, contrary to what is often assumed, the Black ghetto is not a social and cultural monolith. Though criteria of social differentiation and stratification are often quite subtle and may be overlooked or misunderstood by the "outsider," indigenous individuals and families recognize meaningful status hierarchies and distinct social worlds within the ghetto. This was evident in practically every interview conducted in the study of the New Orleans ghetto. For instance, the most general concern

88

expressed by parents was that their children would be negatively influenced by "bad" or "lower class" children in the neighborhood. An interviewer wrote this comment into her report: "This family is obviously lower class in every respect, yet the mother is terribly afraid that she will not continue to be able to prevent her children from playing with 'lower class children' in her neighborhood. As it is now she keeps them in the house as much as possible."

A close examination of social values in the Black ghetto subculture will reveal that meaningful social rankings are often made according to such subtle criteria as marital status of parents, employment status of father and/or mother, the presence or absence of police records for family members, the characteristic way children relate to parents, behavior of children in the school or community, the way parents behave in public, the status of the employers for whom adult family members work, how well children dress when they go to school, how often family members attend church, the religious denomination to which parents belong, the achievements of parents and adult children, and fine differences in the levels of respectability and general style of life.

The central figures in the socialization process in the Black ghetto, as is true in the society at large, are the father and mother. Their formal and informal preparation to cope with prevailing social forces and the personal problems encountered by their children will determine, in large measure, the personality development and social skills of their children. Both the nature of social forces and the personal problems with which parents must deal will vary widely from one family to another and from one time to another with a given family. Consequently, there is no universally established set of norms or role prescriptions according to which the parents can be judged. Black parents, like all other parents, must make many independent, unique decisions about what is "good" or "bad" for their children. Actually, the nature and effectiveness of the parental role seem to vary according to several interrelated factors.

Among the most significant are parents' social background, level of education, economic status, marital status, social outlook, availability of supporting individuals, agencies, and institutions, and the complex of unique experiences they have had. Of course, hardly any two parents, including spouses, ever conceive of the parental role in exactly the same way, nor are they equally prepared to perform that role as they conceive it.

On the basis of information gathered in the study of the Black ghetto of central concern here, we may conclude that *there is a definite correlation between parents' socialization practices and what they perceive as the nature of the primary survival problems with which a particular child may be called upon to deal in the process of growing up*. Thus, in order to better understand socialization in the Black ghetto, it is essential to examine the status of parents in terms of their socioeconomic background, their social outlook, and their ability to perceive and deal with the problems their children characteristically encounter.

The Father

In most societies, especially American society, the father has historically been regarded by law and tradition as head of the household. This status imposes upon him the primary or ultimate responsibility to make decisions regarding the economic, social, and psychological welfare of his wife and children. He is designated as the chief breadwinner and also as the primary or even exclusive link between his family and the larger society of which they are a part and with which they must interact. Despite much rhetoric about the inherent equality of the sexes, the rights of children, and some significant changes in the status and role of women and children during the last generation, the de facto role of the father in American society today is essentially what it has been throughout the history of this nation—he is still regarded by law and tradition as head of the household.

When compared with the ''ideal'' role of the father in American society generally, the specific role of Black fathers in the ghetto varies considerably. (The concept "ideal" as used here is a sociological norm and does not mean to express "superior" or the "best" standard as would be true in philosophy and other disciplines.) In many instances, the term is poorly defined and ineffectual insofar as the socialization of children is concerned. In other instances, fathers seem to make every effort to live up to all of the expected behavior standards prescribed for the ideal father. Yet, no matter how hard they may try, many, perhaps most, fathers in the Black ghetto fail to perform their role according to long-established standards expected of fathers in American society. There are, of course, several reasons for this failure. In this connection let us consider two of the most salient reasons: chronic economic insecurity and inadequate education. Together, these two handicaps render the typical ghetto father relatively powerless in dealing with the ordinary problems of family life and ineffective in protecting family members from the strong, persistent negative pulls and forces they experience in the local community and the larger society.

Chronic economic insecurity. As is well known, throughout the more than 200 years of slavery Black fathers and their families were regarded as mere chattel. They were unable to assume any significant responsibility for their children. They could be completely and permanently separated from their families at the pleasure of their masters. Slave masters usurped the traditional role of the father as the sole provider and protector of the Black family. Black children were robbed of nearly all long-established bases for respecting their fathers. The Black father's role was at best tenuous and informal. The mother, with little help from the father, was expected to socialize the child to fit into the slave society—not to develop its human potentialities, as was expected of white children.

During the 110 years since emancipation, Black men have been continually shackled and frustrated by the deeply entrenched, complex white racism and adverse socioeconomic forces—all of which have seriously militated against their fulfillment of traditional masculine roles, especially fatherhood. The vast majority of them have therefore been relegated to the bottom rung of the economic ladder in American society. They have generally been allowed to hold only the lowest paying of lower status jobs. Any significant move within the Black community or by the federal government to elevate the economic status of Blacks has always caused great anxiety among whites and has generated a counter movement or "backlash" among whites on all social class levels.[2] The basic and tacit rationale that upper-class white employers have for discriminating against Black employees is the doctrine of "white supremacy" to which many conform. This doctrine holds that all white people, in all situations, must be socially superior to all Black people. Accordingly, white employers usually employ Blacks to fill the lowest ranks in all job categories. Though some significant changes are underway, this pattern of discrimination still prevails throughout the economic system, including employment in top business and professional categories. Blacks, as a group, are prevented from achieving the degree of economic success that would be expected in an open, democratic society where they could compete as equals. Therefore, as suggested above, though motivated by somewhat different social class interests, white Americans have participated in an economic conspiracy to keep Black Americans from attaining the degree of economic security normally enjoyed in this country.

According to all formal and popular opinion studies, white upper-class individuals, especially in the South, are essentially conservative. Usually, they can be expected to oppose all basic and even minor changes in the status quo, if they are likely to become a basic force for change. Perhaps the most logical explanation for this opposition is the fact that whites feel that in the present social system they have much to lose and little to gain. They already occupy the highest social class status and thereby enjoy a wide range of special rights, honors, and privileges. They evidently fear that any truly significant change, such as might flow from the equality of economic opportunity for Blacks, would have negative consequences for their dominant position and would interfere with their characteristic affluence.

Closely related to the upper class's conception of itself as deserving special status in society is the deeply rooted belief in the theory of the "mudsill." According to this theory, Blacks should constitute the bottom layer of American society, the extreme top layer being composed of the white upper class. The Blacks' primary duties, then, should be to perform the necessary but unpleasant, less rewarding tasks in a society based upon a hierarchy of statuses and privileges. They should be the proverbial "hewers of wood and drawers of water."[3]

The long economic dependency of the great masses of Blacks upon the upper-class, more affluent, whites has resulted in an unequal, exploitative, symbionic relationship in which upper-class whites have become accustomed to commanding the abundant supply of largely unorganized, cheap, and servile labor found primarily in the Black community. They are predictably disturbed by any federal policy or program that would likely reduce that supply of dependent workers. Myrdal observed this a generation ago when he said: "When the Negro rises socially and is no longer a servant, he becomes a stranger to the white upper class. His ambition is suspected. He is disliked."[4]

In recent years, the persistent fear of losing this vast reservoir of Black labor has been repeatedly manifested in the bitter opposition to federal equal employment proposals, programs, and legislation, existing and proposed welfare programs, as well as all other measures designed to guarantee a decent level of social security to poor people. The majority of upper-class whites, especially the top decision-makers, apparently favor an economic system in which the poor, particularly the Black masses, would be forced to accept the most menial, unpleasant, insecure employment offered them.[5] This has always resulted in what the Kerner Report found to be true in several selected cities with large Black populations:

> Even more important perhaps than unemployment is the related problem of the undesirable nature of many jobs open to Negroes. Negro workers are concentrated in the lowest-skilled and lowest-paying occupations. These jobs often involve substandard wages, great instability and uncertainty of tenure, extremely low status in the eyes of both employer and employee, little or no chance for meaningful advancement, and unpleasant or exhausting duties. . . . The concentration of male Negro employment at the lowest end of the occupational scale is the single most important source of poverty among Negroes.[6]

Historically, the proletarian masses of whites have also employed a variety of strategies calculated to prevent Black men from acquiring equal employment in the United States. Again, the doctrine of white supremacy is the basic rationale. Paul Baran and Paul Sweezy put it this way: "The gratification which whites derive from their socio-economic superiority to Negroes has its counter part in alarm, anger, and even panic at the prospect of Negroes' attaining equality. . . . whites inevitably interpret upward movement by Negroes as downward movement for themselves."[7] However, white workers' opposition to the equality of employment of Blacks is motivated by more than ideological myths. There is much evidence that they believe that any advancement of Black workers will have to be at their expense; that when a Black man is employed on a given job, some white worker will be displaced; that when a Black worker is promoted, some white worker will be passed over or demoted—that in general all equal employment programs will mean immediate and long-range displacement of white workers.

The white worker's fear of Black competition is reflected in the fact that organized labor in this country has always been inherently anti-Black, despite the often-repeated democratic public statements and formal written documents of fair employment policies. Techniques of discrimination range from outright de facto exclusion by some unions and segregated locals to deliberate policies and rules limiting the number and influence of Black workers. The latter is most effectively accomplished through union control of apprenticeship-training programs.[8]

In attempts to counter the powerful anti-Black forces in labor unions, Blacks have employed several strategies. Among the most effective are protest, diplomacy or cultivation of influential white allies within the top labor ranks, litigation, and pressure from well-organized Black caucuses. They have made significant gains but most of the barriers to equal employment for Blacks remain quite formidable. Recent efforts to guarantee racial quotas for certain basic industries—whereby Blacks would constitute approximately the same proportion of employees in all occupational ranks as in the total population —would certainly create an economic breakthrough for Black workers. However, this proposal is meeting very strong opposition, even from some racially liberal whites, because of the traditionally negative connotation of the quota concept. Historically, it has been used to limit the number of minority persons in educational institutions and in certain industries. It is, of course, opposed by management who insists that it should be left alone to employ whomever it pleases. It is also bitterly opposed by white-dominated organized labor because white workers fear they might become victims of a kind of reverse discrimination when it comes to employment and promotion practices, since in practically all industries Blacks fall far short of the number a quota system would require. It is, therefore, very unlikely that there will be, any time soon, an established quota system in industry or government favoring Blacks. However, one conclusion seems certain: until a more equitable system of employment is established, Blacks, especially males, will have to continue to fight formidable opposition from organized labor, management, and public opinion.

The white middle class does not manifest as negative an ideological solidarity regarding the economic progress of Blacks as does the white working class. A powerful segment, however, particularly on the management levels of industry, is still a victim of old, deeply rooted racial prejudices that they have inherited from their working-class backgrounds. Therefore, while several large industries have endorsed "equal employment" ethics in general, little concrete changes have been made in de facto racial employment practices. They have various rationales for not implementing federal guidelines regarding minorities; moreover, a given industry will seldom go beyond minimum compliance. It is rare indeed when management voluntarily moves to equalize employment of Blacks without legal pressure. Thus, after reviewing the many variations of industry's stubborn resistance to equal employment, Herbert Hill concluded: "It is evident that prompt and forceful action is necessary to convince employers and labor unions that the United States government is in fact committed to equal employment opportunity as a basic national policy and the old policy of "voluntary compliance". . . . has come to an end."[9] So far the government has not exerted the force required; consequently, racial discrimination in employment continues, for the most part, as usual. The vast majority of Black men are still perpetually relegated to the bottom rung of the economic ladder; they are still largely employed in unskilled occupations, in dead-end jobs, and in declining industries. Baran and Sweezy summarize what seem to be the major factors involved in the perpetual "subproletariat" status of the Black masses. They contend that the following factors mutually interact to accentuate Black poverty and to keep Blacks locked into the ghetto:

1 Employers benefit from division in the labor force which enable them to play one group off against another, thus weakening all. Historically, for example, no small amount

of Negro migration was in direct response to the recruiting of strikebreakers.

2 Owners of ghetto real estate are able to overcrowd and overcharge.

3 Middle- and upper-income groups benefit from their large supply of cheap domestic labor.

4 Many small marginal businesses, especially in the service trades, can operate profitably only if cheap labor is available to them.

5 White workers benefit by being protected from the Negro competition for the more desirable and higher paying jobs—hence, the customary distinction, especially in the South, between "white" and "Negro" jobs, the exclusion of Negroes from apprentice programs, the refusal of many unions to admit Negroes, and so on.[10]

As suggested, nowhere in American society is economic discrimination and unequal distribution of opportunity as blatant as in Black ghettos, such as the one studied in New Orleans. While the unemployment rate for Blacks in the United States generally is reported to be twice as high as it is for whites,[11] it is perhaps three to four times as high in Black ghettos. The official Labor Department reports do not reflect this statistic primarily because they do not count many who are on relief and thousands of others who are not qualified for or do not receive public aid. Therefore, the National Urban League estimates that the actual rate of unemployment among Blacks is perhaps more than twice as high as the official reports indicate, or about 25 percent of the Black working population in 1963, when the official rate was 10.8 percent for Blacks.[12] If we extrapolate that estimate and apply it to the 1973 census data where Black unemployment was reported to be 10 percent, we would have an actual unemployment rate of about 20 percent, or severe depression insofar as the Black ghetto is concerned.

In the New Orleans ghetto, only 3 percent of the employed fathers were in white collar occupations; 17 percent held skilled jobs; and 80 percent were employed as unskilled or service workers. On the whole, they were not as well off occupationally as the total Black population, where, in 1970, 22 percent were white collar workers; 14 percent were in skilled jobs; and 64 percent were unskilled or service workers.[13]

It should be remembered that Blacks usually hold the lowest ranking jobs in all major categories. Thus, for example it is reported that "in the nine industries with relatively high hourly earnings, Negroes had 8 percent of the total employment but only 1 percent of the higher paid occupations. . . . Negroes had a smaller proportion of the higher paid jobs."[14]

Fathers in the sample, and the Black workers generally, expressed a great deal of frustration because of their feeling of entrapment at the bottom level of their occupational ladder. Some insisted that they were economically worse off now than ever before because of lower take-home-pay and their employment in jobs threatened by automation.

Consequently, a majority of the Black masses are employed in low-status, insecure jobs where the rate of unemployment is always uncommonly high. We found that the actual unemployment rate among the fathers in the sample was 25 percent and that 28 percent were on jobs where they earned less than the 1969 federal standard for poverty (a minimum of $3,743 annual income for a family of four). The median weekly income of the fathers in the sample was just $65, or an annual median of $3,380. This was lower than the 1969 national median income of $3,922 for Black men with less than an eighth-grade education. However, the median for the sample was about 23 percent less than that of all Black husbands in the South, which was $5,059 in 1970 and just a little more than 42 percent of the $7,927 median of white husbands in the South.[15]

It is an understatement merely to report that the majority of Black fathers are unable to support their families, even at the minimum level expected in American society generally or in their community. Thus, we may conclude that *according to available information, it is the chronic economic inadequacy of a majority of Black men—not the inherent dominant personality of Black women—which has compromised and weakened the role of the Black father in the socialization process.* Insofar as the fathers in the sample were concerned, there seemed to have been a definite correlation between their status in the home and the degree to which they contributed to the economic security of their families. Fathers who assumed the major economic support of their families tended also to assume the role as acknowledged head of the household. Those who contributed little, or whose contributions were unstable or sporadic, were usually accorded relatively lower status in the household. Some were treated more like visitors than fathers.[16]

Inadequate education and employment. The average father in the New Orleans ghetto had received only seven years of schooling. This is the same as that reported in a survey sponsored by the Louisiana State Board of Education in 1965. That survey found that the median years of schooling completed by Black males in the state, 25 years of age and over, was also just seven: 9.6 percent had finished high school, 2.8 percent had graduated from college, and 41.6 percent had completed only six years of schooling or less. The others, 46 percent, had dropped out of school between the seventh and twelfth grade. Comparatively, 22.8 percent of white males in that age category had finished high school, 10.1 percent had graduated from college, and the median years of schooling was 11.6, or almost five years more than the median for Black males in the state.[17]

Obviously, in comparison with local white men, with whom they must compete directly for the more stable, better paying jobs, the relatively low level of education or cognitive skills obtained by fathers in the Black ghetto is woefully inadequate. This competitive educational disadvantage is compounded by what seems to be a strong, apparently generally reliable principle: in order for Blacks to succeed in competition with whites their qualifications for the particular position(s) in question must be decidedly better than those of the white competitor(s). As experience shows, practically the only time this principle is not adhered to is when the federal government exerts the leverage of equal employment regulations. Accordingly, it is not at all surprising that when measured by classical white middle-class standards, a majority of Black ghetto fathers are economic failures and their role in the socialization of their children is relatively weak and ineffectual.

The interrelated social forces that tend to prevent many Black fathers from performing their expected role in the socialization process are ultimately the causes for the relatively high rate of deviance among Black youth. This conclusion is based on the fact that economically and educationally disadvantaged fathers are much more likely than more affluent, well-educated fathers to have children who are school dropouts, academically retarded, and delinquent.[18] Therefore, the high rate of "social pathologies" associated with the Black ghetto[19] stems primarily from the fact that a large proportion of Black fathers are seriously handicapped in economic competition. This is particularly serious since American society is becoming more and more industrialized and jobs demand higher and higher levels of skill. As a result, there is an increasingly high correlation between the amount of education attained and the level of employment achieved.

Many, and in some instances most, Black fathers are first- or second-generation urban dwellers. They are directly or indirectly products of small town and rural backgrounds. They were pushed out of farming and related industries by automation and racial discrimination. They migrated to cities that have no use for their simple skills and that have been slow and ineffective in training them for useful industrial occupations characteristic of a highly complex, urban, technological society. This very basic problem was sharply defined by President Lyndon B. Johnson in a nationwide address on April 19, 1964: "We have entered an age in which education is not just a luxury permitting some men an advantage over others. It has become a necessity without which a person is defenseless in this complex industrialized society. . . . We have truly entered the century of the educated man.''

With the notoriously low level of education that migrants received in the generally substandard segregated schools of the South and that their children continue to receive in most Black ghetto schools (where the longer they remain in school the more retarded they are academically),[20] it is to be expected that, without unequivocal government intervention, unemployment and underemployment rates of Blacks will remain high even during prosperity and a shortage of skilled workers. Despite this well-known fact, the government and private corporations sponsor very few effective adult education programs which will train or upgrade the skills of the great masses of subemployed Blacks in the cities. There seems to be no promising concept of dealing with the fundamental domestic problem of this century: the transition from a largely unskilled, relatively simple rural society to a complex, highly advanced technological, urban society. In the meantime it is not surprising that debilitating poverty and ever-sprawling ghettos with their many problems continue to proliferate and threaten the life and welfare of American cities, while some powerful politicians and otherwise enlightened citizens strongly criticize the victims and make only feeble efforts to eradicate the victimizing circumstances.

When asked if they liked their jobs, just 33 percent of the employed fathers in the sample answered ''yes''; 23 percent gave a ''qualified yes'' and 44 percent answered ''no.'' They gave several different reasons why they were generally unhappy about their jobs. As a rule, they mentioned three interrelated factors: the work was too hard and unpleasant; wages were too low and inadequate to live on; and they had little or no opportunity for promotions. Nearly all of the older fathers (45 years of age and over) felt trapped in their low, disesteemed economic position. Almost three-fourths (74 percent) of the employed fathers in that age category had been employed on the same jobs for six years or more. Many had apparently lost hope of ever earning enough money to live a good life according to national standards. They seemed to have resigned themselves to spending the rest of their working lives on low-paying, dead-end jobs. Their only effective motivation for work was survival.

The younger employed fathers often expressed anger and bitterness when talking about their treadmill-type jobs. All of them called attention to low job ceilings for Black men. Over and over they said, in effect, "If I had been white I'd be foreman," "I'd be making twice as much money," "I would not have been laid off." 'And as one man put it: "No matter how hard a Negro man works, he is not respected by his (white) boss and he is always overlooked or passed over when promotion time comes around."

Perhaps the most frustrating aspect of most jobs available to the unskilled Black workers is the fact that they are almost completely devoid of social and psychological gratification. Thus, unlike most white collar occupations where the concept of success is intimately associated with work and becomes a primary source of motivation, the monotonous jobs available to poorly educated Black men provide little incentive to work hard because there is no career pattern with different levels of success. They live in a world where, according to accepted middle-class standards, practically everyone is unsuccessful, and there are far too few examples of those who have somehow managed to escape.

Most of the younger men are also bitter because, in order to earn a living for themselves and their families, circumstances are forcing them to enter available dead-end, low-paying jobs. Just about all of them expressed fear that they would be forever trapped in these jobs as their fathers had been. This fear is manifested in various ways. One father who was 35 years of age said that he kept changing jobs, always "on the look for something better. I have had maybe two dozen different jobs since I became a man with responsibilities." At the time of the interviews, he was very upset because his wife and children had been dropped from the welfare roll because, as he said, "I was *put* on a job by the welfare people. I never liked that kind of work and the people I have to deal with . . . White people expect a grown Black man to get all excited about some lousy job that don't pay enough to feed one person, let alone a big family like mine."

Some of the younger fathers try to avoid being trapped in undesirable jobs by leaving their families and the economic responsibilities involved and attempt to provide for themselves in illegal ways. A considerable number evidently join the world of crime. The large majority, however, regardless of their anger and protest, eventually "settle down," as they often say, and take whatever jobs are available to support themselves and their families. They know that in order "to make ends meet," they must depend heavily upon the income of their wives. Only 57 percent of the mothers interviewed said that their husband, or at least their children's father, provided for "*most* of the financial needs of the children." Only 39 percent of the estranged fathers provided any reliable financial help at all. For the most part, they only gave their children presents, especially on their birthdays and at Christmas and when they happened to get a fairly substantial, unexpected amount of money from some source. Interestingly, several mothers did point out that their children's father could be always depended upon to give them money when a crisis arose or when the children needed new clothes for special occasions, such as graduation from school.

Basically, then, the Black ghetto father's role in the socialization of their children is often seriously restricted because his economic potentialities are limited by institutionalized racial discrimination and their relatively low level of education. The Black mother, by default, must assume the primary responsibility for the socialization process.

The Mother

While about 29 percent of all Black families are headed by women,[21] almost half (47 percent) of the families in the New Orleans ghetto were headed by the mother. In these homes the socialization of children is the exclusive responsibility of the mother. These are the authentic matricentered or so-called matriarchal families that have been a main focus of Black family studies during the last two decades.

The Black matricentered family had its origin during the slave period when the Black father was legally and traditionally prevented from performing the key father role—protector of the family. This protective role is many-faceted and relates specifically to the economic, social, and physical well-being of women and children. The noble performance of this ancient role has been a major source of fictional and nonfictional heroes in literature and life. It is, therefore, important to note that a complex of contemporary unfavorable circumstances have conspired to deny many Black men the economic and social power inherent in the protective role. Almost half of the children in the Black ghetto grow up expecting their mother, not their father, to perform the protective role.

Even when the father is present in the home, it is likely that the mother will have the more secure job, the more clearly defined protective responsibilities, and the greater respect in the community. In such homes, the mother is forced to develop a kind of self-sufficiency uncommon to non-Black women in American society. Almost always this causes conflict between parents. They are often pitted against one another in an unwholesome competition that goes far deeper than simple differences over how a particular socializing problem should be handled. Often, grave differences arise regarding the essential nature and content of the "male" versus "female" roles. In a theoretical sense, the mother is a "sacred" symbol and the father a "secular" symbol in the Black ghetto subculture.[22]

Historically, the concepts male and female have tended to be much more elaborated among the lower socioeconomic class Blacks than in American society at large. In some respects, these concepts have taken on wide philosophic connotations very much like the basic concepts of "Yang" and "Yin" in traditional Chinese culture. *Yang* refers to such virtues as maleness, the source of life, vitality, creativity, light, happiness. In contradistinction, the concept *Yin* connotes femaleness, darkness, evil, destruction, sadness, death. There is, then, in classical Chinese culture the belief that these two major, fundamentally different forces are inherently opposed and eternally engaged in irrevocable conflict.

The male-female principle characteristic of Black ghetto culture is very similar to the Yang-Yin principle in that it, too, recognizes two natural, contrary forces in the human experience. However, it is quite different from the Chinese model in that, in the historically frustrated Black experience, where the Black man has been severely fettered, *Yang* tends to represent the female element in the model and *Yin* the male element. This similar emphasis upon a male-female governing principle in life, and quite dissimilar interpretations of the nature and content of the roles involved, may provide some insights into the unique aspects of life in the Black ghetto. They may also better elucidate the much-talked-about "identity crisis," personality development, social attitudes, and certain behavior patterns characteristic of Black ghetto youth.

Although both roles have been exaggerated almost to the point of stereotypes, there is a glaring difference between this historical image of the Black woman and the white woman in American lore. For many decades, the truly refined, quintessential female was pictured as an upper-class white "lady" who was "well born" but physically weak, basically unstable psychologically, intellectually shallow—even frivolous—and generally helpless and inferior to men. In very sharp contrast, the Black woman has been pictured as physically strong, obstinate, patient, protective, and generally self-sufficient. This classical contrast still exists in some form today. As fundamentally inaccurate as it might be, the traditional image of the refined, delicate, dependent white woman and the stalwart ("Aunt Jemima" type), earthy, reality-oriented, determined Black woman is a primary reason why the Black woman has always been the focus of study by so many white scholars, popular writers, politicians, lay interpreters of the Black Experience, as well as some Black men.

The classical image of the Black man is in many respects quite similar to that of the white woman. He is the perennial *Yin* element in American culture. A complex of strong formal and informal forces in the society have too often prevented him from attaining the *Yang* image of ordinary masculinity. Even now, a majority of Black male adults are relatively poorly educated, subemployed, and have little effective social power. Thus, Professor Kenneth Clark observed that many Black men in the ghetto are ". . . driven to seek status in ways which seem either antisocial, escapist, [or] socially irresponsible . . . The Negro woman, in turn, has been required to hold the family together, to set goals, to stimulate, to encourage and to protect both boys and girls."[23]

The historical forces that created a biracial society in this country, based on the doctrine of white supremacy, functioned to fasten upon Black women the primary, often total, responsibility of socializing Black children. This fact has, in turn, functioned to retard the advancement of Blacks as a distinct social group—not because the mothers have done a poor job, but for a much more subtle reality: traditionally, women and children have inherited the status of the husband and father, with all of the rights, privileges, and respect he was accorded. Thus, it was expected that white women should "marry up" so that they and their children would inherit the higher status of the husband. The circumstances that have so effectively prevented Black men from high social status have thereby prevented most Black women from "marrying up" and passing on to their children the normal advantages enjoyed by white children. In a very real sense, then, the vast majority of Black children begin life with all of the relative deprivations, disadvantages, and lowly social status characteristic of their parents. They are caught up and imprisoned in a sort of "first-generation" trap where each generation is treated more like foreigners than native citizens. This condition is too often overlooked by those who attempt to compare the Black Experience with the experiences of foreign groups in American society: Foreign groups are expected to improve their wealth, social status, and social power from one generation to the next. This has usually happened because American society has been "open" to white foreign groups and has not strongly resisted their upward social mobility. It has been expected that the second generation of foreign-born white children, who have learned to speak English better than their parents and have come to internalize basic values in the culture, would be accorded better jobs and higher social status than their parents. Therefore, after a few generations a given white ethnic group would be accorded equal status with other white groups in the United States.

The privilege of accumulated improvements in social status has been systematically denied Blacks. Thus, while a given Black family may pass on accumulated privileges to its own children, Black fathers are generally caught up in an apparently endless web of economic failures and frustrations from one generation to the next. Their children inherit very little from them. Insofar as the Black ghetto family is concerned, the "apple does not fall far from the tree." Generation after generation, children in the Black ghetto grow up and begin adult lives with about the same disadvantages and disesteem as their parents before them primarily because their fathers are poor and unable to provide them the means of improving their social status.

Education. Mothers in the New Orleans ghetto had received a median of nine years of schooling. Only 19 percent had finished high school and a mere one (1) percent had finished college. Even this was an average of two years more formal education than received by the fathers. Therefore, neither the fathers nor the mothers can pass on to their children the social status and respect that comes from academic achievements. Even more disadvantageous practically is the parents' inability to give their children the level of formal and informal instruction expected of middle-class preschool children. A large percentage of children from such homes, as is also true of first-generation children of foreign-born parents, are a year or two retarded intellectually even before they enter first grade. Since only a very few ghetto schools are organized, staffed, and equipped to deal effectively with this problem, the academic retardation they bring to the school is compounded. They are much more likely to fall progressively behind their national peer group than to catch up. The dropout rate is abnormally high and most who manage to survive through the high school grades usually end up about three years below the national level. This was the conclusion of Professor Clark: "In the third grade Harlem pupils are one year behind the achievement levels of New York City pupils. By the sixth grade they have fallen two years behind; and by the eighth grade they are about two and one half years behind New York levels and three years behind students in the nation on a whole."[24]

In addition to the academic retardation characteristic of many children in the Black ghetto, there is a related condition that often proves to be a serious handicap to their academic achievements: rigid pragmatism. In discussing the vital question of their children's education with their parents (especially the mothers), interviewers were struck by the amount and dimension of crass pragmatism encountered. The majority of mothers regarded education as only an effective economic tool. To them it was simply a means of getting a better job. Seldom did a mother manifest any conception of education as inherently good in itself, as a means of enriching the child's personal life, as enhancing a person's social or cultural status, or as making the individual more useful to society or to his race.

The mothers' pragmatism is, of course, understandable. Most of them had spent their lives working on low-status, low-income, unpleasant jobs. Just about every mother insisted that she was willing to make great sacrifices to send her children to school, especially the girls, because she did not want them to "work hard all of their lives for white folk and end up with nothing as I have done," as expressed in many different ways.

This singular job-oriented argument for getting a "good" education is also voiced by educators in their attempts to prevent dropouts, by representatives of welfare agencies, by the mass media, and by Black leaders. They all insist that the primary cause of economic inequality is unequal academic attainments, that in order for poor children to have a secure future, they must stay in school. (As we shall see later, this thesis has been challenged by Christopher Jencks' recent book, *Inequality.*)

There is some convincing evidence that Black youngsters have been highly motivated by this pragmatic argument for education: an increasing number is remaining in schools on all academic levels. However, there is also some convincing evidence that crass pragmatism functions to militate against their academic success in schools that insist that their students learn a wide range of facts in the liberal arts. All too often, students from pragmatically oriented families become bored and frustrated in the learning of facts that apparently have little or no relevance to the occupations they plan to enter.

Not only do most children from the Black ghetto internalize the pragmatism of their parents, but they have it reinforced by their daily experiences. Except for an occasional toy, Black ghetto children, on the whole, grow up in a reality-oriented world of useful things. Poor families cannot afford to socialize their children to expect or enjoy luxuries, material or nonmaterial. Children soon learn that there is never enough money to buy even what one *needs*. A "Sunday dress," a mother reminded us, must be worn on other than Sunday occasions. "I never put all those frills and stuff on my children's clothes like they want me to, because the next thing I know they want to wear the dress to school or something. They'd look funny out on the street with a frilly dress." Another practical mother said: "My children always want birthday presents. I just wait until then to get them things they need like shoes, sweaters. . . . Their daddy always comes through on their birthdays. Last year he had our T.V. fixed for Joe's (her son's) birthday." Consequently, as would be expected, most teachers in the ghetto schools studied point out that their students manifest little interest in subjects intended for personal and cultural enrichment. One teacher said: "Every time I try to interest them in history, art or some piece of classical literature, they always exclaim 'what good is that? Why do we need to learn some silly stuff about people we never see?' " As a rule, educators seem unable to find effective ways of making a liberal education both relevant and interesting to children from pragmatic environments.

The mothers are not prepared to give the school very much help. Most of the mothers expressed regret that they were not able to do more toward the education of their children. One mother of a sixth-grade daughter was very unhappy because the child was having a problem keeping up with her school assignments and the mother could not help her at all.

Employment. Fully 80 percent of the mothers in the sample, even those with regular full-time jobs, may be classified as subemployed. Despite the fact that 47 percent of the families were headed by the mother, or at least the mother had the primary responsibility of providing for the children, 66 percent of the mothers thought of themselves as primarily "housewives" in regard to employment. Some of them had part-time jobs, while others depended upon welfare. Many of the young mothers had small children they had to care for and could not hold a full-time job. All insisted that they wanted full-time jobs that paid enough to support a family.

The essential crux of the problem is that the kind of jobs available to the majority of the poorly educated women in Black ghettos do not pay enough for them to live on. The disconcerting truth is that it is often much wiser economically to qualify for welfare and find a part-time job to supplement it. For example, 75 percent of the mothers in the sample said that they had only done domestic work. Their average wages for full-time domestic work was from $25 to $30 per week, or only $1,200 to $1,400 a year. This was more than $2,000 a year less than what federal government agencies defined as the poverty level for families of their size.

Mothers on welfare with one child were eligible for a mere $80 per month, or $960 per year. The maximum any family in New Orleans could receive at the time of the study (1968-1969) was $163 per month or $1,956 annually. Even though these incomes were far below the poverty level, they were often more than the mothers could earn from full-time jobs available to them. Many mothers with small children had little choice but to accept welfare in order to stay home and look after their children. A few such mothers organized a baby sitters' pool whereby a mother who worked part-time would leave her children with a mother who had the day off. This arrangement seldom worked effectively among mothers who had full-time jobs unless some worked nights and others worked days. Actually, we saw only one or two such arrangements in the neighborhood studied. Also, some mothers with both small, preschool children and older children (12-18) would depend heavily upon the older children as baby sitters while they held a part-time or full-time job. During the school year, this meant that an older child was kept out of school on days the mother worked or occasionally a teenager would drop out of school to take care of the house during the mother's absence. Grandmothers were also frequently used as baby sitters.

No matter what kind of baby sitting arrangement a given mother chose, it was certain to be unsatisfactory in some important respects. The majority of mothers were caught in a very difficult dilemma: either they had to take full-time jobs that paid less than it took to support their families adequately or they had to accept welfare that also paid less than it took to live on well but did allow them time to care for their children.

Socialization Practices

A 33-year-old mother of seven children, ranging in age from

infancy to 16 years, was asked how she reared her children. After discussing each one at great length she concluded thoughtfully: "Well, come to think about it now, I just play it by ear."

After carefully examining the socialization practices of all of the parents in our sample, the research staff and I were struck with the aptness of that young mother's statement. Even when we take into account the wide range of socialization practices, such as toilet training, feeding, the application of rewards and punishment, the assignment of duties, and informal teaching, socialization practices were generally quite relaxed and unorthodox. They varied from one family to another and from one situation to another in the same family. Generally, socialization tended to be reality-oriented rather than theory-oriented. Parents did, in fact, play it by ear. They apparently established a rather flexible set of simple, basic goals they wanted their children to attain and attempted, as best they could, to encourage them toward these goals. Therefore, when they were asked "What are some of the things you would like most to see your children accomplish?," parents gave numerous answers that may be summarized in three broad categories:

1. *Keep out of trouble.* This negative goal was the most frequently emphasized. All of the parents had a common fear that their children would not be able to resist the constant, ubiquitous temptations and opportunities of becoming involved in the antisocial and socially reprehensible, criminal behavior so characteristic of slum neighborhoods. Somehow they sensed that most of the social-control mechanisms that operate as restraining forces in the lives of more affluent families do not operate for their children. That is, expected rewards for "good" behavior such as respect from successful family members, public approval, recognition of excellence by peer groups, competitive scholarships, admission to prestigious schools and colleges, a high status position, "marrying well," or the inheritance of the family fortune seldom or never operate as social-control restraints among the very poor. Most often, the opposite

is the case: a large majority of them never succeed at anything and have never known anyone personally who has succeeded according to middle-class standards. The fact is, *too often the social system of the Black ghetto is designed to reward what the middle-class person would regard as immoral or antisocial behavior.* In many instances, parents reported that their children had been derided and regularly intimidated by their peers in the neighborhood because they refused to participate in socially and legally disapproved activities. This is an especially strong pull on boys who must often associate with a gang in order to protect themselves.

The gang. [25] The culture of the gang can only be understood in relation to the dominant male-female (*Yang-Yin*) principle mentioned above. In a very realistic way, boys in the Black ghetto constantly attempt to reverse the widely held concept that Black women are strong and creative and Black men weak and irresponsible—just as the matricentered home is organized according to the counter "male principle."

Unlike the matriarchy, where females are bound together by mutual affection and survival challenges, membership in the gang, while implying a limited degree of mutual aid, is highly individualistic and each boy must "prove" himself a "man" before he is fully accepted. The main theme in the ethos of the gang is "prove yourself a man"; "don't be a sissy"; "don't be a woman." The female element in society, as defined by the gang, seems to symbolize refined manners, laws, moral codes, religion, liberal education, and the striving for middle-class success and respectability, while the manhood element tends to symbolize independence, secretiveness, aggressiveness, and sexual prowess. Thus, to be a man means to renounce entirely the female principle as the gang conceives it. It involves fear of women, scorn for middle-class standards, and hatred of established authority, particularly female authority and the police.

The social life of the gang revolves around strictly masculine activities. [26] It usually includes drinking, gambling, "playing the dozens"—a behavior pattern that clearly exemplifies the completeness with which the ghetto male is expected to reject the female principle in the culture by saying derogatory things even about the mother—sports, telling dramatic stories about sexual exploits, and the outwitting of authority. These are the basic elements of what some scholars identify as a counterculture of the Black ghetto.[27]

Not all gangs are composed of juveniles, for there are adult gangs also. They do not necessarily engage in antisocial or criminal behavior. Basically, they are informal associations where men get together away from women. A study of such an adult gang revealed that the members did not belong to or support any community organization; as individuals they were touchy around white people and uneasy around middle-class Blacks; and they violently resented being "pushed around" by employers, their wives or girl friends, and the police. For example, one young man interviewed had just lost his job because he tried to strike an employer who had "dared to holler at me. I am a full grown man," he retorted, "and I don't take that stuff off no one." Another boasted of the time he "told off" a prison guard who "crossed" him, even though he knew that he would be severely punished for doing so. These men also told many stories about fights with police and even about insulting court officials. The touchiness of certain juvenile and adult gang members toward white authority apparently stems primarily from their feeling that their masculinity is being challenged or threatened. This is perhaps the ultimate reason why the most hated symbol of authority in the ghetto is the police. Some police deliberately bait the men by calling them "boy" or some other name that implies weakness.

It is difficult for boys to keep out of trouble in neighborhoods where they are constantly tempted to commit antisocial acts by their peers and where adult males set dramatic examples of social deviance.

Daughters. Girls reared in the Black ghetto are not nearly as likely as boys to get into trouble with the law (the ratio is about

5:1 for boys). Therefore, when pressed to explain what they meant about trying to keep their daughters out of trouble, mothers tended to emphasize three general types of trouble daughters should try to avoid: (1) "Getting tied up with a no-good man," as frequently phrased. This type of problem is complex because it might mean getting hooked on drugs; having a man take money the girl has earned; being dominated by a cruel man who beats her; and, worst of all, having some man force the daughter to reject her mother. As we have seen, nearly all of the mothers wanted children because they offered a measure of security for them in their old age. Therefore, these mothers feel that the daughter who rejects her mother for a man is the most immoral of all people.

(2) Some mothers defined having an illegitimate baby as "trouble." This is particularly true if the girl is quite young so that she must drop out of school. Fully 19 percent of the mothers interviewed acknowledged that they had given birth to at least one illegitimate child. All seemed to have had unusual problems in rearing their children and delighted in telling how indispensable their own mothers had been in helping raise their illegitimate children. Forty-three (43) percent of the mothers who had an illegitimate child were under 18 years of age when their first one was born. (3) Therefore, keeping out of trouble also means not having an illegitimate baby until the girl is old enough to work and support it. This is not an easy goal because girls reared in the ghetto generally do not have as much protection from philandering males as do middle-class girls. As we have noted, most of them must grow up quickly so that they can support themselves or help raise their siblings. Besides, they often live in overcrowded projects where it is impossible to have the kind of protection and privacy needed. The rape rate among girls in the ghetto is believed to be very much higher than is revealed in police records.

2. *Get a good education.* A "good" education as defined by the parents is not so good in middle-class terms. For them it

generally meant a high school or trade school diploma. At least they wanted their children to stay in school until they could get a "steady job."

Some mothers will make almost any sacrifice to keep their children in school. Only a few seemed very concerned with the grades their children made so long as they were able to stay in school. Perhaps every mother interviewed emphasized this point: "I want my children to get a better education than I did, then maybe life for them will be better than my life has been."

3. *Get a good, regular job*. This is indeed the ultimate goal of child rearing. Parents are proud of their children who are well-employed. They like to boast about a child, especially a boy, who works regularly and earns enough money to give presents to other family members.

It is normal for these parents to have such great pride in children with substantial jobs because it is quite an accomplishment considering the fact that the vast majority in their neighborhood are either unemployed or underemployed. For instance, some teenagers in the Upward Bound program studied had never lived in the house with anyone who had a regular job and had seen unemployment as characteristic of the other families they knew personally. Nationally, the unemployment among Black youth in 1970 was 31.8 percent of those in the labor market (16 to 19 years old).[28] It is very much higher in the Black ghetto. There, getting any kind of job is an accomplishment.

Child-rearing practices. Most of the parents relied heavily on corporal punishment as a means of motivating their children toward the goals they had set for them. Fully 68 percent believed that it's the parents' duty to administer corporal punishment to small children. Some even quoted the Biblical injunction: "Spare the rod and spoil the child."

There was considerable difference about how old a child should be before parents stopped punishing it. The distribution was as follows:

Maximum Age of Parental Punishment

Age	Percent Answering Yes
12	18
13-15	60
16+	8
Don't know	14

Since most parents rely heavily on corporal punishment, we asked them what they would do if their teenaged child refused to obey them on a serious issue or became antisocial. They gave several answers which ranged from calling in a strong male relative to assist with discipline, as was often suggested by women family heads, to turning the child over to the police, which a few had done on occasions.

Interestingly, ninety or more of the children were only disciplined by the mother. In most instances, the mothers said they expected the father to intervene only when a child had committed a very serious offense. Fathers often complained about this and tended to agree that the mothers should allow them to assume more responsibility for discipline. In turn, the mothers argued that even when the fathers were expected to punish a child they usually shifted the responsibility to them.

For parents in the Black ghetto, the problem of socialization is uncommonly complex and difficult because their children must be taught to function effectively in two quite diverse, even conflicting, social worlds: one, they must learn how to survive and cope with the constant negative pulls in the ghetto, and two, they must learn how to survive and advance themselves in the more or less unfamiliar world of the middle-class-oriented, powerful white society on which they must depend for jobs and general security. Most of these children will no doubt grow up and remain law-abiding citizens. They will attempt to carve out a secure economic foothold in the Black ghetto and settle down to raise another generation of disadvantaged children. Others, in rapidly increasing numbers, will rebel against the system.

Therefore, unless some very definite measures are taken to guarantee equality of opportunity to all Americans, including the Black masses, Black ghettos in large cities will become more of a "powder-keg" than they are now. Already a large majority of Black youth, including many from middle-class families, are becoming bitter and distrustful of whites and the American social system. They are determined that they will not continue to be treated as second-class citizens as their parents have been.

NOTES

[1]John H. Rohrer, Munro S. Edmonson, Daniel C. Thompson, et al., *The Eighth Generation* (New York: Harper and Brothers, Publishers, 1960), pp. 83-84, 298, passim. For a special analysis of socialization in the different social worlds, see Daniel C. Thompson, "The Formation of Social Attitudes," *American Journal of Orthopsychiatry* 32, No. 1 (January 1962): pp. 74-85.

[2]For a full discussion of this, see Daniel C. Thompson, "Social Class Factors in Public School Education As Related to Desegregation," *American Journal of Orthopsychiatry* 26, No. 3 (July 1956): 449-452.

[3]See James H. Hammond, "The Mudsill Theory," a speech before the South Carolina Senate, March 4, 1958, in Leslie H. Fishel and Benjamin Quarles, *The Negro American: A Documentary History* (New York: Scott, Foresman and Co., 1967), pp. 95-97.

[4]Gunnar Myrdal, *An American Dilemma* (New York: Harper and Brothers, Publishers, 1944), p. 593.

[5]For a comprehensive discussion of job discrimination, see Herbert Hill, "Black Labor in the American Economy," in Pat Romero, *In Black America* (Washington, D. C.: United Publishing Corp., 1969), pp. 182-215.

[6]U. S. Riot Commission, *Report of the National Advisory Commission on Civil Disorders* (New York: A Bantam Book, 1968), pp. 253, 255.

[7]Paul Baran and Paul Sweezy, "Monopoly Capitalism and Race

Relations," in Richard Frucht, *Black Society in the New World* (New York: Random House, 1971), p. 137.

[8]Hill, "Black Labor in the American Economy," pp. 203-204.

[9]Ibid., p. 193.

[10]Baran and Sweezy, "Monopoly Capitalism and Race Relations," p. 136.

[11]U. S. Department of Commerce, Bureau of the Census, *The Social and Economic Status of Negroes in the United States, 1970*, Table 36, p. 48.

[12]Whitney M. Young, *To Be Equal* (New York: McGraw-Hill Book Co., 1964), p. 53.

[13]The comparable percentages for the white population are 43, 21, and 36, respectively. See *The Social and Economic Status of Negroes in the United States*, Table 48, p. 60. (Data adjusted to fit into three distinct, general levels of employment.)

[14]Ibid., p. 63.

[15]*The Social and Economic Status of Negroes in the United States, 1970*, Table 22, pp. 31, 35.

[16]For a discussion of this principle, see Elliot Liebow, *Tally's Corner* (New York: Little, Brown and Company, 1967), pp. 72-101.

[17]Reported in *The Times-Picayune*, March 28, 1965, Section 3, p. 4.

[18]Elbert W. Stewart, *The Troubled Land* (New York: McGraw-Hill Book Co., 1972), pp. 351-353.

[19]Kenneth B. Clark, *Dark Ghetto* (New York: Harper and Row, 1965), pp. 81-110.

[20]Ibid.

[21]*The Social and Economic Status of Negroes in the United States, 1970*, Table 86, p. 107.

[22]For a classical discussion of these concepts, see Emile Durkheim, *Elementary Forms of Religious Life* (London: Allen and Unwin, 1915), pp. 37-62.

[23]Clark, *Dark Ghetto*, p. 70.

[24]Ibid., p. 121. For a recent analysis, see "The Report of the Selected Committee on Equal Educational Opportunity, United States Senate," *Toward Equal Educational Opportunity* (Washington, D. C.: U. S. Government Printing Office, 1972), pp. 9-18.

[25]For a full discussion, see Thompson, "Formation of Social Attitudes," *American Journal of Orthopsychiarty*, pp. 80-81.

[26]See *The Eighth Generation*, pp. 161-185. See also Elliot Liebow, *Tally's Corner*, pp. 161-207.

[27]See Liebow, *Tally's Corner*, pp. 135-160.

[28]*The Social and Economic Status of Negroes in the United States, 1970*, Table 56, p. 68.

5

The Black Ghetto:
Social Organization

The Black ghetto as a distinct social entity is relatively powerless, mainly because it is ineffectively organized. Indigenous social power arrangements are usually unstable and temporary and the power inherent in them is too often dissipated or improperly exercised. Therefore, compared with the machine-like organization of American society at large and the organization of expert power brokers on the local level with which inhabitants of the ghetto must do business, the Black ghetto may be described as a sociocultural enclave in which there is a constant condition of anomie or normlessness. This is a great disadvantage because in stable, productive communities, especially those that are urban and highly industrialized, social organization is the most versatile instrument in getting things done.

It is through effective organization that people in a complex society become united to achieve both the imperative survival goals and voluntary goals such as respect, prestige, pleasure, and social effectiveness. Ultimately, it is through rational organization that a distinct social group generates sufficient power to control the internal and external forces that shape the lives and destinies of individuals composing the group. Since the Black ghetto in New Orleans, as is true of Black ghettos generally, seriously lacks effective organizations through which it can pursue the collective interests of the Black masses and exert pressure on local, state, and national agencies to act in their behalf, it is usually overlooked or given only peripheral or half-hearted concern by power arrangements in the larger society. Seldom, therefore, are the special political, economic, and social views and interests of the Black masses reflected in public policy and programs. This condition is the basic reason for the alienation, bitterness, and threatening unrest so prevalent in Black ghettos throughout this nation.[1]

Not only are the largely unorganized Black masses virtually powerless when it comes to influencing public policy, but they are also relatively powerless when it comes to doing things for themselves. Things that happen to them are usually planned and directed by "outside" organizations and individuals, primarily for the benefit of "outside" interests.[2] Their self-help attempts tend to be compromised as they have little legitimate social power of their own. Moreover, any united, concerted effort to exert power, such as mass demonstrations, boycotts, and rent strikes, is ipso facto regarded as a violation of law and order as defined by representatives of those against whom the efforts are directed. The essential irony is that before the powerless inhabitants of the ghetto can exert any significant control over their own institutions and lives they must first get permission from power groups in the larger community—groups composed of individuals who represent the very interest groups against whom they would bring pressure. In this connection, it is important to note that for the most part indigenous ghetto leaders who are generally far removed from the centers of "legitimate" social power do not understand the intricacies of power arrangements in modern urban industrial society well enough to deal with them effectively in behalf of their people.

Since the lives and welfare of the Black masses are largely controlled by forces outside the ghetto, even agencies and programs designed specifically to benefit them almost always fall far short of their avowed intentions.[3] Just about every time the hopes of the very poor have been raised they have been dramatically shattered. Thus, the much-heralded "War on Poverty" turned out to be little more than a polite economic and political scrimmage that effected very little noticeable change in the stringent lives of the Black masses but did offer some good jobs to middle-class "outsiders." The same was true of the promising Urban Renewal program which, in many cities, was accurately described as a "Black Removal" program. Likewise, practically all job training programs have fallen far short on training and the subsequent placement of individuals who receive the training. Therefore, after a decade of fairly expensive programs to raise the economic level of the Black masses, the unemployment and subemployment rate in the Black ghetto is virtually unchanged, and today (1973) it seems that even the pretense of eliminating poverty and slum living for the Black masses is being abandoned. The poor themselves do not have the resources or the power to improve their own condition. Those who would survive too often find themselves forced into an unwanted, uncomfortable, frustrating, parasitic relationship with the larger social system on which they must depend for public welfare or perpetual subemployment.

The Church

In order to understand the role of the church in the Black ghetto, it must be remembered that one of the oldest and most persistent characterizations of Black Americans is that they are very religious. This belief was given such great, uncritical emphasis that it became a kind of stereotype. This stereotype was perpetuated by some who evidently wished to establish the belief that Blacks are by nature predisposed to be extremely emotional, servile, and mentally childlike. Like most stereotypes, this one is a distortion of facts. It stemmed mainly from the fact that no other people have had to depend so much, for so long, on religion to give meaning to life and sustain their survival efforts as have Black Americans.

Since perennially the Black community has been powerless, next to the family the Black church has had the greatest influence in the social, cultural, and psychological maturation of Blacks. Even now, it is the only truly powerful national organization, including Blacks on all socioeconomic levels, that has been developed and controlled primarily or solely by Blacks themselves.

A careful analysis of available information about the history of the Black church suggests that it has influenced just about every aspect of the Black Experience. It was the only constant source of hope and group identity throughout the almost 250 years of dehumanizing slavery and has continued to be the fountainhead of Black unity and survival throughout the years since slavery. This central role of religion in the life of Black Americans has been recognized by all serious observers of Negro life and history. Thus, Carter G. Woodson, a Black historian and pioneer in the study of Afro-American history from a Black perspective and founder of the "Negro History Week" movement, noted that—

> The Negro church as a social force in the life of the race is nothing new. Prior to emancipation the church was the only institution which the Negro, in a few places in the South and throughout the North, was permitted to maintain for his own peculiar needs. Offering the only avenue for the expressional activities of the race, the church answered many a social purpose for which this institution among other groups differently circumstanced had never before been required to serve.[4]

Woodson went on to point out how the Black church has served as a means of social control and developing Black leadership:

> After the emancipation, moreover, the Negro church

developed a social atmosphere which somewhat strengthened its hold on the youth about to go astray. Not only education found its basis in the church, but fraternal associations developed therefrom. Business enterprises accepted the church as an ally, and professional men to some extent often became dependent thereupon. Most movements among the Negroes, moreover, have owed their success to the leadership of Negroes prominent in the church.[5]

W. E. B. DuBois, writing around the turn of this century, gave a brilliant, succinct summary of the role of the church in the survival of the race:

> The Negro church is the peculiar and characteristic product of the transplanted African. . . . As a social group the Negro church may be said to have antedated the Negro family on American soil; as such it has preserved, on the one hand, many functions of tribal organization, (''Africanisms'' to be discussed subsequently) and on the other hand, many of the family functions. Its tribal functions are shown in its religious activity, its social authority and general guiding and co-ordinating work; its family functions are shown by the fact that the church is a centre of social life and intercourse; acts as newspaper and intelligence bureau, is the centre of amusement—indeed, is the world in which the Negro moves and acts.[6]

Another great Black scholar, E. Franklin Frazier, concluded that:

> The important role of religion and the Negro church in the social organization of the American Negroes has been due to the restricted participation of Negroes in American society. And as a consequence the Negro church has left its imprint upon practically every aspect of Negro life. The

Negro church has provided the pattern for the organization of mutual aid societies and insurance companies. . . . Greek letter societies. . . . administration and control of Negro schools. . . . control and organization of the Negro church has been authoritarian with a strong man in a dominant position. . . . the Negro church and Negro religion have cast a shadow over the entire intellectual life of Negroes.[7]

Benjamin E. Mays, in his very informative and provocative autobiography, vividly portrays the central role of the church among Black people a generation ago:

Old Mount Zion was an important institution in my community. Negroes had nowhere to go but to church. They went there to worship, to hear the choir sing, to listen to the preacher, and to hear and see the people shout. The young people went to Mount Zion to socialize, or simply to stand around and talk. It was a place of worship and a social center as well. There was no other place to go. . . . This was the one place where Negroes in my community could be free and relax from the toil and oppression of the week. Among themselves they were free to show off and feel important.

Preacher Marshall taught the people to be honest and upright, the Gospel he preached was primarily an opiate to enable them to endure and survive the oppressive conditions under which they lived at the hands of the white people in the community.

They believed the trials and tribulations of the world would be over when one got to heaven. Beaten down at every turn by the white man, as they were, Negroes could perhaps not have survived without this kind of religion.[8]

In a recent study of the Black preacher, Charles V. Hamilton, a Black political scientist, pointed out that until roughly World War II—

> The church was pretty much unrivaled in the black community as the major institution of black folk. There were no labor unions; there were few other social, political or economic agencies in the black community among the lower class. Thus the church was the center. . . . If black people wanted to meet, the only available meeting place large enough to hold more than a handful was the church building. . . . Out of this environment came the natural leadership of the black preacher.[9]

Hamilton insists that the Black preacher has been a "natural" leader and as such has performed several different specialized roles—politician, pastor, peacemaker, and general mediator between the Black and white communities. Then he concludes: "One thing is clear, however, about the black preacher over the years: He has known how to survive with his people. He has known how fast and how far to take them, and this is largely because of his developed skills of leadership and his understanding of his followers."[10]

Finally, the author of an empirical study of Black leadership during the 1960s' civil rights revolution concluded:

> The Negro Protestant Church is the first, and in some instances the only major social institution in which a significant number of Negroes with varying talents and academic preparation have found opportunities for self-expression, the development of self-respect and racial pride, professional employment and leadership training.[11]

Throughout the 1960s Black religion constituted the core, the "soul," of the civil rights movement.

Developmental Stages of the Black Protestant Church[12]

Since the Black church has been a key factor in the survival and progress of the race, it has reflected every distinct stage or status Blacks have experienced in American society. For the present purpose, we may call brief attention to the following developmental stages:

Embryonic organization or the "Invisible Church." Ironically, some slave masters were extremely religious people. Not only did they value religion as a personal, moral, and social force for themselves, but they also taught their slaves at least the rudiments of the Christian life. Negro slaves seem to have been quite susceptible to this teaching, perhaps because they had no other sustaining institution or philosophy. Thus, their condition of absolute dependency predisposed them to seek fulfillment in religion.

Even where the slaves were permitted nominal membership in the church of their masters, they attempted to organize themselves for religious purposes. Since there often were definite laws forbidding slaves to assemble, they had to meet in secret. This was done under "Brush Harbours" or in some other secret place where their singing, praying, and preaching would not be overheard. Their efforts eventually resulted in what has been characterized as the "Invisible Church."

Generally, one of the more "educated" slaves, perhaps a house servant or coachman who had had an opportunity to observe how white people worshipped in churches, was given the title of "preacher." He performed at least two comprehensive, far-reaching functions: One, it was his duty to expound the Scriptures in such a way that he could bring some comfort into the miserable, hopeless condition of his fellow slaves. Two, he made it possible for them to learn from him and from one another those things necessary for their survival and development as chattel in a slave society. Therefore, even during the earliest, embryonic stage of the "Invisible Church," several specific needs of the Negro slaves were met, at least to some extent. These basic needs can be generally classified under the rubric *informal education*. They are:

(a) *Syncretization of Africanisms and Christianity*. The slave church functioned as a crucible in which slaves blended the Christian religion of the white masters with the spiritual qualities and selected ritual endemic to their native African religions. Slave worshippers used their religious services, whether clandestine or otherwise, as a focal point around which to reinterpret and adapt every major aspect of the white man's religion—his songs, prayers, sermons, and general ritual. Thus, Gayraud Wilmore argues that

> It was the slave's African past that did the most to influence his style of religion, his rejection of the spiritual and political despotism of the white man, and made the most important contribution to his coming struggle for freedom. . . . the essential ingredient of Black christianity prior to the Civil War was the creative spirituality of the African religions. The defining characteristic of that spirituality was its spontaneous fascination with, and unself-conscious response to, the reality of the spirit world and the intersection between that world of objective perception.[13]

Some scholars, led at first by the writings of Herskovits, have insisted that the Black church has been a repository of Africanisms. Many of the early preachers among slaves were former African priests who had been thoroughly trained in the beliefs, spirit, and ritual of their native African religions. Also, there were usually other slaves who, with varying degrees of success, contributed to the transmission and adaptation of certain Africanisms that had some functional relevance to the slave condition. Apparently, whites observed this phenomenon but generally discounted its importance and derisively interpreted it as a simple manifestation of the primitive superstitions of a heathen people who practiced voodooism and witchcraft. Professor Eugene Genovese writes:

The planters tell us repeatedly that every plantation had its conjurer, its voodoo man, its witch doctor. To the planters this meant a residue of African superstition. . . . But the evidence suggests the emergence of an indigenous and unique combination of African and European religious notions, adapted to the specific conditions of slave life by talented and imaginative individuals, which represented an attempt to establish a spiritual life adequate to the task of linking the slaves with the powerful culture of the masters and yet providing them with a high degree of separation and autonomy.[14]

While DuBois recognized the creative aspects of the slave religion, he, too, was struck by the way "heathen" rites were blended into Christian worship:

Endowed with a rich tropical imagination and a keen, delicate appreciation of nature, the transplanted African lived in a world animated with gods and devils. He called up all the resources of heathenism to aid—exorcism and witchcraft. . . . The witchwoman and the voodoo priest became the center of Negro group life.

The Priest or Medicine-man. . . . appeared on the plantation and found his function. . . . as a bard, physician, judge, and priest, within the narrow limits allowed by the slave system, rose the Negro preacher, and under him the first church. [It] was an adaptation and mingling of heathen rites [with] an early veneer of Christianity.[15]

Herskovits' work tended to reinforce and validate DuBois' contention that the slave religion was shot through with Africanisms.[16] However, E. Franklin Frazier posed a hypothesis that later research has generally invalidated. According to Frazier, the system of slavery was harsh and lasted so long that the African heritage was almost totally destroyed. He argued that contrary to Herskovits' thesis: "Although the area in West Africa from which the majority of the slaves were drawn exhibits a high degree of culture homogeneity, the capture of many of the slaves in inter-tribal wars and their selection for the slave markets tended to reduce to a minimum the possibility of the retention and transmission of African culture."[17] Then, taking direct issue with DuBois' interpretation of Africanisms in the Black church, Frazier asserts: "From the available evidence, including what we know of the manner in which the slaves were Christianized and the character of their churches, it is impossible to establish any continuity between African religious practices and the Negro church in the United States."[18]

Since the 1960s and the tremendously active study of the Black experience, which was stimulated by the proliferation of Black Studies departments and programs in higher education, social scientists have become better informed about the cultures of Africa and how slaves infused it into American culture. Thus, social scientists today are apt to avoid the extreme positions of both Herskovits, who believed that Africanisms were reflected in just about every aspect of American culture —especially in the South—and Frazier, who contended that slavery almost completely destroyed the Blacks' African heritage. They are much more likely to be concerned about how slaves selected certain functional traits and beliefs in their African heritage and blended them with Americanized Christian traits and thinking in order to create a religion, a way of life better suited to their own peculiar social condition and their own survival needs. This approach is summarized by Professor C. Eric Lincoln:

> The blacks brought their religion with them. After a time they accepted the white man's religion, but they have not always expressed it in the white man's way. It became the black man's purpose—perhaps it was his *destiny*—to

shape, to fashion, to re-create the religion offered him by the Christian slave masters, to remold it nearer to his own heart's desire, nearer his own peculiar needs.

Then Lincoln cautioned: "The black religious experience is something more than a black patina on a white happening. It is a unique response to an historical occurrence which can never be replicated for any people in America."[19]

While a significant difference of opinion remains about the exact nature and extent to which African traits and spirit have been retained in American culture generally and in Black religion specifically, all serious analysts of the Afro-American experience tend to agree that the slaves' reinterpretation and adaptation of Christianity was the main reason why they were not completely demoralized and dehumanized by the almost 250 years of the harshest system of chattel slavery ever experienced.

From a careful historical point of view, it is entirely reasonable to conclude that had it not been for the religious syncretism of the slaves, in all probability they would have become a pathetic, normless, unorganized, hopeless mass completely shut outside the traditional Western, American white culture. They would have had no reliable moral standards to judge the evils of slavery and no effective protest against it because effective protest presupposes shared values or norms by the oppressor and the oppressed. Furthermore, slaves would have had no moral or ethical basis for preserving their own personal dignity and integrity. Without the religion they created out of their African and American experiences they would have had no sure foundation for building an autonomous culture or rising above the threatening vicissitudes endemic to their lowly, disesteemed status in American society. As it was, they retained certain selective aspects of their African religion and blended them with Christianity in such a way that it enabled them to withstand the ravages of a long period of slavery and to contribute to the mainstream of American culture, while at the same time maintaining their own individual and racial identity.

The Invisible Church, then, served as a focus around which a degree of racial unity was achieved. It afforded opportunities for Blacks to meet and discuss their common problems and thereby give each other moral and spiritual support. These quasireligious gatherings marked the beginning of a race-consciousness that has continued to manifest itself in various forms throughout the decades and is perhaps most constructively revealed in the Black revolution initiated by Martin Luther King.

(b) *Protest*. The Invisible Church among the slaves helped to define the ethics of race relations and served to give some organization to the dissatisfactions they felt about their oppression. From the very beginning of their religious life, the Blacks tended to identify with the oppressed individuals and peoples described in the Bible. They thought of themselves as representing "God's Chosen People," as they assumed to be true of the ancient Hebrews, and they regarded their oppressors—their slave masters—as "Pharaohs." Thus, their protest was double-edged. On the one hand, the more fearful among them could denounce their masters vicariously by denouncing Pharaoh, for example, who symbolized the slave master, while they identified themselves with the oppressed Hebrews for whom God wrought so many miracles. On the other hand, the more courageous of the slaves actually challenged God to protect and deliver them from the oppression of the slave system just as he had done for the Israelites. Therefore, slave "preachers" created and developed a distinct homiletic style of their own. The most outstanding characteristics of their sermons were picturesqueness and emotional fervor. Such sermons were often delivered with great power. Slave "preachers" told vivid, dramatic stories of the trials and triumphs of Biblical heroes—"Daniel in the Den of Lions," "The Three Hebrew Children in the Fiery Furnace," and especially Moses leading his people through the Red Sea. The more militant preachers extolled the militancy of the ancient Hebrews and urged their fellow slaves to resist oppression at all cost.

The protest of these militant slave preachers frequently led to revolts against slave masters. Most of the revolts were quickly put down. Some, however, lasted long enough to cause widespread fear, even terror, among the whites and to underscore the Blacks' unswerving desire for freedom and dignity. Three of the most notable slave revolts were planned and led by slave preachers: Nat Turner, Gabriel Prosser, and Denmark Vesey. They, and all such slave leaders, thought of themselves as the "Moses" of their people.

Another kind of protest was the Blacks' cooperation on the so-called Underground Railroad, a systematic scheme to smuggle Blacks out of slave states into free territory. Negro preachers served as "conductors" in this effort. The most outstanding of these "conductors," however, was not a preacher but a great Black woman, Harriet Tubman. She entered slave states over and over again to lead about 300 Blacks to freedom. The slaves referred to her also as "Moses" and she identified herself to potential runaway slaves by singing the spiritual "Go Down Moses—away down in Egypt land and tell Old Pharoah to let my people go."

So persistent and threatening became Negro protest stemming from their secret or Invisible Church, that slave states passed laws and brutally enforced rules against such meetings. Slaves attending such "church" meetings were severely beaten and their "preachers" were sometimes executed or severely maimed—tongues cut out or eyes blinded, and so forth.

(c) *Leadership*. Another important need the Invisible Church began to satisfy was the training of leaders. Isolated as they were from all formal institutions and agencies, the more ambitious of the slaves learned to become preachers, organizers, and even spokesmen for their people.

It is interesting to realize that Black leaders, even during the slave period, represented at least three ideal types, just as they do today: the *Uncle Tom* whose main task was that of cooperating with white supremacists to preserve the biracial status quo; the *racial diplomat* who sought to keep peace between the races while attempting to make things better for his people; and the *race man* or "militant" who constantly denounced the biracial status quo and attempted to break down the established slave system at all costs. Therefore, whatever may have been the current philosophy of race relations, the Black church has always trained and provided the greatest opportunity for leadership than any other institution.

(d) *Self-expression and creativity*. Perhaps the most lasting contribution of the Black church, even during its "invisible" state, has been the nurturing of the creative potentials of the Black people. During the embryonic stage, the church was an extremely loose organization. Except for the "preacher," everyone else was considered equal in status. The "members" felt free to sing, pray, shout, or even preach whenever they chose. Out of this freedom of expression came the "preacher's" own interpretation of Scriptures to suit the peculiar needs of his people. These "sermons" were generally short on theology and long on prose. They manifested great imagination and wonderful depths of experience. Some of the rich, poetic flavor of the sermons preached by these informal preachers was caught by James Weldon Johnson in his oft-recited "God's Trombones."[20] It is his vivid impression of the slave preacher's interpretation of the creation story: dramatic, moving, and profound.

Another great creative achievement stemming from the "invisible" slave church are the Negro spirituals. Some believe that the Negro spiritual is the only true American music —except jazz, which is a secular interpretation of the moods, philosophy, and protest expressed in spirituals. Here again, we find that the spirituals functioned to satisfy several needs. Two of the most important were protest and faith in God. Take, for example, the spiritual "Nobody Knows the Trouble I've Seen. . . ." It is a protest against the oppression Blacks experienced, and as do all spirituals, it ends on a high, triumphant note —"Glory, Hallelujah."

The Invisible Church among the slaves set a pattern of worship that has persisted to the present time; that is, it endeavored to provide maximum opportunities for the generation of race pride, protest, leadership, and creativity among its members.

Baptism into white faiths. Stage two in the development of the Black church existed simultaneously with the invisible slave church. Some of the leaders of the Invisible Church attended established white churches. Two denominations in particular—the Baptists and the Methodists—did intensive missionary work among the slaves.

Masters often allowed slaves to sit in a segregated area of their churches and listen to the services. About the only participation allowed them aside from singing with the congregation was communion, which they had to partake alone, after everyone else had finished.[21] Free Blacks in the North did likewise. There is evidence that Blacks were never really satisfied in the churches of their masters because their most pressing needs were not satisfied there.[22]

(a) There was no opportunity to develop race pride; the opposite was more often true. White preachers told them that they were childlike and inferior and that their greatest duty in life was obedience to their masters.

(b) There was no opportunity to voice their dissatisfaction with the slave system. Protest was severely frowned upon. The "good Nigger" was expected to accept his lot in life without protest.

(c) There were few or no opportunities in the white churches for Blacks to develop their leadership potentials. Occasionally a "good Nigger" in the congregation might be asked to perform a service relating to other Negroes. There was no opportunity to play a leading role as "preacher" or church officer or to get a committee appointment.

(d) White churches offered little or no opportunity for

Blacks to nourish their capacity for creativity or to develop the self-respect and pride they so badly needed.

One indication that Blacks did not get the religious satisfaction they sought in white churches is a fact mentioned above: they maintained connections in their Invisible Church while they were "members," so to speak, of the white churches. After leaving the churches of their masters, Black preachers would give their own versions of the sermons and hymns they heard to their fellow slaves. In this way they were able to transmit what they had learned.

A second indication that they did not receive religious satisfaction in white churches is that they finally broke away from them completely, even though they were afraid that the whites would punish them for doing so. The most dramatic of these breaks came in 1816 when Richard Allen, a free Black, walked out of a white Methodist church in Philadelphia in protest of discrimination. He later formed the AME church.[23] This walking-out process was repeated time and again and led to the firm establishment of the traditional Negro church.

The independent Black church. The third stage in the development of organized Black religion was the setting up of independent Black churches. Most of their effort was confined to the North. Yet, some slave states did allow Blacks to have their own churches. Remarkably, these independent churches were less militant than the Invisible Church had been among the slaves. Most of them became what some scholars described as completely "other-worldly."[24] There was little attempt to change the status quo or even to organize social protest. This was an understandable position because these churches would not have been allowed to exist if they had openly opposed the traditions of the communities in which they were located. Thus, many Black preachers, like leaders of other Black institutions, notably education, became *accommodation leaders*.[25]

There were some outstanding exceptions to the general social apathy of the independent Black church. Some congregations

assisted on the Underground Railroad and supported slave revolts; several preachers could only be silenced by beatings,
threats, and other punishment.[26] Also, the sermons, songs, and
prayers characteristic of the Black churches identified Blacks as
"God's Chosen People" and those who oppressed them as
enemies of God. Therefore, despite the generally "other-
worldly" stance of the Black church during the latter years of
the nineteenth century until recent decades, it has made a
significant contribution to Black progress.

(a) It fostered race pride. It had a virtual monopoly of the
race leaders: practically all of the most prominent Black leaders
in every community were ministers or outstanding laymen.

(b) It sponsored most of the colleges for Negroes. There
were times, even until now, when church-related Negro colleges offered the highest quality of education for Negro youth
available.

(c) It encouraged business. Not only were Blacks advised to
organize their own businesses when possible, but Negro people
were taught that they had a sacred duty to support one another's
efforts.

Not only did it encourage the founding of businesses (many
insurance companies actually began as church burial aid
societies), but practically all of the community life among
Blacks was centered in the church.[27]

(d) It continued to nurture creativity. Many creative activities were sponsored by the church. Highest priority, of
course, was given the ministry. Preachers vied with one another
in developing oratorical techniques and unique homiletic styles
in order that they might communicate with the untrained masses
who constituted most of their memberships. Some of them
became highly skilled and set standards of oral communication
that even now are revised and copied by top television commen-
tators.

Other creative activities made available through the church
were in the areas of music, public speaking, and leadership.[28]
There were also some opportunities for creative writing, usually

in connection with church literature used for Sunday Schools, young people's meetings, and like activities.

(e) It engaged in protest. Most people who criticized the Negro church from the Reconstruction period to World War II as being entirely "other-worldly" have failed to understand the strong, though subtle, protest in which it was engaged throughout the years. For the most part the protest was on a symbolic level. That is, it was not overtly pointed at any individual or any system; rather, it attempted to subvert or undermine the oppressive system of race relations in terms of overall principles. Sometimes this was done through prayers, singing, or preaching. But, for those who would hear, the message was always there: God hated sinners and loved the humble. God was with Blacks in their struggle for dignity and human rights.

The Ghetto Church. In order to understand and appreciate the role of the church in Black ghettos of large cities, it is first necessary to recall that the period between World War I and World War II may have represented the ultimate nadir in the Blacks' long, painful struggle since emancipation to survive and to achieve a significant level of dignity in American society. Although Black soldiers as a distinct, segregated group had acquitted themselves well in the European war—whose avowed primary aim was "to make the world safe for democracy"—and many had received high praise and citations as good soldiers, on their return to the United States they soon found out that the democracy for which they had fought so valiantly had "escaped" them. There had been a great revival of the Ku Klux Klan throughout the South and in several communities outside the South. White mob violence and the lynching of Blacks continued unabated. In 1919, the first year after the close of World War I, more than seventy Blacks were lynched, including at least ten soldiers, and Black intimidation and oppression were characteristic aspects of Black-white relations in the South. The hopes and eventual frustration and disappointment on the part of Blacks were eloquently voiced by W. E. B. DuBois in July 1918. Speaking as editor of *The Crisis* and as the most respected interpreter of the Black Experience, he admonished Blacks to participate fully in the war:

> That which the German power represents today spells death to the aspirations of Negroes and all other darker races for equality, freedom and democracy. Let us not hesitate. Let us, while this war lasts, forget our special grievances and close our ranks shoulder to shoulder with our white fellow citizens and the allied nations that are fighting for democracy.

After the war was over (May 1919), DuBois noted the plight of the "returning soldiers." Recalling how Black men had bled and died in France in the struggle against "the threat of German race arrogance," he said angrily:

> But today we return! We return from the slavery of uniform. . . . We stand again to look America squarely in the face and call a spade a spade. We sing: This country of ours, despite all its better souls have done and dreamed, is yet a shameful land. . . . It *lynches*. . . . It *disfranchises* its own citizens. . . . It encourages *ignorance*. . . . It *steals* from us. . . . It insults us. . . . *We return*. . . . We *return from fighting*. . . . We *return fighting*.[29]

To all sympathetic observers of race relations DuBois' assessment of the social status of Blacks following World War I was penetrating and altogether accurate. But it was obvious that Blacks themselves were too powerless to do much about it. DuBois, in sheer desperation, suggested "we *return fighting*." Several bloody race riots erupted during the two or three years after World War I, yet in all instances Blacks lost, not gained, civil rights. Those who fought, as DuBois had suggested, were quickly put down and both the legitimate and illegitimate aspects of established white power increased the restrictions and repressions placed upon the social and civic mobility of Blacks in every aspect of community life. In most instances, white police either joined the white rioters or refused to enforce the law. In some cases they simply allowed the white mobs to have their way. One such incident was vividly described by an anonymous Black man who was caught up in a bloody riot in Chicago in July 1919. This riot left 38 dead, 500 or more injured, and over 1,000 homeless: "Blacks were taken from streetcars and beaten. Bands of whites roamed black neighborhoods, shooting randomly. . . . A major riot was put down that summer, but skirmishes continued. . . . Any black who entered white territory became fair game for an attack by whites."[30]

In 1918 about 91 percent of the Black population lived in the South and 75 percent of them were engaged in agriculture. They had therefore already begun to feel the crushing blow of the depression several years before the 1929 stock market crash. Myrdal pointed out that:

Almost three-fourths of all Southern cotton farms and more than half of the crop-specialty farms (tobacco, potatoes, peanuts, and so on) were operated by tenants. About two-thirds of all tenants in the South, and almost three-fourths of the croppers, worked on farms. . . . Negro farmers have always been dependent on the cotton economy to a much greater extent than have white farmers of the South.

Cotton production in 1922 was only one-third of the average for the period 1905-1914.[31]

The drastic decrease in the production of cotton, the ravishes of the boll weevil which made the production of cotton difficult, the rapid mechanization of agriculture, as well as some very oppressive social conditions—including mob violence—Blacks encountered in the South, resulted in the great exodus of Blacks from farms and small towns to large cities, especially in the North.

The major reason, then, for the Black migration was a desire for greater freedom and security than they had had in the South. Perhaps their appreciation of even the restricted freedoms of the North is best reflected in a well-known Black verse "I'd rather be a lamp post in Harlem than the mayor of New Orleans." However, most who went North were destitute and had no salable skills the industrialized North needed. Their economic plight in cities, North and South, was often more desperate than it had been in the agricultural communities they had left. Unemployment rates were tremendously high. "In 1935 around half of all Negro families in the North were on relief."[32]

During the 1920s and 1930s, the great majority of Blacks found themselves quite unprepared to cope with the many complex problems they faced in urban America. The traditional survival tactics that they had developed to cope with southern rural problems proved to be ineffective in the impersonal, industrialized cities. Even the urban institutions Blacks had developed, such as the NAACP, Urban League, and the church, were inadequate when it came to solving the day-to-day problems of urban living. The traditional Black church was especially disappointing because it had apparently lost its power to give them the moral and spiritual uplift they needed. Outwardly the Black population seemed crushed and demoralized. Some scholars and lay experts began to declare that Blacks were irrevocably condemned to general poverty and second-class citizenship. The most informed sociologists tended to agree that Blacks constituted the lowest caste in American society, and like the "Untouchables" in India, they would forever occupy that disesteemed, disadvantaged social position. Some of the most imaginative white liberals, as well as some Black social scientists, expressed little realistic hope that Blacks would ever become equal citizens in American society.

It is, therefore, quite significant that it was during this nadir in the history of free Black Americans that Blacks in large numbers attempted to "turn back the clock" and revive a form of religious behavior that had sustained them during slavery. From what is known about the slave religion, the "storefront" churches that sprang up in large cities during the 1920s and 1930s were little more than a form of the slave religion adapted to modern urban settings. Thus Frazier said:

> The migrations of Negroes to cities, especially to northern cities, produced a crisis in the life of the Negro similar in many respects to the crisis created by the Civil War and Emancipation. . . . The most important crisis in the life of the Negro migrant was produced by the absence of the church which had been the centre of his social life and a refuge from a hostile white world.[33]

Black migrants attempted to reestablish the traditional religion of the past in such ways that it would serve their new, more complex survival needs. Frazier called this process "secularization." The most obvious manifestation of this new, urban adaptation was the "storefront church." The Blacks had no special desire to hold religious services in old, abandoned stores and rundown houses, but chose these places simply because they could not afford to rent, buy, or build regular churches. This point is well made by St. Clair Drake and Horace Cayton:

> In 1933, Chicago Negro churches were carrying the second highest per capita indebtedness among all urban Negro churches in the country. . . . Seventy-five percent of Bronzeville's churches are small "storefront" or house churches, with an average membership of fewer than twenty-five persons. . . . Competition between congregations for the abandoned white churches (after whites moved out of Black neighborhoods) and synagogues resulted, on the one hand, in the paying of exorbitant prices for church property, and, on the other, in the proliferation of makeshift churches.[34]

Consequently, those congregations that could afford to do so acquired traditional churches and those who couldn't moved into 'storefront'' facilities. A survey of Black churches in twelve cities, as reported in 1933 by Benjamin Mays and Joseph Nicholson, revealed that 777 out of a total of 2,104 Black churches (almost 37 percent) could be classified as storefront.''[35]

Professor Clark summarizes the role of the storefront churches in this way:

> . . . the many storefront churches, and the sporadic Negro quasi-religious cult groups, like Father Devine's and the late Daddy Graces' followers, play chiefly a cathartic role for the Negro. These churches and cults and their leaders provide an opportunity for their followers to ''let off steam'', to seek release for emotions which cannot be expressed in overcrowded homes or on the job.[36]

While the storefront churches undoubtedly provided Blacks with opportunities to ''let off steam,'' this psychological interpretation does not take other important functions into account. It must be remembered that these churches drew their membership from the most impoverished, disorganized segment of the Black community. Many of them had been socially uprooted from rural communities where, despite their poverty and white intimidation, they were recognized as persons by their fellows. In the large cities where they had migrated, they desperately needed to find a basis upon which to reestablish community. Without a common basis of identification they would have been doomed to live in a state of anomie with all of its inherent psychological and social problems. All of their traditional ties to others in the rural communities from which they had migrated were either severed or severely strained. Their family life was too often shattered or disorganized, their lodges and informal social groups were no longer functional, and many were lonely, frustrated, and socially lost in complex urban surroundings.

Like the original slave churches, of which they were modern, urban descendants, the storefront churches helped poor, frustrated, disorganized, and disesteemed Blacks to establish a reliable basis for community. In these tenuous, alienated communities, the individual preserved a sense of dignity and worth, participated in shared experiences, and reestablished the foundation for racial pride and unity.

Nationalistic Organizations

Certainly one of the most dramatic and historically significant experiences Blacks have had in American society has been their unprecedented rapid urbanization. Within a generation, between World War I and World War II, the Black population was transformed from a predominantly peasant to a predominantly urban people. Some made this transition smoothly and a few found their new urban environment a land of opportunity and prosperity. The great majority, however, found life in big city ghettos disappointing, threatening, and frustrating. As a rule their neighborhoods were ugly, overcrowded, and in a constant state of disconcerting anomie. The institutions, voluntary associations, and the network of informal social relationships they had developed as survival mechanisms in the rural South proved to be ineffective in dealing with the infinitely more complex urban-adjustment problems. The Black masses found themselves alienated from their fellows, powerless, and crushed by the white society in which they were helplessly enmeshed.

To say that the Black masses came to lose faith in the so-called white establishment is an understatement. The great majority began to feel as if they were aliens in American society and regarded established white individuals and institutions as their enemy. This feeling was forcefully expressed by the great Black poets, writers, and spokesmen during the critical period in Black survival, the 1920s and 1930s. The poet Claude McKay may have best captured the Black nationalists' mood in his poem, "If We Must Die":

> If we must die, oh, let us nobly die,
> So that our precious blood may not be shed
> In vain;[37]

All available evidence shows that nationalism among Blacks has been a counter-response to white separatism. It has always been based on the belief that organized white society is their enemy and that Blacks must find a way of defending themselves against it. James Turner expresses this response:

> The black nationalist recognizes himself as belonging to an out-group, an alien in relation to the white society which controls the total universe in which he moves.
>
> Becoming a black nationalist seems to involve a realization that persons of African descent are treated categorically by the dominant group. Subsequently, there develops the firm conviction that Afro-Americans must become transmuted into a conscious and cohesive group. Race, color and mutual resistance to the oppression of the dominant group and its imposed assumptions and definitions about the minority, become the vehicles for realizing conversion from category to group. . . . Black nationalists argue for the exclusive right of members of the group to define, establish, and maintain their own group boundaries.[38]

All Black nationalistic organizations share at least three main traits: they have been mass-oriented, separatist, and have emphasized self-help and self-protection. These central, distinguishing characteristics are best reflected by three of the most successful of the Black nationalistic groups: the Universal Negro Improvement Association (the Marcus Garvey Movement of the 1920s and 1930s); the Black Muslims, which reached its greatest development during the 1950s and 1960s; and the Black Panthers, which was in the eye of the racial revolution of the late 1960s.

Garveyism. The Garvey movement, which flourished during the decade or so after World War I, was the first nationally significant Black nationalistic organization. E. David Cronon insists that: "up to this time no Negro organization had either seriously attempted or succeeded in the organization of the Negro masses. None. . . . had directed much attention to lower-class Negroes, but had instead depended upon the upper classes, both white and Negro, for intellectual and financial support."[39]

Garvey, a flamboyant man, relied mainly on intense emotional appeal and emphasized Black separatism and Black supremacy. He insisted that Blacks could never expect justice and dignity in white America and zealously attempted to unite Blacks in a movement calling for the renunciation of American citizenship and the establishment of an All-Black African Nation.

Garvey's Black racial chauvinism and "back-to-Africa" appeal made full use of the suspicions, prejudices, aspirations, frustrations, and limited intellectual attainments of the Black masses. Garveyism played into the hands of white supremacists because it criticized Blacks for attempting to integrate into American society. The movement was endorsed by the Ku Klux Klan. Small wonder, then, that it was repudiated by Black intellectuals and leaders. DuBois best expressed the opinion of the Black middle class regarding Garvey: "Marcus Garvey is, without doubt, the most dangerous enemy, of the Negro race in America and in the world. He is either a lunatic or a traitor."[40] DuBois also took sharp issue with Garvey's insistence "that no person of Negro descent can ever hope to become an American citizen. . . . That forcible separation of the races and the banishment of Negroes to Africa is the only solution of the Negro problem. . . . That race war is sure to follow any attempt to realize the program of the N.A.A.C.P."[41]

Despite criticism from all segments of the Black middle class and constant harassment from legal authorities, Garvey was able to attract a large following. The exact number is unknown, though Garvey estimated it to be more than two million and even DuBois admitted that it was perhaps 80,000. He was able to establish a considerable network of varied business enterprises, including the famous Black Star Shipping Line and a widely read paper, *The Negro World*. However, the best acknowledged, most far reaching of Garvey's contributions was the creation of genuine race pride among the disesteemed, downtrodden Black ghetto masses. They were organized as never before into cohesive subgroups—including a rather pompous military unit— and indoctrinated with the idea that Blacks constituted a superior people. Garvey taught Blacks to be proud of their African heritage and to recognize their own special beauty.

The Black Muslims. As the story of the rise and development of the Black Muslims is quite well known to students of the Black Experience, there is little need to repeat it here.[42] It is, however, apropos to point out some of its most salient nationalistic characteristics. This may be done by recalling some key statements by two of its most illustrious leaders, Elijah Muhammad and Malcolm X.

Arthur Littleton and Mary Burger report a speech made by Elijah Muhammad in 1965 entitled a "Message to the Blackman." In this speech or "message," he sets forth the essential nationalistic stance of the Black Muslims. It included the following key principles:[43]

1. *Appeal to the masses.* The Muslims depend upon the Black masses for their prime support, yet Muhammad appealed to the total Black population to unite. He denounced the Black middle class in these well-chosen words regarding Black unity:

What actually is preventing this unity of 22 million or more of us is the ignorance and foolish love and fear of our enemies in the professional and leadership class of this nation of 22 million black people up from slavery. . . . There are disgraceful "Uncle Toms" in a world of freedom, learning and advanced science of every branch of study.[44]

Therefore, Muhammad very cleverly appealed for unity, while at the same time clearly identifying with the masses.

2. *Separatism.* Muhammad said: "A prime requisite for freedom and independence is having one's own land. There can be no freedom without a people having their own land. . . . The Black people throughout the earth are seeking independence for their own, not integration into white society."[45] There have always been some unanswered questions about where the Muslims plan to establish an independent state of their own. This has yet to be definitely set forth. Muhammad leaves that very central problem unresolved even when he insists that ". . . we cannot demand recognition until we have some land that we can call our own." Then he adds: "You might argue that this is impossible, but I say to you, with Almighty Allah (God) on my side this is not only possible but is in the working for our people and will manifest itself soon!"[46] Muhammad concludes by saying that "integration means self-destruction, and the means to this end is exactly that—death and nothing less."

During recent years, Black Muslims have been voicing what they evidently regard as an ultimate eschatological answer to the question of where and how they will eventually establish a state of their own. Under Muhammad they have advocated withdrawal from the dominant society and claim that they are waiting for the "white devils" to destroy themselves. Presumedly, when this is done they believe that the nation of Islam will then inherit the earth and declare its independence.

3. *Self-help.* In this same "Message to the Blackman," Muhammad emphasizes the need for Blacks to help themselves and not depend upon help from white society:

It is time for you and me, the so-called Negroes, to start doing for ourselves. We must not let our children be as we are, beggars of another man. . . .

As a people we must become producers and not remain consumers and employees. . . . We must stop the process of giving our brain power, labor and wealth to our slaveren. We must eliminate the master slave

According to all reliable information, including advertisements in their own publication, *Muhammad Speaks*, the Black Muslims have gone far beyond any other Black nationalist group in achieving the self-help goals they set. They have established a nationwide network of varied business enterprises offering jobs and steady incomes to many of their members. These enterprises include farms, manufacturing, retail trade companies, and service agencies. Their efforts, however, have not stimulated the proliferation of new Black business enterprises as they might have if the Black middle class had taken their philosophy of self-help seriously.

Malcolm X. Malcolm X was one of the most charismatic Black leaders in history. No other spokesman articulated the Black experience more forcefully during the restless, turbulent ghetto crises of the late 1950s and early 1960s. He was much more than a Black Muslim preacher; he was a creative interpreter of the Black Experience. He extended the Muslims' goal to include all Blacks, regardless of their social or ideological persuasions. This is revealed in his "Message to the Grass Roots":

What you and I need to do is learn to forget our differences. . . . you don't catch hell because you're a Baptist or Methodist. . . . a Democrat or a Republican, a Mason or an Elk. . . .You catch hell because you're a black man. You catch hell, all of us catch hell, for the same reason.[48]

Malcolm X developed a tremendous rapport with the frustrated, angry Black masses by lambasting established, middle-class Black leaders, on the one hand, and by feeding their hatred of whites on the other. This double-pronged oratorical attack is revealed in the following, caustic statement:

There is no such thing as a nonviolent revolution. The only kind of revolution that is nonviolent is the Negro revolution. The only revolution in which the goal is loving your enemy is the Negro revolution.

Then he challenges: "Revolution is bloody, revolution is hostile, revolution knows no compromise, revolution overturns and destroys everything that gets in its way." And more pointedly: "Whoever heard of a revolution where they lock arms singing "We Shall Overcome." . . . These Negroes aren't asking for any nation—they're trying to crawl back on the plantation."[49]

Malcolm X clearly showed his preference for the Black masses over the Black middle class in his statement emphasizing the basic difference between two slave statuses, the "field hand" and the "house Negro." He glorified the field hand and interpreted his hatred of the white master as heroic. He pictured the house Negro as morally weak and a traitor to his race: "The field Negroes—those were the masses. . . . That house Negro loved his master, but that field Negro—remember, they were in the majority, and they hated the master." The context in which this statement was made leaves no doubt that Malcolm X pictured educated Blacks and traditional Black leaders as house Negroes or modern Uncle Toms. He charged that such leaders as Martin Luther King, Jr., Roy Wilkins, and James Farmer were being used by powerful whites to prevent the Black masses from fighting for their rights. He accused them of "selling out the Black revolution" as house Negroes had done during slavery. He then identified what he regarded as the Black man's enemy: "We have a common enemy. . . . We have a common oppressor, a common exploiter and a common discriminator. . . . whether he's in Georgia or Michigan, whether he's in California or New York. He is the same man—blue eyes and blond hair and pale skin—the same man."[50]

Finally, Malcolm X evaluated the role of the Black Muslim

movement in the fight for civil rights during the 1960s. In his "Prospects for Freedom in 1965," he claimed that: ". . . . Its contribution to the black struggle for freedom in this country was militancy. . . . The Muslim groups gave respectability to the civil rights groups."[51]

In conclusion, then, we may say that the Black Muslims' appeal to the masses in Black ghettos has encouraged Black self-respect and self-reliance, strengthened family life, and inspired traditional civil rights organizations to adopt a much more militant stance than they had hitherto expressed.

The Black Panther party. The Black Panther party has been a natural, endemic product of life in the big city ghetto. It was founded in Oakland, California, in 1966 by Huey P. Newton and Bobby Seale, at a time of widespread ghetto unrest and violence. Thus, the ideological stance of the organization articulates a peculiar synthesis of the Marxist-Leninist conception of social change and the revolutionary nationalism of Malcolm X.

From the very beginning the *raison d'être* of the Panther organization has been to deal with the insecurities, fears, and powerlessness characteristic of Black ghettos. It was designed to appeal to the millions of angry young Blacks who feel disesteemed, alienated, and persecuted by the white establishment. Therefore, for the most part, its members have come from the ranks of the rootless, restless, disillusioned Black youth who feel ignored or "written off" by established social institutions and programs. Its organizers and charter members were, in fact, bona fide representatives of this element in the Black ghetto subculture.

More than any other of the Black nationalistic groups, the Panthers addressed themselves directly to the problem of powerlessness and the sense of helplessness in the ghetto. This may be so primarily because, more than any other segment of the Black population, the disinherited Black ghetto male is subjected to the most frequent confrontations with the police—the most tangible symbol of white power in the ghetto. It is a well-known fact that Black young men generally tend to regard the police as a foreign army whose only designated purpose is to force Blacks to obey "white man's laws."

The most authentic evidence of the extent to which the Black Panthers feel alienated from the mainstream of American society is reflected in their formal declaration of "What We Want," in the 1966 Panther party's platform. Among the most pertinent of the ten official "wants" listed are the following:

1. "We want freedom. We want power to determine the destiny of our Black community."

Robert M. Fogelson believes that the insistence upon community control of the ghetto sets the Panther party apart from other brands of Black nationalism:

Before his assassination Malcolm X concluded that racism and capitalism were so intertwined that one could not be abolished without eliminating the other. And more recently. . . . the members of the Black Panthers insisted that blacks cannot expect social justice under the prevailing economic and political conditions.[52]

Fogelson concluded that

from this perspective the militants' demand for community control is fundamentally different from the Garveyites' quest for an independent African nation and the Muslims' demand for a separate American state. It is more realistic and yet more radical; it is, above all more political. . . . there is little doubt that with the emergence of community control, black nationalism has come of age politically.[53]

2. "We want all black men to be exempt from military service. We believe that Black people should not be forced to fight in the military service to defend a racist government that does not protect us."

3. "We want freedom for all black men held in federal, state, county and city prisons and jails."

4. "We want land, bread, housing, education, clothing, justice and peace. And as our major political objective, a United Nations-supervised plebiscite to be held throughout the black colony in which only black colonial subjects will be allowed to participate, for the purpose of determining the will of black people as to their national destiny."

The particular brand of nationalism advocated by the Panther party was further revealed in a listing of twenty-six Rules. One especially is apropos: "No party member can join any other army force other than the Black Liberation Army."

The overall influence of Malcolm X's Black militant ideology on the organization and outlook of the Panthers has been well expressed by Eldridge Cleaver, who was described by William Hedgepeth (*Look*, January 7, 1969) as "the ultimate in pantherdom. . . . author, editor, agitator, self-educated ex-convict, parole breaker and the hottest piece of radical merchandise on the market." Cleaver writes: "When I decided to join the Black Panther Party the only hang-up I had was with its name. I was still clinging to my conviction that we owed it to Malcolm to pick up where he left off. . . . For Huey, it meant implementing the program that Malcolm advocated." Then Cleaver indicated the direct influence of Malcolm X:

> For the revolutionary black youth today, time starts moving with the coming of Malcolm X. Before Malcolm, time stands still.
>
> Huey P. Newton is the ideological descendent, heir and successor of Malcolm X. Malcolm prophesied the coming of the gun to the black liberation struggle. Huey P. Newton picked up the gun and pulled the trigger, freeing the genie of black revolutionary violence in Babylon.[54]

Despite its militant nationalistic stance and the eloquent manner in which its leaders have articulated the fears, hates, anguish, alienation, and hopes of the young ghettorized Blacks, the Panther party has never attracted a significantly large following. Though no definite number or reasonable current estimate exists, close observers tend to agree that the membership was never more than a few thousand and generally numbered only a few hundred.[55] At no time has the Panther party developed the rational social organization or the effective self-help programs comparable to the Garvey movement or the Black Muslims. On the one hand it may be that its members have had to spend too much of their time, energy, and resources in confrontations and clashes with the police and in prolonged, costly court cases. On the other hand, its militant ideology —which emphasized what they called "revolutionary suicide"—tended to discourage a large devoted following. Throughout the centuries Black Americans have been obsessed with survival, not suicide; therefore, the great majority of Blacks rejected the Panther-type militancy which insisted that "power grows out of the barrel of a gun." They saw how this philosophy led to near genocide of the Panthers during the late 1960s, when several of its top leaders were killed in police shootouts and others were jailed or forced underground. The Black masses seem to agree with the Panthers' definition of the problems of the ghetto and tend to sympathize with their plight vis-à-vis the police. Yet, they have been unwilling to participate, in large numbers, in their bloody confrontations.

Perhaps the greatest contributions of the Black Panther party to Black liberation and advancement have been (1) its unequivocal, realistic definition of the survival problem faced by relatively powerless Blacks in a racist society, and (2) its assistance in firmly establishing the sociological and political perimeters of the Blacks' perennial struggle for equal citizenship and dignity. Thus, at one extreme we find the disciples or followers of Martin Luther King, Jr., who espouse a radical, Christian-oriented, nonviolent, peaceful approach to Black liberation and progress. This approach celebrates the body of values we refer to as the "American Creed" and sanctions existing American institutions. At the other extreme are the Black Panthers, who express serious doubts about, or even contempt for, some of the basic values inherent in the American Creed and frequently advocate the overthrow of some basic institutions.

James Baldwin sensed this set of alternatives in regard to the "problem of the color line" in American society and stated the two clearly divergent approaches to its solution:

> If we—and now I mean the relatively conscious whites and the relatively conscious blacks, who must, like lovers, insist on, or create, the consciousness of the others—do not falter in our duty now, we may be able, handful that we are, to end the racial nightmare, and achieve our country. If we do not now dare everything, the fulfillment of that prophecy, re-created from the Bible in a song by a slave, is upon us: *God gave Noah the rainbow sign, no more water, the fire next time.*[56]

Since effective social organization is the ultimate source of social power, it may be instructive at this point to examine some basic social organizations in the New Orleans ghetto.

The Church in the New Orleans Ghetto

About the only organization espoused and supported by the very poor in the Black ghetto studied is the church. Fully 90 percent of the heads of families in the study claimed to hold membership in some church or at least identified with some religious denomination (see tabulation on page 157).

A careful examination of the information interviewees gave about their religious beliefs and practices revealed at least two important findings:

1. *Individuals who live in the Black ghetto are likely to cling to the faith of their rural forebears.* Though New Orleans is a predominantly Catholic city, only about a fourth of the Blacks

Denomination	Percentage
Baptist	60
Catholic	27
Methodist	7
(all branches)	
Others	6
	___
Total	100

in the sample identified with the Catholic church.[57] Like their parents and grandparents, they are usually Baptists. Only about 8 percent (7 percent Methodist and 1 percent "others") belonged to what is generally regarded as traditionally middle-class churches. Most in the "other" category were formerly Baptists who joined esoteric religious sects or cults. Only 11 percent of the adult respondents reported a different denominational affiliation than their parents.

There are several reasons why religious Blacks are still predominantly Baptist, despite the many pulls to identify otherwise in the urban ghetto, which is far from the plantation culture of their ancestors:

(a) The Baptist ritual is relatively informal and does not presuppose the level of literacy that is ordinarily needed to participate in the services of some other churches.

(b) Despite avowed institutionalized mission programs, the more formal, white-controlled denominations have made only weak, sporadic attempts to "save" the very poor in the Black ghetto. Some Blacks insist that they cannot really worship in such churches, which they identify with what one interviewee described as a "white man's religion and a white man's way of thinking."[58] They object primarily to the lack of freedom provided to give spontaneous expression to their own "soul."

(c) Blacks have more control of Baptist churches than they do over the other traditional churches. The pastor of a Baptist church is selected or "called" by the members themselves and does not answer to any other authority. Therefore, members are the unmistakable "boss." They make all decisions pertaining to the church's organization and operation.

(d) More than any other institution in the ghetto, the Baptist church has perpetuated and celebrated the religious heritage of Black people. It has done much to preserve Negro spirituals and the artistic style of preaching that complements the imagery and freedom of the spiritual.[59] It is not surprising that, when asked why they attended church, practically all of the older interviewees gave the same simple answer: "I enjoy the services." This is quite different from the Catholics in the sample who gave answers suggesting duty to God, family, or themselves.

The enjoyment expressed by many of the Protestant devotees stems from their feeling of being in a familiar social setting. The congregation, including the minister, is usually uniclass, in the sense that all of the members are poor and live in the same community. In such a setting they can feel free to express themselves through active participation in the more or less informal church services: they can escape, for a time, the feeling of alienation and insecurity inherent in their daily lives.

2. *The Black masses, on the whole, are not as religious as they were once believed to be.* When asked how often they attended church the parents in the sample replied as follows:

	Fathers	Mothers
Regularly	38%	60%
Occasionally	41%	25%
Seldom or Never	21%	15%
Total	100%	100%

Most who reported attending church regularly were older parents, usually women. Characteristically, they complained that other members of their households displayed little or no interest in the church's programs and only attended on special occasions or when pressured to do so. Interviews with pastors in the neighborhood revealed that very few young adults or youth ever become meaningfully involved in the church's interests and programs. One pastor estimated that about 90 percent of his church's budget and program support "come from grand-mothers." On days when research personnel attended churches in the target area, from two-thirds to three-fourths of the con-gregations were women. There were four occasions when up to 85 percent of the congregations were women. Most of the women who attended church regularly had practically no other significant social outlet. Upon close, probing questioning, 73 percent of the women, compared with just 37 percent of the men, revealed that they had no "real friends" outside of their church circle.

Despite the strong, indispensable support women give to churches in the ghetto, they seem to be contented to support men for the top positions of authority. Only one church in the New Orleans ghetto had a woman as pastor, and this was an esoteric sect with only a few men in attendance and none in positions of authority. The fact that only a few women hold major church offices does not mean that they are not important in decision-making. They certainly are. Pastors of ghetto churches recognize the influence of women and tend to act according to their wishes. This might be the basic reason why most churches in the ghetto are still primarily concerned with "other-worldly," purely ritual procedures and interests rather than with the knotty, mundane, practical problems with which their members must deal. Apparently, most of the women who support these churches have given up hope that the socioeconomic problems characterizing their daily lives can be solved by any effort on their part. Their main efforts, then, are directed toward escaping these problems for a few hours each week as they "enjoy" the services in their churches. According to an earlier study: "Rarely do Negro women in New Orleans initiate, stimulate, coordinate, or direct the activities of the Negro masses in the solution of major social problems affecting them. None has [in 1963] become a symbol of the Negro's struggle to achieve equality of citizenship."[60] To the extent that older women influence decision-making in certain Black churches, we would expect these churches to be "other-worldly" in their pattern of commitments. Consequently, even though some ministers in ghetto churches have distinguished themselves as civil rights and community leaders, for the most part their churches, as institutions, have remained outside the Blacks' struggle to acquire equal citizenship. This aloofness has caused severe criticism in some quarters because it is felt that the Black church could be much more effective in racial advancement than it has been.[61] This may be an important reason why some of the more activist-oriented Black youth are turning to the Black Muslim religion and to certain antireligious, militant organizations in the ghetto.[62] Some are evidently seeking organizations through which they can actively participate in the survival and progress of the Black masses.

Secular organizations. Individuals in the Black ghetto are not usually joiners. Only 12 percent of the heads of families in the sample belonged to any organization outside the church. A mere 1 percent claimed membership in any civil rights organization at a time (1968) when the civil rights movement was at its zenith. Again, to underscore the relative powerlessness of the Black masses, while nearly all of the individuals employed had "blue collar" jobs, only 1 percent was active in labor unions and just five of these held any leadership position. These individuals were affiliated with a powerful, predominantly Black longshoremen's union.

The most significant nonreligious organization in the ghetto studied was the local Parent-Teachers Association. Ten percent of the parents claimed membership in that organization. Other mothers said that they attended meetings of the PTA once or twice a year. The local PTA is not concerned with community power as such; rather, it is narrowly concerned with the children enrolled in specific schools.

Fraternal organizations and their once-popular women's auxiliaries seem to be disappearing in the ghetto. Only a few adults (3 percent) claimed membership in the Masons, Odd Fellows,

Elks, Eastern Star, and other organizations. These groups were quite prestigious in rural communities until the great migration of the 1940s and 1950s and tended to hold their own in urban communities prior to World War II. The Masons, who conducted rites at a funeral in a church in the target neighborhood, were all men in their sixties and over.

At the time of the study, there was very little political interest among the adults studied. After a long, hard struggle to become enfranchised, the 1965 Voting Rights Act was regarded by civil rights leaders as a major accomplishment. All artificial barriers to registering and voting that Blacks had always encountered were swept aside. Registering to vote was a simple task requiring little time. Nevertheless, three years after the act had been in effect only 10 percent of the parents in the sample were actually registered voters. Since then, however, Blacks have been running for public office in increasing numbers. Their campaigning in the ghetto has brought about a considerable increase in the number of Black voters. The proportion voting, however, is still believed to be far below the city's average.

When asked why they did not register to vote, the interviewees gave several reasons. Among the most plausible is that they have little substantive faith in traditional politics or professional politicians. This was expressed by every person in the sample. A young truck driver put it this way: "I have always voted because I believe it is a part of being a man. It's my duty as a citizen. Yet I feel that politics is a crooked game. Some good guys become crooks when they get into politics. One thing for sure—Blacks never get anything out of politics. Politics is a white man's game. He knows how to win."

Some of the antipoverty programs operating at that time in the ghetto did have an important effect: they involved indigenous individuals in discussions of public policy. This experience has indirectly led to a greater political awareness among the masses as they have had to relate to federally sponsored agencies. Increasingly, the politically hopeless or complacent have begun to become interested in politics as they are related to their personal welfare. Some of the younger, politically oriented Blacks are cultivating this new interest in politics in the hope of launching their own political careers. If this trend continues, the Black ghetto could become a great force in local politics. As yet, the political organization of the Black masses is, at best, in its embryonic stage of development.

The most frequent and obvious reminder of powerlessness in the Black ghetto is the naked display of police power. When parents were asked to express what they believed to be the prevailing attitude of the people they knew regarding the police, they gave the following answers:

	Percentage
Favorable	38
Neutral	21
Definitely unfavorable	41
	———
Total	100

Even those who felt that the police had a favorable image among the people they knew agreed that the police practiced unnecessary brutality in dealing with Blacks. Some of the interviewees, especially those who had been victims of crime, argued that much of the brutality was necessary because the criminals police must deal with are also brutal and dangerous. However, the frequent display of power by the police was resented by the ghetto residents. A group of community leaders discussed this problem at length on two occasions during the research. They agreed that the police department tended to assign the most discourteous and racist police to their neighborhood. While these leaders wanted much more police protection than the community was receiving—because so many persons in the community were victims of crimes—they contended that the police were characteristically insulting and used unnecessary force, even during routine action. These leaders expressed fears that eventually there would be open conflict between the police and certain Black youth. A pastor said: "Every boy I know hates the police. Some of these boys are just plain bad and are always in trouble. Most, however, are good boys whom the police harass just because they have the power to do so." Fundamentally, it seems that the ghetto Blacks resent the police because they are often insulting and punitive and so constantly remind them of their own powerlessness. This was the central suggestion of the Kerner Report: ". . . to many Negroes police have come to symbolize white power, white racism and white repression. And the fact is that many police do reflect and express these white attitudes."[63] Black youth and young adults in the ghetto have such a negative image of the police that, despite their need for employment and the repeated efforts to recruit them by the police department, few of them seek to become policemen.

The ultimate Black experience is the Black family. A strong, viable family anywhere presupposes strong, reliable social institutions and agencies to bolster it. Without this support from the larger society the family cannot achieve its own unique goals. The Black ghetto family has not had the community support it needs; it can seldom depend upon sustained support from other community institutions. The Black family is frequently exploited and victimized by the very agencies established to assist the poor. This is an important reason why an increasing number of Black leaders are insisting that ways must be found to give Black people control over the institutions and agencies essential to their welfare.

The concept of control over indigenous institutions is not as simple as some assume. For instance, control of ghetto schools by ghetto people would be of little if any benefit to the inhabitants unless they also had significant representation on school boards and in state legislatures which determine overall educational policy and funding. The same is true of other institutions and agencies operating in the Black ghetto. To get control of structures and programs without gaining control of funding could be an empty victory.

In the final analysis, the Black ghetto is an integral part of the larger community and must be treated as such if its people are to benefit from the economic and social advancement in the larger society. Community separatism is hardly a satisfactory approach. Problems of the Black ghetto can be solved only by a fair and effective integration of indigenous Black leaders in original policy-planning and the central administration of organizations that deal with these problems. Blacks, through their representatives, must have equal participation in the mainstream of social power in the larger community.

NOTES

[1]For a detailed analysis, see *U. S. Riot Commission Report* (New York: The New York Times Co., 1968), pp. 135-148.

[2]See Kenneth B. Clark, *Dark Ghetto* (New York: Harper and Row, 1965), pp. 154-198.

[3]See Lee Rainwater, *Behind Ghetto Walls* (Chicago: Aldine Press, 1970), pp. 406-425.

[4]Carter G. Woodson, *The History of the Negro Church* (Washington, D. C.: The Associated Publishers, 1921), p. 266.

[5]Ibid., p. 267.

[6]W. E. B. DuBois, *The Philadelphia Negro* (New York: Schocken Books, 1967—first published in 1899), p. 201.

[7]E. Franklin Frazier, *The Negro Church in America* (New York: Schocken Books, 1966, 1972), pp. 85-86.

[8]Benjamin E. Mays, *Born to Rebel* (New York: Charles Scribner's Sons, 1971), pp. 13, 15.

[9]Charles V. Hamilton, *The Black Preacher in America* (New York: William Morrow and Co., Inc., 1972), pp. 13-14.

[10]Ibid., p. 227.

[11]Daniel C. Thompson, *The Negro Leadership Class* (Englewood Cliffs, N. J.: Prentice-Hall, Inc., 1963), p. 34.

[12]See, for instance, Hart M. Nelsen, *The Black Church in America* (New York: Basic Books, Inc., 1971); E. Franklin Frazier, *The Negro Church in America*; Benjamin E. Mays, *The Negro's God* (New York:

Atheneum Press, 1968); and Major J. Jones, *Black Awareness: A Theology of Hope* (Nashville: Abingdon Press, 1971).

[13]Gayraud S. Wilmore, *Black Religion and Black Radicalism* (New York: Anchor Books, 1972), pp. 36-37.

[14]Eugene D. Genovese, *In Red and Black* (New York: Vintage Books, 1971), p. 108.

[15]W. E. B. DuBois, *The Souls of Black Folk* (New York: Washington Square Press, 1903 and 1970), pp. 159-161.

[16]Melville J. Herskovits, *The Myth of the Negro Past* (New York: Harper and Brothers, 1941), p. 225, passim.

[17]Frazier, *The Negro Church in America*, p. 1.

[18]Ibid., p. 6.

[19]C. Eric Lincoln, "Preface" to James H. Cone, *Liberation* (New York: J. B. Lippincott Co., 1970), p. 8.

[20]Abraham Chapman, ed., *Black Voices* (New York: A Mentor Book, 1968), pp. 364-366.

[21]Benjamin Quarles, *The Negro in the Making of America* (New York: Collier Books, 1964), pp. 99-102.

[22]Eugene Genovese, "Origins of The Folk Religion," An Unpublished Manuscript, now in publication.

[23]Quarles, *The Negro in the Making of America*, p. 100.

[24]Gunnar Myrdal, *An American Dilemma* (New York: Harper and Row, 1944), pp. 858-861.

[25]Ibid., pp. 720-724.

[26]Quarles, *The Negro in the Making of America*, pp. 78-82.

[27]John Hope Franklin, *From Slavery To Freedom* (New York: Vintage Books, 1969), p. 227.

[28]Ibid., p. 227.

[29]Henry Lee Moon, *The Emerging Thought of W. E. B. DuBois* (New York: Simon and Schuster, 1972), pp. 254, 259-261. See also Franklin, *From Slavery to Freedom*, pp. 477-497.

[30]Jay David, ed., *Black Defiance* (New York: William Morrow and Co., Inc., 1972), pp. 85-86, 87-91. For a general discussion of race riots following World War I, see Franklin, *From Slavery To Freedom*, pp. 475-497, and Myrdal, *An American Dilemma*, pp. 1004-1008.

[31]Myrdal, *An American Dilemma*, pp. 233-235.

[32]Ibid., p. 197.

[33]Frazier, *The Negro Church in America*, p. 48.

[34]St. Clair Drake and Horace R. Cayton, *Black Metropolis* (New

York: Harper and Row, Publishers, 1945 and 1962), Vol. II, pp. 415-416.

[35]Benjamin E. Mays and Joseph W. Nicholson, *The Negro's Church* (New York: Negro University Press, 1933), p. 313.

[36]Clark, *Dark Ghetto*, p. 174.

[37]Arna Bontemps, ed., *American Negro Poetry* (New York: Hill and Wang, 1963), p. 31.

[38]James Turner, "The Sociology of Black Nationalism," in Joyce A. Ladner, ed., *The Death of White Sociology* (New York: Vintage Books, 1973), pp. 235-236.

[39]E. David Cronon, *Black Moses: The Story of Marcus Garvey* (Madison: The University of Wisconsin Press, 1969), p. 37.

[40]Henry Lee Moon, *The Emerging Thought of W. E. B. DuBois* (New York: Simon and Schuster, 1972), p. 325.

[41]Ibid., p. 325.

[42]For a systematic analysis of the Black Muslims, see C. Eric Lincoln, *The Black Muslims in America* (Boston: Beacon Press, 1961), and E. V. Essien-Udom, *Black Nationalism* (New York: Dell Publishing Co., Inc., 1962).

[43]Arthur C. Littleton and Mary W. Burger, *Black Viewpoints* (New York: A Mentor Book, 1964), pp. 152-158.

[44]Ibid., p. 155.

[45]Ibid., p. 157.

[46]Ibid., pp. 155-156.

[47]Ibid., pp. 152-153.

[48]Malcolm X, "Message to the Grass Roots," in Richard P. Young, ed., *Roots of Rebellion* (New York: Harper and Row, Publishers, 1970), p. 347.

[49]Ibid., pp. 351-352.

[50]Ibid., pp. 348-349.

[51]Ibid., pp. 359-360.

[52]Robert M. Fogelson, *Violence as Protest* (New York: Anchor Books, 1971), p. 12.

[53]Ibid., p. 159.

[54]For a full presentation of this discussion, see Robert Scheer, ed., "Eldridge Cleaver: Post-Prison Writings and Speeches," in Jay David., ed., *Black Defiance* (New York: William Morrow and Co., 1972), pp. 222-237.

[55]Edward Peeks, *The Long Struggle for Black Power* (New York: Charles Scribner's Sons, 1971), p. 401.

[56]James Baldwin, *The Fire Next Time* (New York: The Dial Press, 1967), pp. 119-120.

[57]The Catholic Church has not had great success in recruiting Blacks in the ghetto. Blacks remain primarily Protestant. See Clark, *Dark Ghetto*, p. 179.

[58]See a discussion of this by Frazier, *The Negro Church in America*, pp. 53-67.

[59]Hart M. Nelsen, Raytha L. Yorkley, and Anne K. Nelsen, *The Black Church in America*, pp. 135-137.

[60]Thompson, *The Negro Leadership Class*, pp. 25-26. Since the latter part of the 1960s, some middle-class Black women have distinguished themselves as community leaders.

[61]See, for instance, Nelsen, Yorkley, and Nelsen, *The Black Church in America*, pp. 299-314.

[62]Clark, *Dark Ghetto*, pp. 214-217.

[63]*U. S. Riot Commission Report*, p. 206.

6

Education

The Blacks' struggle to acquire a "good" education has been long, frustrating, and dangerous. Motivating the struggle has been the conviction that education is the key to individual dignity, social status, and equal citizenship. Even during the slave period when the education of Blacks was prohibited by law and when those who violated that law were severely punished, many slaves dared to attend "clandestine" schools and learned to read and write whenever and however they could manage to do so.

Henry A. Bullock gives an excellent description of the determination of some slaves to get an education:

Historical literature is replete with cases of slaves who struggled to gain literacy (by defying state laws). Old slaves give mixed accounts of these educational escapades. In the experience of some, learning was the expected thing—an apparently formal course, of plantation life; for others, it was a forbidden and clandestine undertaking into which only the young would venture.[1]

Despite heroic efforts to gain literacy, according to the most reliable estimates, at the close of the Civil War only 2 or 3 percent of the 4 million freedmen were able to read and write.

For the most part whatever education they had received was informal, unsystematic, and superficial.

The movement to provide formal education for Black Americans began during the Reconstruction period. All concerned observers—the President, certain congressmen, heads of religious bodies, and some influential educators—agreed that it was urgent that schools for Blacks be established if they were to retain their tenuous freedom or even survive in the prevailing anti-Black atmosphere of the bitter, defeated post-Civil War South. Therefore, northern church bodies, with some important assistance from the Freedmen's Bureau, which was established by Congress in 1865, and private philanthropy, began to establish separate schools for Blacks because schools for whites would not accept them.

From the beginning, schools for Blacks met strong opposition from southern whites. Some powerful whites objected to the education of Blacks per se. Others suspected northern white teachers of subversion, and there was a widespread fear that educated Blacks would become too independent and not make good workers and servants. In some communities, white planters and employers used the threat of firing and eviction from houses to prevent Black parents from sending their children to the "missionary schools." Also, it was not uncommon for marauding bands of whites to attack teachers and burn down schoolhouses.

> Many of these incidents were mischievous pranks, but most were overt expressions of an intense resentment of any action taken to educate Negoes. Since they were more or less common to the entire South, they combined to keep the freedmen's school movement unstable and the pupils and teachers insecure. They set a pattern that would prevail for almost one hundred years.[2]

Throughout the hostile, dangerous years of Reconstruction and during the more than seventy years that followed, Blacks continued to struggle against powerful anti-federal, anti-Black forces in their attempts to establish and maintain schools for their children. Despite the many handicaps and frustrations inherent in the biracial system, in which they were regarded as innately inferior, the Blacks' faith in themselves, their abilities, and the efficacy of education never wavered. There was evidence of their increasing determination to get a good education, even at great sacrifice. This unremitting thirst to acquire an education was dramatically recounted by Benjamin E. Mays in his autobiography:

My prayers were all variations of the same theme: a petition to God to enable me to get away to school. My desire for an education was not only a dream but a goal that drove and prodded me, day and night. . . . I accepted the prayer Jargon of the older people. I asked God to move out of my way "every hindrance and cause" which kept me from getting an education.[3]

At first Blacks attempted to find ways to make their own segregated schools truly equal to white schools in the same communities. Eventually, it became obvious that they would never attain equality of educational opportunity in the biracial society in which they were disesteemed and powerless. Thus, their strategy to acquire equal educational opportunity gradually, but definitely, shifted from attempts to equalize their own schools to the persistent use of this nation's legal machinery, especially the federal courts, in an outright abolishment of racial segregation.

Finally, on May 17, 1954, almost 100 years after the Emancipation Proclamation, the U. S. Supreme Court decided that:

In these days it is doubtful that any child can reasonably be expected to succeed in life if he is denied the opportunity of an education. Such an opportunity. . . . is a right which must be made available to all on equal terms. . . . We conclude that in the field of public education the doctrine of "separate but equal" has no place. Separate educational facilities are inherently unequal.[4]

The Court's decision outlawing racial segregation in public schools was regarded by many civil rights advocates as the most revolutionary national event since the signing of the Emancipation Proclamation by Abraham Lincoln on January 1, 1863. But that decision was almost as vigorously opposed by southern whites as was the freeing of slaves. It stimulated a powerful, well-organized white backlash that not only successfully resisted the Supreme Court's decision but also succeeded in taking away from Blacks some of the status gains they had already won.

In 1956 Harold Fleming, of the Southern Regional Council, estimated that at least 20 such [resistance] groups had appeared on the southern scene since the Supreme Court's 1954 decision.

Although they can claim only a small minority of the total white population of the South as members, these groups still comprise the largest body of southern whites who mobilize for the expression of their opinions on the question of desegregation. The opinions they express by words and action are, of course, unequivocally pro-segregation.[5]

These influential white resistance groups generally molded public opinion and policy regarding race relations throughout the nation, particularly in the South. According to election results, they actually controlled at least four southern states.

Significance of the 1954 decision.[6] The 1954 Supreme Court decision deliberately rejected the "separate but equal" doctrine of race relations that was legally established by the 1896 decision. These two contradictory constitutional interpretations emphasize two basic roles the Supreme Court has played in changing the status of Blacks. (1) It has legitimatized patterns of race relations already established by customs and state laws. This was essentially the nature of the 1896 decision. (2) It has occasionally rendered decisions that were intended to give direction to changes in race relations. This was certainly inherent in the 1954 decision.

The U. S. Supreme Court gave constitutional sanction to an already deeply entrenched, discriminatory biracial system for more than 50 years. It was not until the late 1930s that it even looked beyond lower court rulings to find out if segregated facilities for Blacks were in fact unequal to those provided for whites, as numerous Blacks had constantly contended. Yet, after World War II the Court began to shift its position to the point where it did look into Blacks' charges of discrimination and ordered states to live up to their "separate but equal" commitment in the area of race relations, and eventually, in 1954, it declared segregation unconstitutional altogether. The main question is—why did this basic change take place?

The interpretation of the spirit of the law by the 1954 Court was completely different from that of 1896. The basic reason for this change was the fact that these decisions were made in response to very different stages in this nation's development. This was specifically noted by Mr. Chief Justice Warren who read the unanimous opinion: "In approaching this problem, we cannot turn the clock back to 1868 when the 14th Amendment was adopted, even to 1896 when the Plessy v. Ferguson was written. We must consider public education in the light of its full development and its present place in American life throughout the nation."[7]

In 1896 ours was a predominantly agrarian society, and the economic, political, and social aspects of life articulated conservative, even "folk" values. By 1954 only 13 percent of the U. S. population was engaged in agriculture. Blacks were in the midst of a great rural exodus, with about 40 percent already living outside the South and only about 16 percent still in agriculture. The Blacks' migration to urban areas had created new racial problems as cities were strained to provide jobs, housing, education, and other public services. Thus, American society in 1954 had become predominantly urban and industrial and large cities outside the South had become increasingly more powerful economically and politically. Although the eastern cities were not the "promised land" Blacks sought, they were considerably more liberal than the nation was in 1896. Their relative liberalism reflected the fact that Blacks in cities outside the South were generally enfranchised and exerted far more political strength within their states and districts.

In 1896 the U. S. government adhered strictly to its policy of isolationism.[8] Even as late as the 1920s, isolationism characterized our basic foreign policy. By 1937, however, the United States had become significantly involved in foreign affairs. It could no longer discount the rise of Communism in Russia, Fascism in Italy, Nazism in Germany, or Japan's bid for international power.

By 1940 it was obvious that the United States could not continue to maintain its policy of isolationism. President Franklin D. Roosevelt warned that such a policy would lead to this nation becoming "a lone island in a world dominated by the philosophy of force," and concluded later, that we should become the "arsenal of democracy."

The United States emerged from World War II (which ushered in the nuclear age) as the leader of what was termed the "free world." Some of the nations we proposed to "lead" were represented by nonwhites. These nations immediately began to express suspicion of the United States because it had maintained a biracial society.[9]

This nation's role as world leader became crucial when Russia became her close competitor. Through her top representatives, Russia clearly challenged the United States to competition in all fields, including the military. This challenge was echoed in Russia's propaganda of her own brand of "democracy" versus America's undemocratic racial policies and practices. By 1954 some very influential Americans had begun to insist that this nation should revitalize its commitment to achieve a society based on equal citizenship.

In 1896 the literacy rate in the United States was much lower than in 1954. Less emphasis was placed on education: only 7 percent of the children of high school age were in school. By 1954, approximately 80 percent of all children of high school age were enrolled in school. Further, in 1896 there were only about 150,000 college students in the nation; in 1954 there were nearly 3 million.

Not only had the level of education of Americans generally increased, but the relative level of education among Blacks had improved even more. In 1896 more than half (57 percent) of the Black population ten years old and over were illiterate. By 1954 less than 10 percent were illiterate and there were 100,000 Black college students.

The great increase in the education of Blacks signaled a better educated and sophisticated Black leadership. No longer was the burden of Black leadership resting almost exclusively on Black ministers, as was the case in 1896. Strong, competent Black leaders could be found in education, government, law, labor, business, literature, sports, as well as religion. After World War II, Black leaders, representing all aspects of the Black community, organized to fight for civil rights.

In 1896 more than two-thirds of the jobs in the nation could be done by unskilled laborers. Just before 1940 the percentage had shrunk to 36, and by 1954 it was estimated that only about 19 percent of this nation's jobs could be done by illiterate or unskilled workers. And even a large proportion of these jobs were being threatened by automation. Therefore, Mr. Chief Justice Warren observed, in the *Brown* decision, that unlike what was true in 1896, "Today education is perhaps the most important function of state and local governments. . . . [it] is required in the performance of our most basic public responsibilities, even service in the armed forces. It is the very foundation of good citizenship."[10]

In 1954, then, the U. S. Supreme Court decision drew upon

the most reliable findings and interpretations of some of the most reputable social scientists, political experts, lawyers, and leaders in all major walks of life, and concluded that old laws and customs requiring segregated schools not only limited the development of the individual but also weakened and threatened our national life and security. The Court decided that there was no legal or moral alternative but to strike down the infamous and inherently discriminatory "separate but equal" doctrine of race relations.

Responses to the 1954 Decision

As constitutionally logical and just as the 1954 decision was, it triggered a chain of explosive responses throughout the American social system that have continued until today— twenty years later. The justices evidently sensed the revolutionary nature of their decision and attempted to mitigate the harsh response and rebellion expected from white segregationists. Therefore, they inserted a key phrase in the decision: "with all deliberate speed." In essence, this phrase modified the decision by clearly indicating that compliance could be evolutionary rather than revolutionary, so that each segregated school and each biracial school system would be permitted to design its own plan of change and set its own timetable.

The Court's modified order to desegregate public schools gave white opposition leaders ample time to organize more extensively and effectively. In communities throughout the South, an almost invincible white backlash rapidly developed, which actually "turned back the clock" in the field of education and in the area of race relations. Strong, resourceful antidesegregation forces emerged which employed every conceivable resistance tactic from peaceful persuasion, persistent legal procedures, blatantly unconstitutional legislation, to vicious anti-Black propaganda, economic reprisals, flagrant terror and lynchings, and the closing of public schools. Thus, by applying a wide variety of legal, extralegal and illegal strategies, an-

tidesegregation forces have had disconcerting success in circumventing and frustrating both the letter and the spirit of the
1954 decision. Even now, after more than two decades of
planning, constant litigation, confrontations, sporadic violence, endless studies, and contradictory findings and interpretations, the constitutional issues regarding school desegregation
are still unsettled. In the meantime, according to the recent
report by a congressional committee:

> . . . the plain fact is that full educational opportunities—so
> fundamental to success in American life—are denied to
> millions of American children who are born poor or non-
> white. [And that] Nationally . . . of a total of 9.3 million
> minority-group students—5.9 million, or more than 60
> percent, attended [in 1970] predominantly minority-group
> schools. At the same time, 72 percent of the Nation's
> nonminority-group students attend more than 90 percent
> nonminority schools.[11]

The report also points out that Black students are still isolated in
twenty-one key states and the District of Columbia where 50.5
percent are attending schools that are 80 to 100 percent Black.
From 1954 until 1969, the desegregation of schools was almost
completely stymied by one legal technicality after another.
Thus, as late as 1968, 68 percent of all Black students in the
nation were attending schools that were 80 to 100 percent
Black, with 78.8 percent of Black students in the South attending schools where 80 to 100 percent of the students were Black.
In 1968, 68 percent of the South's Black students were in
all-Black schools. *This was fourteen years after segregated
schools were declared unconstitutional.*

The desegregation of schools was greatly accelerated in 1969
when the U. S. Supreme Court was finally convinced that the
concept "all deliberate speed," in the 1954 decision, functioned to take the enforcement teeth out of the order to desegregate. The 1969 order was to desegregate "at once." This new

language was directed at school districts where segregated schools were supported by Jim Crow laws. School districts in northern and western states where widespread de facto racial segregation exists were not significantly affected. The new language of the Court, then, placed uncommon pressure upon the eleven southern states to whom the mandate to desegregate implied legal, not simply sociological, changes. Consequently, in 1968, 57.4 percent of the Black students outside the South attended schools that were 80 to 100 percent Black. There was little or no significant change in response to the new 1969 decision. In 1971, 57.1 percent of Black students in schools outside the South were still in schools that were 80 to 100 percent Black.

The 1969 decision, directed at the South, had a very significant effect in bringing about school desegregation. In 1968, 78.8 percent of the Black students in the South were in schools with 80 to 100 percent Black students, *with 68 percent in all-Black schools. By 1971, only 32.2 percent of Black students in the South were in 80 to 100 percent Black schools, and just 9.2 percent were in all-Black schools.* [12] This is a very important sociological fact because it emphasizes the creative role of law in social change, even when change runs counter to deeply entrenched mores.

As we look back upon the more than twenty years of costly litigation, community disruptions and crises, student dislocation, widespread bitterness, and violence related to the issue of school desegregation, we can observe a new, challenging dimension of the Black Experience. Apropos to an understanding of this dimension is an analysis of this basic question: Why, in a nation avowedly dedicated to the principles of democracy, where every child is guaranteed an equal right to the best education available, has the process of school desegregation aroused so much antagonism, division, and pain? The answer to this question is, of course, quite complex and buried deeply in the ethos of American civilization, where notwithstanding the sincere belief in a democratic society, there also exists the belief in the myth of white supremacy. The biracial system is the most obvious manifestation of this belief. Any threat to this traditional myth is also a threat to the biracial system that dispenses numerous special privileges and rewards to whites, while it provides an intriguing contradictory ideological rationale for discrimination against Blacks. This rather synthetic ideology, based on a sociological myth, makes it entirely possible for white individuals and institutions to espouse both democratic principles and systematic discrimination against Blacks without experiencing the *dilemma* Gunnar Myrdal claimed to have observed. One of the classic examples of how democracy and extreme racism can be synthesized is what Seymour Lipset and Earl Raab call the "New Nativism" of George Wallace of Alabama.[13] In order to win votes in the 1968 presidential campaign, he skillfully exploited racist issues in what he alleged to be a defense of basic democratic principles. Accordingly, he attempted to suppress dissent and thwart every aspect of the civil rights movement by constructing a conspiracy theory in which desegregation was defined as a process of destroying "true" American democracy. Thus, in his governor's inaugural address, he had promised "segregation today, segregation tomorrow, segregation forever."

> Wallace laid the basis for the most comprehensive ideology of monism the country had seen since World War II, including the element of majoritarian disruption of the democratic process. "There is one thing more powerful than the Constitution . . ." he said, "That's the will of the people . . ." His speeches were replete with statements that would eliminate the sources of evil in society without regard to due process of constitutional rights.[14]

Wallace's enunciation of the "new nativistic" ideology, which was designed to synthesize the basic principles of democracy with the doctrine of white supremacy, was quite convincing: "George Wallace secured almost 10,000,000 votes, or about 13.5 percent of the total voting electorate. He captured five states with forty-five electoral votes. All of them were in the Deep South. . . . Mississippi, Arkansas, Georgia, Alabama, and Louisiana.''[15]

Just as Martin Luther King, Jr., became the symbolic head of the new civil rights movement of the 1950s and 1960s, George Wallace became the symbolic head of the new white backlash opposing the civil rights movement. Also, just as the new civil rights movement generated a much more united and powerful thrust than ever before, the white backlash became a powerful force in national politics. And even though Wallace did not win the presidency, he defined the political issues in such a way that he became a major force in shaping American politics on race relations, especially regarding the desegregation of schools.

Let us turn now to an analysis of the role of the civil rights movement and the white backlash as a means of understanding the nature of the social struggle triggered by the 1954 and 1969 U. S. Supreme Court decisions.

The National Association for the Advancement of Colored People

Any valid interpretation of the process of school desegregation must take into account the initiatory action and constant vigilance of the NAACP. Without the NAACP's relentless legal prodding and extensive efforts to cultivate a positive public opinion, there would have been no Supreme Court decision outlawing racial segregation in public schools. There is absolutely no reason to believe that local school boards, state legislatures, or Congress would have voluntarily taken steps to eliminate racial segregation in public school systems. As a rule, they would not acknowledge, officially, that the biracial system was inherently discriminatory, even when confronted with convincing evidence that it was. Instead, they had stubbornly insisted, despite overwhelming contrary evidence, that schools for Blacks were ''equal'' to schools for whites. They paid no serious official attention to the well-known fact that some school systems appropriated from three to twenty times as much per capita for white children as they did for Black children.[16] Forcing official recognition that Black children were discriminated against was for decades a major legal action of the NAACP.

Since its founding in 1910, the NAACP has been constantly whittling away at the roots, as well as the obvious manifestations, of racial segregation. It has attempted to advance the civil rights of Black Americans on several key fronts. During the late 1930s, it began to attack segregation at what it deemed to be its core—public tax-supported education. This campaign was carefully calculated to accomplish both major interrelated goals of the civil rights movement: the removal of a fundamental barrier to equal citizenship and the facilitation of the Blacks' desire for self-improvement. The campaign against racial segregation began to show some success in 1938 when the NAACP won its first major victory in the battle against blatantly unequal and separate facilities in higher education. It was then that Lloyd Gaines charged that the law school of the University of Missouri had refused to admit him because he was Black.

> Gaines protested that he was being deprived of "equal facilities" since the state maintained a law school for whites but not for Negroes. The Supreme Court, in a strong opinion by Chief Justice Hughes (two of the conservatives dissenting), upheld this claim, reiterating that his right to a law school education in Missouri was a personal one unaffected by the fact that few Negroes sought to exercise it.[17]

From 1938 to 1950, the NAACP brought a series of cases before the Supreme Court that were designed to eliminate the "separate but equal" doctrine under which the Court continued to operate. In case after case, the NAACP-sponsored litigation attempted to prove that segregated schools were inherently discriminatory and thereby a violation of the "equal protection of laws clause" of the Fourteenth Amendment. The central aim of these suits was to force school systems in the South to equalize educational opportunity for Blacks. It was assumed that this would be such a costly endeavor that states would voluntarily abandon their dual system of education.

> This hope of attacking segregation by a flank movement proved to be fanciful, for the southern states began to appropriate additional funds for Negro schools. . . . The South was in effect strengthening "Jim Crow" by establishing gilded cathedrals of segregation. . . . They [the NAACP victories] were failures concealed by success.[18]

In 1945, the NAACP committed itself to a difficult, direct frontal attack on segregation in public schools. After about five years of extensive research and preparation, in May 1950 the attack was formally launched. A suit was filed in the federal court in Charleston, South Carolina, on behalf of sixty-seven Black children. These children were asking to be admitted to Clarendon County public schools without regard to race. This case and other similar ones eventually came before the U. S. Supreme Court and all of them were entitled *Brown v. Board of Education of Topeka*. The decision in this case, as discussed above, had some far-reaching implications, not only for all levels of education; it also opened the door for the desegregation of all publically operated facilities. Professor Quarles expressed it in this way:

> The Supreme Court's Decision in the School desegregation cases created a sense of crisis in the South. Ever since Reconstruction its social structure had been buttressed by both social and legal sanctions. Now the latter had received a body blow, one that threatened the whole social pattern of the South.[19]

Even before the Supreme Court rendered its unequivocal decision outlawing segregation in the use of public facilities, segregationist forces in the South had begun to organize and retrench in anticipation of the imminent constitutional threat to the biracial system. Already, some old anti-Black, anti-federal organizations had increased their membership and support and had prepared to make an all-out bid to create an antidesegregation public opinion, and through it exert economic and political control throughout the South. The most militant of these groups, such as the Ku Klux Klan and the White Citizens Councils, became the shock troops in the fight to "maintain segregation forever, at all costs," as they vowed to do. Their two main targets were the NAACP and the U. S. Supreme Court.

The disconcerting organization and strength of the segregationist forces and the magnitude of their potential for resistance, even to federal court rulings, became clearly evident in March 1956. It was then that nineteen Senators and eighty-one House members issued a "Southern Manifesto" calling for total resistance to school desegregation and pledging themselves "to use all lawful means to bring about a reversal of this [1954] decision which is contrary to the Constitution." Also, by the end of 1956 southern states had passed 106 new Black codes designed to strengthen and reinforce the biracial system. In effect, southern white leaders, while unconvincingly opposed to segregationists "taking the law in their own hands," as they often put it, tacitly approved of violence against civil rights advocates—white and Black—by their own intemperate efforts to resist the federal courts' desegregation orders. They openly advocated, "within the law," economic reprisals, all forms of anti-Black legislative actions, the most severe police action, and constant challenges through the courts—all deliberately intended to frustrate federal court desegregation orders and to intimidate those who were pressing for the implementation of these orders.

While segregationists tended to single out the federal courts

and the NAACP for the brunt of their vicious opposition to
school desegregation, all civil rights organizations and leaders
were suspected, frequently threatened, and legally restricted by
the new Black codes. The NAACP was especially harassed
during the early years of the new white backlash. It was the
object of intense investigations and numerous prohibitions in
one southern state after another. Its activities were seriously
hampered. For instance, it was fined $100,000 in Alabama,
outlawed, and had to carry on its limited operations as an
underground organization.[20] Some of the most powerful southern leaders publicly vowed to use all means at their disposal to
"kill" the NAACP. Accordingly, it was accused of being a
subversive, "Communist-front" organization and actively involved in a conspiracy to overthrow the government of the
United States. This charge instigated continuous local, state,
and federal investigations of NAACP members and activities.
The charge itself was skillfully designed and timed in order to
serve two interrelated functions: to cultivate a strong anti-
NAACP public opinion that would likely diminish much-
needed financial support and force the NAACP to curtail some
of its major activities (especially expensive desegregation
suits); and to confuse the issue of desegregation with the
much-publicized, alleged "Communist conspiracy," which
Senator Joseph McCarthy had made a national *cause célèbre* for
several years.[21]

Perhaps no other issue in American history so clearly marked
the ideological division between Blacks and whites as did the
program and stance of the NAACP in regard to the issue of
public school segregation versus desegregation. The more persistent, and even violent, anti-NAACP propaganda became, the
stronger and more influential the NAACP emerged. This was,
of course, an unanticipated consequence of the white backlash.
It was during this severe crisis period that membership in the
NAACP became most highly prized. Black leaders and white
liberals began to recognize that membership was a necessary
credential if they would be effective among Blacks. NAACP

membership became a symbol of racial loyalty the Black masses expected of their leaders. The Black masses themselves swelled the NAACP's membership rolls as never before. For instance, in 1962 the NAACP reported: "A membership of 370,000 in 1,200 local branches in forty-four states and the District of Columbia . . . By the end of 1964 its membership was given as 455,839 in 1,848 branches in forty-eight states and the District of Columbia. An unaudited budget indicated that income for 1964 was $1,116,565.68."[22] Not only did the Black community expect its leaders and white liberals to be "card-carrying" members, but they generally expected them to hold a life membership, which cost $500. Roy Wilkins, its national secretary, insisted that "life members in the NAACP are the bedrock of the fight for freedom." Life membership was extended to organizations as well as to individuals. Some organizations had several life memberships. By 1964, the NAACP had over 10,000 individuals and organizations with life membership certificates.[23] Furthermore, in addition to formal membership fees all race conscious Black individuals and organizations were expected to contribute funds to support NAACP activities. Blacks mounted campaigns throughout the country to raise money for the crucial civil rights program spearheaded by the NAACP.

While the membership roll and economic strength of the NAACP greatly increased in response to the segregationists' efforts to kill it, the threatening anti-American image they sought to pin onto it was successful to the extent that it diminished the leadership role the NAACP might have played in establishing creative communication between Black and white leaders. Specifically, this prevented the NAACP from making the contribution it was capable of in developing feasible, progressive school desegregation plans. Pragmatically, this was unfortunate because the long history of the NAACP's fight against segregation and discrimination had provided its leaders with a clear understanding of the problems and strategies of race relations. Logically, no other group of leaders was as capable of developing just and feasible plans for the desegregation of public schools as those who had been trained by the NAACP. For thirty years or more, its professional staff had carried on extensive research and had gathered mountains of information about the nature and consequences of segregated schools. Its lawyers had developed the most advanced methods and procedures of analyzing, interpreting, and applying this information in scores of cases presented before special investigating committees and courts on all judicial levels, particularly the U. S. Supreme Court. The NAACP staff and lawyers had thoroughly analyzed nearly every conceivable approach and serious proposal ever offered in regard to school desegregation. They had themselves developed numerous desegregation plans designed for different schools, school districts, and comprehensive school systems. Nevertheless, on the whole, the great expertise NAACP leaders and professionals had achieved over a long, difficult period was either ignored altogether, drastically discounted, or summarily rejected by those who had the authority to design school desegregation plans and procedures. There are at least three main reasons for this attitude:

First, the stance of school boards on the issue of desegregation has been historically negative. Even the most compliant school boards have indicated reluctance or opposition regarding forthright desegregation such as advocated by the NAACP. Seldom, if ever, have school boards attempted to go beyond minimum compliance according to the "letter of the law," as conservatively interpreted by their lawyers.

The conservative stance of school boards stems mainly from the fact that very few school board members have been elected or appointed for the avowed purpose of promoting desegregation. The very opposite has been the case. Since 1954, school board members have too often attained their positions precisely because they could be depended upon to take a conservative posture on desegregation. Thus, even the more liberal school boards are likely to have a substantial number of members who will impede, not implement, school desegregation plans.

Second, school boards have rejected NAACP plans, even when they were later adopted under different sponsorship. This has been largely the result of the fact that the NAACP has been a perennial protagonist in the segregation-desegregation drama. It has been the hated "outsider" with whom segregated school systems have had to deal. Its dedication to the proposition that extensive, depth changes in the biracial status quo are needed presents a constantly disturbing threat to the very foundation of racial segregation based upon the theory of white supremacy. The NAACP has been the most identifiable protagonist in the Blacks' struggle for equality under the law. As such, plans designed by the NAACP would have to be rejected on their face by conservative school board members, who could hardly afford to sanction the validity of the NAACP as a legitimate leadership group in the community.

The need to oppose the NAACP, no matter how constructive its desegregation plans may be, has disturbed some school officials who were willing to acquiesce to court orders to desegregate. Besides the fact that school officials have been reluctant to accept the NAACP as a bona fide community organization, some opposed its desegregation plans, even when they were obviously the most logical and creative available, because they feared they would activate a powerful white backlash. A notable example is the position taken by Dr. Omer Carmichael, who was superintendent of the Louisville school system during the early years of the desegregation crisis. He acknowledged that he deliberately timed the starting of desegregation because "I wanted desperately to be ahead of the NAACP. I wanted to have a tentative plan. I knew NAACP would be in very promptly, and sure enough, they were before the next board meeting—within less than two weeks."[24]

Third, on a subtle sociological level, it is a well-understood proposition that the identity of the planner directly influences the response a social system will make to a given plan. Therefore, desegregation plans submitted by persons or groups of high social esteem and power in a given community are much

more likely to be accepted and implemented than plans origi-
nated and sponsored by low-status, relatively powerless individuals or groups. Though certain leaders of the NAACP are
acknowledged to be high-status individuals with considerable
social power, the NAACP itself has always been identified with
Blacks who represent a lower status, more or less powerless
racial group. Also, the NAACP has championed causes that are
ignored or opposed by certain influential white community
leaders and organizations. Here again, it would have to be
expected that no matter how sound NAACP-sponsored plans
might be, they would be rejected or effectively disguised by
conservative school officials. To accept the NAACP as a
legitimate community organization would in essence amount to
endorsing its avowed principle of total desegregation. This
would be a symbol of significant social changes which the
majority of school officials are expected to resist.

It is unfortunate that the NAACP, which has been the initiator
of the school desegregation process, has had little opportunity
of making it work to the advantage of all students, Black and
white. In several instances, community leaders and school
officials have opposed desegregation primarily because they
interpreted it to be NAACP-inspired and -engineered social
change. This grows out of the fact that for at least ten years,
1954-1964, the NAACP was almost totally responsible for
prodding stubborn school districts to desegregate or at least
comply with the letter of the law as enunciated by the Supreme
Court. Throughout those years, it was bitterly opposed by a
very well-organized, well-financed, dedicated white backlash
that made every slow step toward eliminating a discriminatory
dual school system both socially disturbing and costly. Therefore, after ten trying years, in 1964 only 2.25 percent of Black
children in the eleven old Confederate states attended schools
with white children.[25]

The NAACP, as the initiator and advocate of constant court
action to force compliance with the ''law of the land'' as
interpreted in the Brown Decision, became the inherent enemy

of the biracial system. This automatically pitted it against official public policy-makers in community after community. Its lawyers were dutifully opposed by status quo-oriented lawyers who represented recalcitrant school boards in all sections of the country, particularly in the South where discrimination was supported by the legal system. Desegregation cases were so hard fought and bitter that even when the NAACP won, school officials, backed by strong anti-Black, anti-Supreme Court sentiment in the local community, generally refused to acknowledge the validity of the courts' verdicts and attempted to do business as usual. This noncompliance stance triggered community disruptions, demonstrations, school boycotts, racial antagonism, and violence.

By 1964 the U. S. Department of Justice had finally become convinced that the NAACP should not be expected to assume the total burden as "watchdog" of the federal court-ordered desegregation process. In the first place, it was too vulnerable to hostile state legislatures, which, as noted above, were able to place disabling restrictions upon the organization and thus prevent it from performing its role. In the second place, the massive resistance mounted by so many school districts was much too costly for the NAACP to assume alone. The legal cost was staggering. The Brown case alone is estimated to have cost in excess of $100,000.[26]

Thus, the NAACP did not have the resources or the social power necessary to exert the pressure to change the social system as radically as demanded. What power it had stemmed directly from the support of federal courts. Even this support proved insufficient because state legislatures and leaders in school districts found a variety of ways of delaying, circumventing, and otherwise ignoring court orders stemming from individual cases. Consequently, in 1964, Congress acted to put "teeth" into desegregation orders. It established a Civil Rights Act.

Title VI of the Civil Rights Act prohibits the extension of Federal financial assistance to any dual or segregated system of schools based on race, color, or national origin. To be eligible to receive, or to continue to receive such assistance, school officials must eliminate all practices characteristic of such dual or segregated school systems.[27]

The full force of Title VI was brought to bear through the federal judiciary "which grants authority to the Attorney General to initiate school desegregation lawsuits."[28] This made it unnecessary for the NAACP to enter suits where flagrant resistance on the part of school districts was obvious. Though it has stayed in the fight for desegregation, its main task has been to prove noncompliance with federal court orders. Enforcement itself is in the hands of federal agencies.

White Racism

In direct opposition to the goals and actions of the NAACP were white racists who insisted upon the maintenance of complete, total segregation of schools. While many reasons were given to justify and even to glorify the status quo in education, upon close examination white racism was the obvious primary cause for community resistance. A functional definition of racism has been presented by Anthony Downs, who insists that "racism is an attitude, action or institutional structure which subordinates a person or group because of his or their color."[29] As used here racism is the tendency to interpret all individual and social events according to deeply imbedded racial attitudes and beliefs. As such, racism pervades just about every facet of community life, especially in long-segregated southern communities. Thus, some form of racism is obvious in the political life, courts, economic system, churches, as well as schools in all communities faced with the problem of desegregation.[30] In communities where racial segregation has always been a fact of life, all social decisions become essentially racist in nature. That is, any decision having to do with public affairs is very likely to be influenced overtly or tacitly by the fact of race. The

NEA Special Committee on Teacher Displacement concludes: "For the white establishment to admit equality of opportunity anywhere would be to undermine racial discrimination everywhere. This would mean the end of a way of life, with all of the cherished advantages for some and all of its hardships for others."[31]

One fact that becomes increasingly evident in a study of the consequences of racism in communities undergoing desegregation is that officially none of the communities has seemed to understand the nature of racism well enough to deal with it effectively. The main reason is that racism is much more than a personal attitude; it is an ideology, a way of life. It is an oversimplified philosophy of human relations and is often so subtle that even the racist himself is not fully aware of his racism. As will be discussed subsequently, school desegregation, certainly integration, will be hampered until responsible community leaders and educators understand the essential nature of racism and how to deal with it more effectively than has generally been the case.

Degree of racism. To begin with, it is necessary to emphasize that some individuals and organizations involved in school desegregation are much more racist or prejudiced than others. Perhaps no other issue in American history has more clearly revealed the depth, intensity, and nature of racism as has that of school desegregation. The degree of racism on the part of individuals and groups is likely to vary in time, intensity, and expression. At one extreme are avowed bigoted chauvinists and at the other are some erstwhile white liberals who strongly disavow overt racism in their personal and social life. There are at least four classifiable types of racists: militant, nonviolent, apologetic, and "liberal" racists.

1. *Militant racists.* Included in this classification are persons and groups who are actively engaged in the preservation of white supremacy. Most would prefer to operate within the law, but there are usually fringe elements who are always ready and willing either to interpret the law as they would like it

to be or to go beyond the law when necessary. The great influence that militant segregationists have in most desegregating communities stems primarily from the nature of their formal and informal organization. Their influence is not so much attributable to the large number who join antidesegregation organizations as it is to the fact that varied talents are enlisted to oppose school desegregation.

One of the useful talents widely employed by militant racists is that of speechmaking. Among such orators are noted segregationsists from several southern states who make a career of speaking before mass meetings where school desegregation is the major concern. In addition, there exists a cadre of top business and professional men, particularly candidates for public office, available to propagandize popular anti-Black and anti-federal issues. Thus, in each of the communities where desegregation of schools has been a major issue, the case of the segregationist has always been eloquently presented. In almost all instances the most effective of these speakers have adopted some version of the oratorical style of the old-fashioned southern demagogue. Such speakers are highly emotional, play upon traditional emotionally packed symbols, make maximum use of racial stereotypes, and have appeared at mass meetings in communities where school systems were in the first traumatic stages of developing desegregation plans in response to or in anticipation of federal court orders.

Between 1954 and 1964, when most federal cases for desegregation were filed by the NAACP, militant speeches made by segregationists were usually given wide publicity in local newspapers. Herbert Wey and John Corey observed that "mass communication media . . . are a stick swinging a mighty wallop in helping 'make or break' preparation programs for desegregation."[32] It is quite difficult, of course, to give an accurate assessment of the role of the mass media except to say that wherever it has supported militant segregationists the process of school desegregation has been slow and widespread community disturbances have occurred. For example, with the cooperation of the mass media militant racists have been able to propagandize in the total community. In the beginning of the desegregation movement, even the most avowedly "neutral" mass media in the South tended to give a disproportionate amount of coverage to anti-Black, anti-desegregationist ideas, rationales, and points of view. (The antidesegregation tone of most southern newspapers has changed considerably since the Civil Rights Acts of 1964 and 1965.)

In New Orleans two television stations—WWL and WDSU—carried live broadcasts of the debates in the state legislature concerned with the problem of desegregating the public schools. Whereas this more comprehensive news coverage was interpreted as a desirable innovative public service, its actual effect was that it gave wide, convincing publicity to militant racist attitudes and opinions. This was especially disconcerting to the Black community because at that time there were no Blacks in the state legislature to counter the diverse propaganda and it was regarded as politically dangerous for white politicians to present a positive view on the problem of desegregation. Some even refused to take a positive stand on "open schools," even if desegregation was the "price to pay."[33] In nearly all instances the mass media in southern communities tended to propagandize the ideologies and activities of militant segregationists. It was usually after the communities had entered the critical stage in race relations and some crippling social disruptions or violence had occurred that the news media would begin to assume positive leadership. A notable exception was the *Little Rock Gazette*, under Editor Harry Ashmore. Immediately after the 1954 Supreme Court decision, he took a firm stand for desegregated schools. As a result, during the grave school crisis in Little Rock, the *Gazette* lost about 20 percent of its readers.[34] Most papers did not choose to run this risk until it was absolutely necessary for general community welfare.

In addition to the use of mass media, militant racists have used a variety of other means of propagandizing their anti-school desegregation views. In most communities they had no compunction of "standing up to be counted." For a decade (1954-1965), both planned and impromptu speeches denouncing desegregation were frequently made before PTA meetings, church groups, professional associations, and in any gathering where public education was discussed. The White Citizens Council made wide use of one of the most unique propaganda techniques. It had convincing speakers to tape succinct antidesegregation speeches to be automatically relayed when a certain telephone number was dialed. These messages always dealt with crucial issues in desegregation. They particularly denounced the Supreme Court, civil rights organizations, Black leaders, and white liberals who identified with the desegregation movement. Always the character, citizenship, and intelligence of Blacks were impugned.

All in all, the militant racists developed strong, viable organizations to oppose desegregation. Not only did they manage to enlist a relatively large number of followers, but they also included and made use of a wide variety of specialized "talents" and influences. This would include a "surging, jeering mass of teenagers shouting 2-4-6-8, we don't want to integrate,"[35] and state and national political figures who formulated top-level school policy and influenced legislation. Small wonder that militant segregationists were able to successfully spearhead massive resistance to federal court orders to desegregate for more than a decade and still wield considerable negative influence in the formulation of desegregation policy.

2. *Nonmilitant racists.* This very broad category includes individuals and groups of all social statuses, ideological postures, and temperaments. Their basic common denominator is that they value "white supremacy" (with all the special privileges that status implies) above general community welfare—to say nothing about the welfare of Black Americans.

In communities throughout the United States, these people constitute a large segment of that unnumbered mass certain politicians have referred to as the "silent majority." In some quarters, the concept "silent majority" has become synonymous with racism or those who oppose changes in the biracial system. Though no systematic study has been done of this group of citizens, sufficient evidence exists to conclude that, for the most part, they are known in their communities as "law-abiding, hard-working, God-fearing, family people," who deeply believe in the rural-oriented, white Protestant, middle-class values handed down to them from their ancestors. They are basically conservative and would likely oppose any significant changes in the social system. This would be true especially if a social change such as desegregation might have widespread reverberations.

The main difference between the militant and nonmilitant racist is the difference between a politician who campaigns for public office on a racist platform which he aggressively propagandizes and the citizen who can be relied upon to vote for him or support his campaign because he promises to maintain racial segregation. In this category are numerous white parents who would not lead a boycott of a desegregated school but who would find a reason to support it in endorsing his segregationist programs. This happens when the nonmilitant racist is one with high prestige or social power. In each community where a considerable amount of information on the subject is available, such individuals have set standards of race relations and the acceptability or nonacceptability of key social policy. They have been referred to as the "silent elite." The racial stances they take set the tone for the community response. For example, if a prestigious, socially powerful family refuses to send its children to a desegregated school, that act is likely to become a symbol of rejection for the less-prestigious families. In the same way members of the elite community may withhold endorsement of basic school desegregation plans, thereby jeopardizing both the initiation and the probable success of such plans. In some communities, such as Atlanta and Houston, with identifiable elite leaders, the school boards were reluctant even to submit a plan without their prior endorsement. The failure of the elite to respond to desegregation demands may lead to community disruption and interfere with the operation of the total school system.[36] Herein lies the great negative influence of the nonmilitant racists, especially the "elite," who have the social power to extend or withdraw the sanction of legitimacy to school desegregation plans and procedures. They have served as an influential nonmilitant racist element because even their nonaction has been an important factor in subordinating Black people and frustrating creative desegregation plans.

3. *Apologetic racists.* We may label a distinct, powerful antidesegregation element found in nearly every community with a relatively large number of Blacks as "apologetic." Their most salient characteristic is the tendency to give nonracist reasons for their racist opinions and acts. They, like their militant and nonmilitant cohorts, have been dependable opponents of school desegregation without attempting to justify their actions on strictly racial grounds. Generally, they give as their reasons for objecting to desegregation the fear that "it will lower academic standards"; "it will cause the deterioration of neighborhood schools"; "it will require inconvenient, expensive bussing"; "it is a violation of states rights"; or "it is a Communist-inspired movement to overthrow the government of the U. S."

This group wields so much influence because it generally includes professionals with legitimate credentials in the field of education. Sometimes they are teachers reporting on actual classroom experiences; principals who formally report the lowering of academic standards or increased disciplinary problems; school board officials who insist that a given desegregation plan is unfeasible; scholars who raise questions about the abilities of Blacks; and pollsters who come up with pseudoscientific evidence that desegregation is not wanted by the vast majority of people. Particularly damaging have been evaluations of certain schools and school districts by "teams of experts." These persons have usually been commissioned by school officials or state government agencies bent upon proving that desegregation would in fact bring about a deterioration in academic standards and school management. They have studied school systems such as those in Washington, D.C., and have attempted to blame all of the problems there on desegregation.

This process of arriving at policy decisions was emphasized by Henry A. Kissinger, now Secretary of State. He was a professor at Harvard when he made the following evaluation of the role of the intellectual in policy-making:

> Our Executives are shaped by a style of life that inhibits reflectiveness. For one of the characteristics of a society based on specialization is the enormous work load of its top personnel. . . . Decision making is increasingly turned into a group effort . . . In our society the policymaker is dependent to an increasing extent on his subordinates' conception of the essential elements of a problem . . . Many organizations, governmental or private, rely on panels of experts. Political leaders have intellectuals as advisers . . . The intellectual is rarely found at the level where decisions are made; his role is commonly advisor . . . Since the American intellectual is so strongly committed to the same pragmatic values as the rest of society, it produces a tremendous overspecialization.

Kissinger also perceptively pointed out that policy-makers are likely to choose experts who give them the advice they want:

> It is the executive who determines . . . whether he needs advice. He frames the questions to be answered . . . He decides who is consulted and thereby the definition of "expertness" . . . The "expert" not uncommonly is the person who elaborates the existing framework most ably (segregated schools, in this instance), rather than the individual charting new paths, (or desegregating schools.)[37]

In many cases "experts" in the field of education chosen to

evaluate desegregation plans and programs were segregationists themselves. As anticipated, their findings always "validated" the proposition that school segregation was the best policy. Therefore, when top politicians and school administrators were called upon to justify their resistance to court-ordered desegregation, they inevitably turned to the findings of "experts" they had selected and commissioned. Their findings emphasized the problems and failures of a democratic school system and tended to ignore its successes and promises.

4. *The "liberal" racists.* No other group in a desegregating community faces the dilemmas and stresses of social change as much as do liberals. Before 1954, when the objective of Black leaders was to achieve "equal rights" within the biracial system, white liberals functioned as go-betweens or negotiators for Black leaders. This was necessary because whites had a monopoly of official social power. Black leaders could get little or nothing done unless they established a workable relationship with white men of power.[38] Therefore, the most effective channel of communication between Black leaders and white men of power was the small group of liberal whites who performed a distinct, functionally necessary liaison role. It was essential, then, for white liberals to be respected by white men of power and trusted by Black leaders. Within a more or less rigid set of proscribed, well-understood principles, this group was to some extent successful.

The Supreme Court's decision in the Brown Case redefined the role of the liberal. Originally, the white liberal advocated "separate but equal" treatment of Blacks. The new white liberal had to identify with desegregation efforts and advocate equal, integrated education. Such a stance was very precarious during the crisis period of the late 1950s and throughout the 1960s. Truly liberal whites were labeled "renegades," "integrators," "left wingers," "Communists," and "nigger lovers." Faced with a relentless barrage of criticism and ostracism, most white liberals were unable or unwilling to remain identified with the Black thrust for total integration. This fact was stated by a prominent Louisiana segregationist who observed that ''most white liberals have run for cover.'' There were other white ''liberals,'' however, who retreated from Black causes, not because of fear of the white backlash but because they did not believe in integration. They were unable to serve ''two houses,'' as the traditional liberals had done. No longer could they ''walk in two worlds,'' as one described her role. In other words, *identification with the Black cause after 1954 has implied identification with the forces of change and not those striving to achieve the best possible compromise in a biracial society.* This ideological redefinition of the liberal's role made that status uncomfortable. Most became marginal, not really belonging in any one world, Black or white. They suffered all of the suspicions, frustrations, and criticisms of a marginal group that is never quite accepted by either the white racists or the Black community.

During the civil rights revolution, the erstwhile white liberals played very different roles, ranging from martyr to racist.[39] During the height of the civil rights movement, some of the most flexible white liberals joined sit-in demonstrations and otherwise supported the dangerous confrontations between Blacks and the white ''Establishment.'' They suffered all of the insults and violence meted out to Black people, including assassinations. There were others, usually the most established, powerful liberals, who began to complain that Black people were ''pressing too hard,'' ''being influenced by outsiders,'' ''using the wrong strategies,'' ''following illogical patterns of race relations,'' and ''elevating the wrong Blacks to leadership positions.'' Therefore, while Black leaders and dedicated white liberals were fighting for school desegregation, white liberal racists were emphasizing the importance of ''community control of public schools,'' making schools in the Black community equal to those in the white community, and constantly expressing the fear that direct action against segregation would result in the alienation of ''white friends.'' Where there were unequivocal federal court orders to desegregate public schools, the erstwhile white liberals usually championed a policy of gradualism and tokenism. For example, when school districts were forced to submit desegregation plans, instead of championing an all-at-once plan, as advocated by the NAACP, influential individuals in this category developed or supported plans for gradual desegregation, such as "from the bottom up, from the top down, from both ends at the same time, selected schools, pupil assignment."[40] Liberal racists thus sanctioned the actions of the more rabid racists which were calculated to frustrate the desegregation process. Even though some have continued to support such uplift organizations as the NAACP, Urban League, and Black colleges, they tend to function as racists in the sense that they make the "Negro Cause" a thing in itself rather than a total community or national cause. Their actions suggest that desegregation is a concession to be bestowed by whites—not an inalienable right.

Official Leadership

As noted above, in any large community there are likely to be several more or less well-organized social groups competing for social power. When a major community decision is to be made, a number of such groups will feel compelled to identify with one alternative or another. If the decision is basic, in the sense that it threatens the status quo, some of the groups will identify with the forces making for change (pro) and others will identify with forces seeking to maintain the status quo (anti). The great masses of people in a community express their wishes as pro or con in three fundamental, ideal ways. (1) As individuals they may write "Letters to the Editor," their congressmen, local officials, etc., and engage in other forms of personal protest to express their opinions. (2) Individuals may join together in public protests or demonstrations, in which their summary opinions are expressed in slogans and some form of action. And (3) the masses of individuals may express their opinions through their official representative leaders.

Prior to a discussion of these three methods, we should keep in mind that the issue of school desegregation is of such great consequence to individuals as well as to the social system that even citizens who ordinarily do not participate in social action have felt called upon to express their personal opinions. They have used all of the three means just cited. In regard to the first form of protest, for several years during the desegregation crisis I carried on some informal research regarding "Letters to the Editor," as published in a few selected big city newspapers in the South. The opinions expressed in the vast majority of the letters may be classified as negative in regard to the issue of desegregation. I was never quite sure whether the antidesegregation opinions of the editors led them to select for publication those which most mirrored their own personal opinions or whether the vast majority of their readers were in fact segregationists. It may also be that segregationists were more willing to express their opinions in this form. In any case, the fact remains that many individual citizens find this as the most tangible way of identifying themselves for or against proposed school desegregation plans.

The individual citizen has also resorted to personal protest of an abusive nature. In nearly all communities where there is a large percentage of Black students in the school system, certain individuals have used the telephone and other personal means to harass school officials whose stand on desegregation is contrary to their own. Some white community leaders whose stand on desegregation was not known also found themselves harassed and abused, even threatened constantly by individuals who wanted to know their views and to dissuade them from supporting plans for desegregation. Similarly, certain citizens would visit key officials in order to express their segregationist views or criticize moves toward desegregation among their peers.

A second level of individual expression has been organized action. In most cities where competing groups are strong, there have been mass meetings, mass marches, boycotts, and/or other forms of mass behavior designed to express strong community displeasure. These demonstrations are tenuous, irregular, and bring together many individuals who may have only this one salient social issue in common. They often differ in age, social class, and political ideology but commonly oppose some specific desegregation proposal.

While all of the means above have been used by individual citizens to express their opinions on desegregation, the influence they exert is generally indirect. Even so, this indirect influence is often decisive in that official leaders may respond positively to it. In actual fact, officials in some communities such as in Cairo, Illinois, Greenbriar, West Virginia, and Bay City, Texas, responded to citizen pressure by vacillation, inaction, and changing decisions because they met opposition.[41] Interestingly, where official leaders vacillated under mass pressure, communities experienced a kind of "anomie" or normlessness. The issues were thoroughly confused and respect for law and order descended to a low ebb. Invariably, the issue of "good" education was lost and decisions were made to please one group or another and not for the good of the school system itself.

A third level at which individual citizens may express their opinions is through duly organized group behavior, especially through political action. In St. Louis, for instance, the citizens deliberately elected a school board with a majority of its members sympathetic to desegregation. The very opposite was true in New Orleans, where school desegregation was an extremely traumatic experience. The majority of its school board members during the crisis were elected primarily because of their segregationist views.

The Role of Law

The key question, then, is this: *After carefully examining communities that have undergone the process of desegregation for almost twenty years, what have we learned that may help us to make this process more orderly and rewarding in the future?*

The answer is quite complex. Its complexity lies primarily in the nature of American society itself. It is inherent in the democratic process that individuals, groups, and communities must be accorded freedom to pursue their welfare according to the dictates of their own consciences so long as it does not violate the civil rights of others. This was indeed the spirit of the 1954 Supreme Court decision in the Brown Case. The justices recognized that school desegregation in some communities would be more complex and difficult than in others. Their language, "all deliberate speed," recognized this fact and suggested compliance in accord with local situations. The spirit of this decision has been violated by states and local communities which, instead of transcending traditional barriers to desegregation, proceeded to expand old barriers and erect new ones designed to make desegregation more difficult than it would have been ordinarily. Thus, in 1963, the justices agreed that they "never contemplated that the concept of 'deliberate speed' would countenance indefinite delay."[42] What then seems to be the best procedure? The following is suggested:

1. *Court decisions regarding desegregation must be clear and unequivocal*. The many and varied community responses to school desegregation seem to underscore at least one fundamental principle. During times of widespread social crises and revolutionary social changes, citizens need to be guided by the *letter* of the law and should not be expected to respond to the spirit of the law. This is particularly true when the masses of citizens have been led to believe that the courts are in conflict with established cultural values or do not represent the people. Therefore, when already confused citizens and communities give their own interpretations of the law, as implied in the spirit, their interpretations will likely reflect their own personal prejudices. Thus, "all deliberate speed" has been translated in several ways:

As an *administrative problem* in some communities such as Louisville, where officials asked for time to make certain administrative changes.

As an *intellectual problem* in several communities where only a token number of "intellectually acceptable" Black children were admitted to white schools. This step was regarded as necessary to maintain traditionally high academic standards, which some believed would be lowered by an influx of Blacks.

As a *psychological problem* in a few instances whereby it was contended that Black and white children would have to come to know each other and become accustomed to associating with one another. Thus, some officials suggested that desegregation should begin in the first grade, gradually including a grade a year through the succeeding grades. The process then would take twelve years.

As a *community acceptance problem* in some places where it was deemed necessary first to convince at least a majority of the white citizens that desegregation could work before a general desegregation plan should be accepted.

A fifth interpretation of the concept, and certainly the most frustrating, is that based on the doctrine of "community schools." This doctrine holds that the school should be controlled by, and available to, those who live in the community in which it is located. Consequently, in places where there is a rigid ecological separation of races, schools would remain segregated until the neighborhoods became desegregated. Proponents of this doctrine naturally oppose the bussing of Black students from other neighborhoods to their community schools or vice versa.

It follows that, when citizens are expected to translate the spirit of the law during times of grave community crises, their interpretation of the law is likely to be quite contrary to the letter of the law or established justice in terms of the law. Accordingly, local officials so translated "the law" in school desegregation situations that they could maintain the status quo essentially intact for several years in some instances and "forever" in other instances, as pledged by some officials.

Fortunately, the federal courts and the U. S. Department of

Health, Education and Welfare (HEW) acknowledged that the spirit of the law, as applied to desegregation, was not sufficient to produce even minimal compliance with the letter of the law. In some cases, resegregation had begun to take place more rapidly than desegregation. Beginning with its revised decision in 1969, which definitely changed the "all deliberate speed" concept to "at once," the Supreme Court restored order to the desegregation process. This decision, which is strongly supported by HEW, has provided definite guidelines in communities where formerly anomie existed. For example, prior to 1969 in the eleven southern states where school segregation was sanctioned by state laws, school desegregation encountered the greatest resistance. In 1968, fourteen years after the Brown Decision, 81.6 percent of Black school children were still attending predominantly Black schools and 68 percent were attending all-Black schools. However, after the unequivocal desegregation position taken by the Supreme Court in 1969, the desegregation tempo in the South increased rapidly. By 1971, just three years later, only 56.1 percent of Black students in the South were in predominantly Black schools and just 9.2 percent were in all-Black schools.

In thirty-two states outside the South where there were no laws requiring school segregation, the 1969 Supreme Court decision was not clear in regard to school desegregation. Consequently, almost no gains were made between 1968 and 1971. In 1968, 72.4 percent of Black children in these thirty-two states were in predominantly Black schools and 12.3 percent were in all-Black schools. Very little change had been made by 1971: 72.2 percent were still in predominantly Black schools and 11.2 were still in all-Black schools.[43]

2. *An attitude of compliance with constituted law on the part of top school officials.* The desegregation process is disturbing in all communities, even under the best of circumstances. It is particularly disturbing and most frustrating in communities where it is opposed by top political and/or official school leadership. The key role of official leadership has been demon-

strated over and over again. For instance, in communities such as New Orleans, where race relations had been generally amicable, the failure of the official community to respond decisively resulted in school boycotts and near social chaos. In contrast, in other communities where race relations have been traditionally inflexible and top leadership has taken a definite compliance stance, school desegregation seems to be progressing smoothly and serious community disruptions have been avoided.

At this point, it must be understood that the compliance stance by responsible officials may be the result of personal convictions, public opinion, or federal guidelines. The immediate reason for advocating compliance is not an important consideration here. The best example of how the individual official can contribute to orderly desegregation is the leadership assumed by several superintendents of school districts. Perhaps the most publicized of these was Omer Carmichael of Louisville. Such superintendents have assumed the responsibility of not only developing feasible desegregation plans, but also of selling their plans to their school boards, administrative staffs, and the general public. All evidence indicates that, wherever school superintendents have assumed a positive, clear-cut, vigorous leadership, role desegregation has proceeded with relative calm and effectiveness.

What has been said about superintendents of school districts also applies to school boards. Wherever school boards have been opposed to or seriously divided in regard to basic desegregation issues, the community and the schools have suffered disruptions and conflict. This has been so whether the school boards were elected or appointed. The most effective school boards have been the mixed ones—those that represent the basic social elements in the community, such as the business elite, the existing government, the major social classes, and particularly the Black community.

When school board members are hopelessly divided or persist in opposing court-ordered desegregation, the only agency that can restore order and progress is the federal government. This is because a divided school board seems always to indicate a divided community and/or divided political leadership. In the first instance, when elected school boards are seriously divided, it is likely that the electorate is divided. In such cases, various pro and antidesegregation forces will endeavor to select their own representatives to champion school issues as they interpret them. This has often meant that there was no recognized leader on the school board who was able to command respect or effectuate a working consensus. On crucial issues, individual representatives of special interest groups frequently make non-negotiable demands that result in nonaction. Furthermore, whatever action the majority of the board takes is usually strenuously opposed by the minority. Their differences, then, serve to reinforce already existing conflicts in the larger community.

In the second instance when an appointed school board is unreconcilably divided over the issue of desegregation, it usually reflects a comparable division among top political decision-makers. Here again, the fact that responsible political representatives are divided on crucial community issues may in turn indicate a divided electorate. It may also indicate that a prolonged desegregation crisis has brought about rifts in an otherwise homogeneous, apparently monolithic community power structure. Such rifts have been reflected in debilitating, hate-filled political campaigns, punitive action, a general breakdown in community consensus, paralysis of the educational process, and/or violence. The most notable example was Little Rock, Arkansas, in 1957 when mobs virtually sabotaged the public school system. They created a state of anomie and federal troops had to be used to restore order.

It seems, therefore, that both the quality of leadership furnished by school officials and the timing of their actions are crucial. While vacillating leadership has inevitably led to community disturbances and school paralysis, positive, wise leadership by school officials has often proven to be ineffective when exerted after divisions and chaos had occurred in the larger community. Likewise, when vigorous community leadership is too long postponed, it eventually becomes ineffectual and it is necessary to turn to federal leadership in order to establish order and proceed with desegregation plans.

3. *The support of the white elite or "power structure" is essential.* As noted above, in communities where total racial segregation has always been the way of life and where the doctrine of white supremacy has been accepted by the great masses of white people, federal court orders to desegregate public schools can be a very traumatic experience. When such a community has not been honestly prepared to comply with desegregation orders, records show that a large majority of its white citizens interpret such orders as an unfair, even unconstitutional, invasion of their civil rights and tend to regard all parties to the act as their enemies.

Such a response has two interrelated negative consequences. First, it destroys confidence in, and allegiance to, constituted authority. Thus, the court, which must be the ultimate source of impartiality and justice in an organized, stable society, becomes suspect. Its motives will be questioned and its decisions will be resented, rejected, and, when possible, flaunted. When this happens, the very foundation of justice, and even social morality, is compromised. Community consensus on major social issues will be shattered and long-established social and moral norms will divide rather than unify key individuals and groups. Eventually, old patterns of interpersonal, intergroup relations will deteriorate and conflict rather than order will become characteristic of the community. A true state of anomie will begin to emerge.

Second, when a large proportion of citizens lose faith in the court or the system of justice to which they must submit, they tend to exalt their own personal, prejudiced concept of "right" and "wrong," "just" and "unjust" above duly-established laws and legal procedures. There is always a grave danger that this individualistic interpretation of constituted law will deteriorate to the point where small groups of disgruntled citizens will attempt to "take the law into their own hands." The inevitable result is publicly proclaimed bigotry, the polarization of erstwhile cooperating individuals, groups, and interests, and, often, open violence. This is the advanced stage of anomie—community paralysis—which has occurred to some degree in all communities where the white elite (powerful business and professional men) either sought to remain neutral on school desegregation (in which case they were generally assumed to be opposed to desegregation) or tended to oppose it openly in their personal and/or public lives.

One of the clearest examples of how the failure of the elite to take a firm stand for desegregated schools as ordered by federal courts may lead to anomie and a serious degree of social paralysis and conflict is the New Orleans experience. In that city, the dominant newspaper, the *Times-Picayune*, best reflected the attitudes of the elite. Its official stand on the school desegregation issue was regularly presented in such editorials as this:

> Public education, unquestionably, is a foundation of democracy, but whether public education can survive the forced integration of schools in a community like ours, with a large Negro population and ingrained customs, remains to be seen. Forced integration. . . . is a tragedy just as closing the schools would be a tragedy.

A later editorial concluded: "The choice as to whether closed schools are to be preferred to integrated schools is one which the people themselves must make."[44]

The uncompromising, noncompliance attitude of the elite in New Orleans, as expressed by the *Times-Picayune*, continued to worsen during the more than three years of crisis following the court order to desegregate its public schools (*Bush v. Orleans Parish School Board*, 1956). No change was evident until

December 14, 1960, when 105 influential business and professional men in New Orleans signed a three-quarter page advertisement which was carried by the *Times-Picayune*. Though their stand for "open schools," even if desegregated, came very late (after there was widespread disruption and violence), it did restore some measure of community order by redefining the issue of school desegregation. In the first place, it sanctioned the supremacy of constitutional law as interpreted by federal courts over personal prerogatives, no matter how unpleasant the law might be. Second, that elite redefined the issue as "no school versus desegregated schools." Faced with this clear choice, other less established community leaders began to seek ways to bring about minimum compliance rather than continued "massive resistance." Therefore, just as an uncommitted or opposition elite can and does cause community disruption and violence, committed, positive leadership by the white elite has been an indispensable force in orderly school desegregation. According to published records, in all communities where the white elite acted quickly and firmly in favor of a definite desegregation plan, the plan was adopted with a minimum degree of community division and conflict.

The prime question, of course, is this: What motivates the elite to take positive action for desegregated schools? Any valid answer to this question must be complex and many-faceted because the elite is seldom, if ever, a social monolith. The different segments of the elite are likely to adopt different approaches and require different motivations in regard to basic social changes. However, the community elites have at least one thing in common: their elite status is accorded or legitimized by an organized social system. Consequently, when that system experiences anomie, there are no longer recognized, established norms according to which individuals can be considered as "elite." After all, the elite are those who symbolize certain highly valued, widely shared norms. When respect for these norms is destroyed, the elite, by definition, cannot continue to exist as a meaningful social category. This holds whether the norms regard private property, official authority, or freedom of the individual. Basically, then, the elite is motivated to act positively for desegregated schools when it is convinced that its inaction or negative action may destroy certain basic norms undergirding its privileged status. Again, the motivation to act may be public enlightenment through the mass media, enlightened self-interest stemming from an objective analysis of its own welfare, or force as exerted by federal courts.

4. *Finally, there must be a well-organized, respected Black leadership class.* Traditionally, Black public schools have been notoriously inferior. Therefore, original desegregation plans assumed that desegregation would be a "one-way street." That is, Black children were expected to desegregate white schools; white children were not expected to desegregate Black schools. Consequently, preplanning for desegregation involved the white community. Little or no attention was given to the fact that desegregation is a more traumatic experience for Blacks than for whites. In many instances, Black parents were expected to submit their children to the hostile environment of white schools where they would encounter insults, ostracism, and, in some cases, physical abuse. Also, the Black community was frequently called upon to participate in direct action calculated to bring pressure on public officials in order to force them to obey federal court orders. Finally, for several years it was common for Black Americans to experience various forms of economic, civic, and social retaliation when they advocated or participated in desegregation efforts, and it was always the Black school personnel who were in the greater danger of experiencing demotion or loss of jobs.[45] Therefore, while no precise figures are available on the extent to which Black educators have experienced the negative consequences of desegregation, HEW reports that in one year, 1970-1971, at least 4,207 Black teachers and administrators were demoted or dis-

missed in only six southern states where substantial school desegregation was taking place.[46]

Since Blacks were expected to be the sole initiators of desegregation before 1969, and are still expected to furnish most of the leadership for the civil rights movement and social change, strong Black leaders are indispensable in the comprehensive, orderly desegregation of public schools. Ordinarily, they carry the total responsibility of gearing the Black community to initiate specific desegregation action and to give sustained support to the civil rights movement when Black security is threatened. Black leaders perform another essential function: they must facilitate creative communication between the Black community and the white power structure. In this very important sense, they have operated on the frontier of race relations. In this capacity they have had to develop the skills necessary to negotiate successfully with the most knowledgeable, powerful, often hostile white community leaders.

The kind of skills Black leaders must have if they are to perform a creative service in school desegregation can only be developed by extensive experiences in other areas of desegregation. Therefore, in communities where early efforts for school desegregation had the greatest success, such as St. Louis, Louisville, and Atlanta, much of the success was the result of astute leadership by Blacks who had had previous experiences in other desegregation efforts. Where such leadership had been lacking or disorganized, desegregation was a much more disturbing and disrupting experience as in Little Rock, New Orleans, and Cairo. Black leadership is necessary in helping to prepare the Black and white communities if desegregation is to have a fair chance of success.

Today, after more than two decades of litigation, disruptions, and conflicts, de jure school desegregation is a generally accepted principle throughout the United States. Nevertheless, all is far from well. The more illusive problem—racial resegregation—is now the major threat in school systems where there is a relatively large Black population. This resegregation process is extremely difficult to deal with legally because it is enmeshed in the total socioeconomic fabric of American society. That is, white families in exercising their inalienable right to live where they choose are rapidly abandoning the central cities and are enrolling their children in public schools in more or less "lily white" suburbs. A large proportion of other white families who choose to remain in or near the central city are sending their children to private schools in increasing numbers. Consequently, eighteen of the largest public school districts throughout the United States, even some that were once functionally desegregated, have become predominantly Black.

With Blacks concentrated in central cities, virtually locked out of lily white suburbs, and white families constantly moving into these suburbs, some observers predict that it is only a matter of time—a few years—before the vast majority of white and Black children will again be attending segregated schools. At present the only serious solution offered for this problem is bussing. This approach is meeting much strong resistance from parents who claim the right to send their children to nearby neighborhood schools. The controversy is likely to hamper the process of desegregation until federal authorities and local public school officials find a way to resolve it.

The long-range solution to school desegregation is, of course, open housing and open neighborhoods. This long-range issue is now muted and very little effort is being made to achieve this goal. In the meantime the only promising approach to equalizing educational opportunity is to make all schools, whether in the Black ghetto or the wealthy suburb, equal in every respect. While this principle is accepted in theory, little in fact is being done to implement it. Commenting upon this nation's failure to provide equal educational opportunities for disadvantaged and minority group children, the U. S. Senate Committee concluded:

The schools which our Nation's low-income children attend are often those with fewer and lower quality educational services. They are the schools where educational dollars are either fewer or purchase less . . . money for education is raised and distributed inequitably. The children who need the most often have the least.[47]

Therefore, children in Black schools are still being short-changed and their efforts to use education as an avenue to social mobility are being constantly frustrated.

NOTES

[1]Henry A. Bullock, *A History of Negro Education in the South* (Cambridge, Mass.: Harvard University Press, 1967), p. 11.

[2]Ibid., pp. 43-44.

[3]Benjamin E. Mays, *Born to Rebel* (New York: Charles Scribner's Sons, 1971), p. 36.

[4]*Brown v. Board of Education of Topeka*, 347 U. S. 483 (1954).

[5]Lewis Killian and Charles Grigg, *Racial Crisis in America* (Englewood Cliffs, N. J.: Prentice-Hall, 1964), p. 11.

[6]Daniel C. Thompson, "The Role of the Federal Courts in the Changing Status of Negroes Since World War II," *Journal of Negro Education* (Spring 1961): 94-101.

[7]*Brown v. Board of Education of Topeka*.

[8]Elgin F. Hunt, *Social Science* (New York: The Macmillan Co., 1966), pp. 752-753.

[9]Jacob K. Javits, *Discrimination U.S.A.* (New York: A Washington Square Press Book, 1962), pp. 228-245.

[10]*Brown v. Board of Education of Topeka*, 347 U. S. 483 (1954).

[11]Select Committee, United States Senate (Senator William F. Mondale, Chairman), *Toward Equal Educational Opportunity* (Washington, D. C.: U. S. Government Printing Office, 1972), pp. VII and 102.

[12]Ibid., p. 111.

[13]Seymour Martin Lipset and Earl Raab, *The Politics of Unreason* (New York: Harper Torchbook, 1970), pp. 340-358.

[14]Ibid., pp. 355-356.

[15]Ibid., p. 378.

[16]E. Franklin Frazier, *The Negro in the United States* (New York: The Macmillan Co., 1957), pp. 43-431.

[17]*Missouri ex rel. Gaines v. Canada*, as reported in Monroe Berger, *Equality by Statute* (New York: Doubleday and Co., Inc., 1968), p. 141. See also pp. 141-150 for a summary of other cases dealing with segregated schools.

[18]Benjamin A. Quarles, *The Negro in the Making of America* (New York: Collier Books, 1964), p. 237.

[19]Ibid., p. 239.

[20]Langston Hughes, *Fight for Freedom: The Story of the NAACP* (New York: Norton, 1962), pp. 129-147, and passim.

[21]See an analysis of "McCarthyism" by Lipset, *The Politics of Unreason*, pp. 209-245.

[22]Kenneth B. Clark, "The Civil Rights Movement: Momentum and Organization," in Richard P. Young, ed., *Roots of Rebellion* (New York: Harper and Row Publishers, 1970), p. 298.

[23]Langston Hughes, *Fight for Freedom*, pp. 131-134.

[24]Herbert Wey and John Corey, *Action Patterns in School Desegregation* (Bloomington, Ind.: Phi Delta Kappa, 1959), p. 31.

[25]See Southern Education Reporting Service (SERS), *Statistical Summary*, No. 2, November 1964.

[26]Langston Hughes, *Fight for Freedom*, p. 129.

[27]U. S. Office of Education (Department of Health, Education and Welfare), "General Statement of Policies under Title VI of the Civil Rights Act of 1964 Respecting Desegregation of Elementary and Secondary Schools," April 1965.

[28]Ibid.

[29]Anthony Downs, "The Nature of Racism in America, and How to Combat It," unpublished manuscript written for the U. S. Civil Rights Commission, November 1968, p. 4.

[30]For a systematic study of this, see Robert L. Crain, *The Politics of Desegregation* (Chicago: Aldine Publishing Co., 1968).

[31]The Mondale Report, part 3A, *Desegregation Under Law*, p. 1067.

[32]Wey and Corey, *Action Patterns of School Desegregation*, p. 36.

[33]*The New Orleans School Crisis*, Report of the Louisiana State Advisory Commission on Civil Rights, 1961, pp. 31-37.

[34]Wey and Corey, *Action Patterns of School Desegregation*, p. 36.

[35]*New Orleans School Crisis*, p. 33.

[36]Crain, *The Politics of Desegregation*, Chapter 15.

[37]Henry A. Kissinger, "The Policymaker and the Intellectual," *The Reporter*, March 5, 1959.

[38]For a systematic discussion, see Daniel C. Thompson, *The Negro Leadership Class*, pp. 58-79 and 160-164.

[39]For a comprehensive discussion of the white liberal, including the martyr role, see Killian and Grigg, *Racial Crisis in America*, Chapter 5, pp. 92-104, especially p. 100.

[40]Wey and Corey, *Action Patterns of School Desegregation*, p. 102.

[41]Ibid., pp. 158-159; and Crain, *The Politics of School Desegregation*, pp. 48-50.

[42]U. S. Supreme Court Decision. *Watson v. Memphis*, May 27, 1963.

[43]U. S. Senate Committee, *Toward Equal Educational Opportunity*, p. 111.

[44]Quoted in Crain, *The Politics of School Desegregation*, p. 247.

[45]For an accounting of this very basic problem, see Robert W. Hooker, "Displacement of Black Teachers in the Eleven Southern States," *Race Relations Information Center Special Report*, December 1970.

[46]*Toward Equal Educational Opportunity*, p. 201.

[47]Ibid., p. 141. See also pp. 145-153.

7

The Black
Middle Class

The Black middle class may be defined as a distinct socio-economic category in American society, composed of individuals and families who are regarded as successful in terms of their education, occupation, and income. They are characteristically engaged in occupations that require high school or college education, or serve as owners or managers of stable business enterprises. Their annual income is above the national median.

Some who measure up to these criteria may be accorded upper-class status in the segregated Black community because there is widespread poverty among Blacks and the median family income was only $6,279 in 1970. This was $3,957, or 39 percent less than the $10,236 for white families.[1] Yet, they would not belong in the middle class in the larger white community where they live or in American society generally where prestigious family background, inherited wealth, and significant social power or top-level decision-making are criteria of upper-class status.[2]

When education, occupation, and income are used as criteria of middle-class status, we find that there has been a significant increase in the size and composition of the Black middle class in the United States since 1955. At that time only 3 to 5 percent of the Black population could be classified as middle class. The great majority of those who did place in the middle class represented a very narrow range of occupations: teachers, ministers, physicians, and a few of the more successful businessmen. Today, on the basis of income, the Black middle class is almost ten times as large, including from 28 to 30 percent of the Black population. It is also much more complex in that it now includes individuals and families representing a variety of occupations and occupational statuses once closed to Blacks, who today possess a greater variety of interests, talents, and academic backgrounds than was the case in 1955.

The upward social mobility of Blacks has been especially pronounced since 1960.[3] In 1960, just 36 percent of Black males and 41 percent of Black females 25 to 29 years of age had completed high school. By 1970, 54 percent of Black males and 58 percent of Black females in that age group were high school graduates. Of additional importance to a study of the Black middle class is the fact that in 1960 there were 192,344 Black college students in the United States. Ten years later, in 1970, there were almost three times as many—522,000. Within a four year period, 1964-1968, the Black college student enrollment increased from 234,000 to 434,000, or by 85 percent. When this rate of increase is extrapolated, it is estimated that at present there are approximately 680,000 Black college students, if we include those in community colleges.

Again, in 1960, 4.3 percent of Blacks between 25 and 34 years of age had graduated from college; by 1970, 6.6 percent in that age group were college graduates, and it is estimated that at present about 7.3 percent in that age group have graduated from college. This represents significant intraracial progress. But in 1970 almost three times as many whites, 17 percent, had graduated from college.

Another indication of the increasing size of the Black middle class is the proportion of families whose income is above the national median. In 1960, only 9 percent of Black families had an annual income of $10,000 or more. By 1970, about 28 percent of Black families were in this income category. Furthermore, in 1960 only 2 percent of Black families had an annual income of $15,000 and more; by 1970, 9 percent of Black families placed in that category. Since consumer prices have risen considerably since 1960, a more reliable indication of the upward social mobility of Blacks is the progress they have made relative to whites in terms of median income: In 1960, the median income of Blacks was just 55 percent of whites; by 1970, their median income was still only 64 percent of whites.

Finally, the most universally accepted index of social class differences in the United States is occupation. Even when multiple indexes are used by researchers, occupation is generally regarded as the most reliable single test or measure of social class differences.[4]

Between 1960 and 1970, Blacks made considerable progress in terms of occupational categories and levels of employment. The number of Blacks in white collar, craftsmen, and operative occupations—''the better paying jobs''—increased by about 72 percent, or from somewhat less than 3 million to approximately 5 million; the number in managerial positions increased from 178,000 to 298,000, or by 67 percent; and those in professional and technical occupations increased from 331,000 to 766,000, or by 131 percent. Thus, here again, intraracial progress has been noteworthy. Nevertheless, while about 60 percent of employed Blacks hold ''better paying jobs,'' over 81 percent of whites are engaged in such employment.

Evidently, Black scholars and white liberals have chosen to deemphasize the rapid growth and affluence of the Black middle class primarily because, while this progress has been very significant in terms of intraracial comparisons, it has not been nearly as rapid to achieve true racial equality. This challenging lag between Black accomplishments and the socioeconomic status of whites was well stated by Dr. Martin Luther King, Jr., who often said: "We have come a long, long way, but we still have a long, long way to go."

Some of the most perceptive Black leaders, such as Vernon Jordan, head of the National Urban League, fear that Blacks may be headed toward another period of oppression, neglect, and frustration such as they encountered during the "First Reconstruction" after the Civil War. He analyzed the state of race relations today and concluded that it is very similar to the period which began in 1865, continued for about a decade, and "ended with the infamous Hayes-Tilden Compromise" in 1877. It was then that the newly emancipated Blacks were abandoned by their former friends in the North. The South was left free to reinstate its former Rebel leaders of the Confederacy and Blacks were promptly reduced to a serfdom akin to slavery. Jordan concludes:

> Now, in 1972, there is persuasive evidence that the Second Reconstruction—the dismantling of segregation and the further extension of basic civil rights to Black people—is coming to an end. Once again, the North seems weary of the struggle. Once again, the righteous cause of Black people seems relegated to national neglect. Once again, a period of national reconstruction and reform seems doomed to be unfinished and uncompleted. . . . The Second Reconstruction has been as incomplete as the First.[5]

Therefore, today most Black leaders and scholars feel compelled to insist that the nation complete the new drive toward equality, and they seem to believe that boasting about success is premature and perhaps unwise.

Differentiations Within the Black Middle Class

Observations and hypotheses in some of the literature to be

cited subsequently strongly suggest that the Black middle class is not a monolith. For instance, in a recent article by Joseph Scott there is an analysis of certain fundamental differences to be found within the Black middle class. He concludes that:

> Black individuals of the middle range have been at the forefront of all organized efforts at black liberation . . . There does not seem to be one typical bourgeois response (as Frazier insisted). There does seem to be the fact that the bourgeoisie does respond to changing historical conditions.[6]

Scott is one of the few recent Black scholars who call attention to the flexibility of the Black middle class. This in effect contradicts Frazier's scathing description of the ''Black bourgeoisie'' on the whole as superficial, insecure, alienated from the Black masses, and rejected by the white middle class.[7]

Sidney Kronus' 1970 study of eighty Black ''middle class'' individuals in Chicago is the only empirical study of the Black middle class published in over ten years.[8] Even previous empirical studies did not focus on the middle class per se, but on social stratification in the Black community generally.[9]

Kronus selected his interview sample from those Blacks whose annual income was $7,000 and more, and who were engaged in a white collar occupation. With $4,000 per year as the more commonly accepted level of ''poverty,'' the $7,000 income level may be seriously questioned.[10] Anyway, the author is primarily interested in class attitudes and not in the role of the Black middle class in urban society. He does, however, divide the Black middle class into four analytic types according to their scores on an anti-white, anti-Black continuum:

(a) ''Benevolents''—those who are pro-white and pro-Black.

(b) "Uncle Toms"—those who are pro-white and anti-Black.

(c) "Race men"—those who are anti-white and pro-Black.

(d) "World haters"—those who are anti-white and anti-Black.

While Kronus has been accused of too loosely defining the middle class, manipulating raw data, and differentiating the Black middle class into easy, pat segments, he does warn against the overgeneralization, even stereotyping of the nature and social role of the Black middle class as most other writers are prone to do. There is still a critical need, however, to discover and interpret empirically verifiable differentiations within the Black middle class and to interpret this class as a viable social category in the larger society, as well as in the Black community.

Theoretical Orientation: Basic Hypotheses

Theoretically, one should be aware of at least four distinct "social worlds" within the Black middle class: the Black elite, stable middle class, upwardly mobile, and downwardly mobile:[11]

1. *The Black elite.* Those who belong to this social world within the Black middle class are usually highly educated professionals, who hold academic or professional degrees from prestigious universities outside the South, and highly successful businessmen. Nearly all male heads of families in this group are accorded top leadership status in the Black community and are recognized as legitimate leaders by whites who have significant social power.[12]

A considerable proportion of the Black elite who constitute the 15 percent or so of the Black middle class are second or third generation. That is, they come from families where one or both parents, and occasionally one or more grandparents, are/were engaged in professional, technical, or managerial occupations. Horace Mann Bond emphasizes the importance of family background among the Black elite. In a study of top Black scholars (those who hold the Ph.D. or some other doctorate and have made significant contributions to their special fields and leadership), Bond concludes that these elite "were derived overwhelmingly from what one can identify as a Negro upper class."[13]

Older members of the Black elite attempt to effect a degree of national unity by joining high-status, national professional, business, and social organizations. The Negro National Medical Association, the Negro Bar Association, on the one hand, and the "Boule," Links, and Jack and Jill on the other hand, are prime examples. In speaking of "Boule," Kenneth Clark says: " Sigma Pi Phi, founded in Philadelphia in 1904, and known informally as the Boule, is a conscious attempt to bring together Negroes who have manifested outstanding ability to compete successfully with whites . . ."[14]

These organizations not only facilitate national social relationships among the Black elite, but they also make regular contributions to other organizations and programs designed to improve conditions among the Black masses and to advance the education of Black youth.[15]

2. *The stable middle class.* Those who compose this social world are usually first-generation middle class. They are successful in their occupations, but do not strive for social recognition or leadership. Some continue to live in the Black ghettos in which they were raised or to which they migrated, despite their ability to live in more affluent neighborhoods. There is little evidence that they place a high value upon "conspicuous consumption" and affluent display, as E. Franklin Frazier (*The Black Bourgeoisie*) insisted was the case of the Black middle class generally.

3. *The upwardly mobile.* This social world is composed of

younger members of the Black middle class who are "trying to get ahead." They have the "proper" credentials for professional and community leadership and are striving to become recognized and accepted. They challenge traditional institutional structures and procedures and are among the most vocal advocates of social and professional changes. A major contention of Black leaders and civil rights organizations is that agencies and enterprises in both the public and private sectors of American life tend to discriminate against this segment of the Black middle class. They insist that a vast amount of talents and potentials in this group are underutilized and underdeveloped.

4. *The downwardly mobile.* In practically every large city, there is likely to be a social world within the Black middle class composed of individuals who once belonged to the Black elite but are now losing influence and status. Their high social and occupational status of previous years—such as the ministry, high school principalship, the "first" Blacks in some administrative positions in government, private agencies, etc.—has been neutralized, so to speak, by a relatively large number of Blacks who hold even more prestigious, well-paying positions in occupations that were closed to Blacks only a few years ago. Along with losing the prestige of being the "first" or best employed Blacks, they often find themselves losing out to younger Black professionals and managers who are strongly bidding for public recognition and community leadership. This is the social segment that is most criticized by Black militant intellectuals.

Some Current Views of the Black Middle Class

Eldridge Cleaver has recently given a caustic, and perhaps exaggerated, description and interpretation of how the older Black elite—"the bourgeoisie"—has responded to the challenge of the new, "Black militant" leaders. Traditionally, he charged—

No matter what storm beset the black masses, the black bourgeoisie felt itself to be above it, and outside the circle of harm . . . What put them uptight was the fact that the black masses had turned black. At first the black bourgeoisie tried to ignore the phenomenon as a passing fad. [Later] they fought a running battle of sabotage against all black-oriented organizations.[16]

He concluded: "The magic word was black. Their every third word was black. Black, black, black. They had discovered their new thing. Now they were ready, again, to become the running dogs for their white masters."[17]

Cleaver's bitter criticism of the Black middle class, especially the elitist element, is simply an echo of E. Franklin Frazier. Frazier's provocative and controversial interpretation of the Black middle class was adopted by Black power advocates during the 1960s. They made the overthrow of top middle-class Black leaders a *cause célèbre*.[18] However, one of the latest and perhaps most bitter criticisms of the Black middle class is by a Black woman—Trellie Jeffers. In analyzing the plight of the black woman (referring here to skin-color), Jeffers offers the following:

The black middle class has for generations excluded the black black woman from the mainstream of black middle-class society, and it has, by its acts of discrimination against her, induced in itself a divisive cancer that has chopped the black race in this country into polarized sections; consequently, the black middle class has devoured its own soul and is doomed, a large number of black working class people believe, to extinction. [Further] What it is, is an insanity that has helped whites turn blacks on themselves and has caused the black middle class to claw itself into a form of psychic annihilation.[19]

This kind of criticism is no doubt one of the primary reasons why Black scholars and civil rights leaders have deliberately ignored successful Blacks and emphasized Black poverty. It has been unpopular to recognize the contributions made by middle class-oriented Black leaders or a successful middle class per se. Therefore, following the pattern of criticisms set by Frazier, young Black militants and some established Black intellectuals have constantly accused the Black middle class of being a superficial imitation of the white middle class—obsessed with feelings of inferiority and inadequacy, deeply frustrated at their alienation from the Black masses and rejection by the white middle class, and preferring to live in "a world of make-believe."[20]

One of the best examples of the Frazier-style critics of the Black middle class is Harold Cruse, who has said:

> The economic philosophy of the black bourgeoisie . . . reflects a kind of social opportunism . . . . The black bourgeoisie is self-seeking but in a shortsighted, unsophisticated, unpolitical and cowardly fashion. It is one of the rare bourgeois classes of color that will sell itself out to white power without a principled struggle for its economic rights . . . Because the masses do not support the black bourgeoisie, the latter is powerless as a class . . . The black bourgeoisie sells skills and abilities, the products of education."[21]

Samuel D. Proctor, an established elitist scholar and administrator (professor at Rutgers University and now pastor of Abyssinian Baptist Church, successor to Adam Clayton Powell), answered some of the criticism of the Black middle class: "It is alleged that the black middle class is shot through with apathy, cowardice, or both. But the black middle class is not quite that naive. It has only a survival strategy. . . . the idea of a blood bath looked like genocide. They rejected it."[22] He concluded that:

most middle class blacks cannot find themselves in E. Franklin Frazier's work . . . The gap that is alleged to exist between the black masses and the "bourgeoisie" is largely a myth and a lazy description of a complicated phenomenon . . . Let's face it, there are places where we need blacks that can be filled only with blacks who may be classified as middle class.[23]

Proctor states that the Black middle class is composed mainly of individuals who are "prudent": "They made it on safe bets, hard work, self-confidence, skillful manipulations, and brutal competitiveness."[24]

Professor Kenneth B. Clark emphasizes another vital role the Black middle class plays vis à vis the Black masses:"The competitive demands of the growing Negro middle class, if successful, would open more doors for all Negroes." Clark reasoned that successful Blacks would neutralize the negative image whites generally have of Blacks. "The tendency of whites to lump all Negroes together could lead ironically to major social advances, as Negroes in high status jobs prepare the way for gradual acceptance of all Negroes."[25]

Clark then emphasized a common characteristic of successful Black professionals that may seriously militate against their functioning as effective leaders and symbols of Black Americans: the tendency to flee from the Black ghetto and find homes in formerly white communities. This is one of the reasons why some mass-oriented Black leaders and scholars criticize the Black middle class and accuse successful Blacks of being alienated from the Black masses.

Black Success: A Civil Rights Strategy

During recent years, especially since the mid-1950s, most of the research and writings about Blacks have focused on conditions and problems of the Black masses whose income is near or below the poverty level.[26] Very little scholarly attention has been given to the Black middle class. Ben Wattenberg and Richard Scammon attribute this scholarly neglect of the Black middle class to a kind of spontaneous conspiracy by civil rights leaders and white liberals who ". . . have insisted that conditions for American blacks are not improving at all, but actually deteriorating . . . It will be a great and tragic irony if this insistence on failure should in the end prove a hindrance to the continued upward progress of American blacks."[27]

In order to understand why Black intellectuals have chosen to focus on the plight of the masses rather than on the successes of the Black middle class, it is necessary to know that most Black professionals and businessmen, in response to the dictates of institutionalized racism, have had to build their economic and social existence almost totally on the resources of the segregated Black community. Those who have insisted on support from the larger white society have risked activating an oppressive white backlash and accusations of "pushing too hard." Thus, no matter how well educated or affluent individual Blacks may become, the network of social forces stemming from racism reminds them that they share a common identity and a common destiny with all other Blacks, even the most economically disadvantaged. This phenomenon was perceptively stated by Myrdal a generation ago:

> The Negro genius is imprisoned in the Negro problem . . .
> In the existing American civilization he can grow to a
> degree of distinction but always as a representative of "his
> people," not as an ordinary American or an individual in
> humanity. . . . That is the role awarded him, and he cannot
> step out of it. He is defined as a "race man," regardless of
> the role he might wish for himself. . . . To the ordinary
> members of the Negro middle and upper class, even the
> window shutters of the prison are closed.[28]

The Black condition in American society has obviously changed significantly since 1944, for more and more Blacks are managing to escape the prison of racism Myrdal described. Yet, the prison still exists; it is very real. The vast majority of Black professionals and businessmen must still depend for their economic and social support from the Black community, or from white institutions, through pressure. As long as this situation continues, Black intellectuals are likely to agree that boasting about Black successes is premature because the opportunity structure in American society today falls far short of its egalitarian commitment. Unemployment among Blacks remains about twice as high as it is among whites; almost four times as many Black families have incomes below the poverty level (29 percent for Blacks compared with 8 percent for whites); and Blacks who do manage to succeed must generally sacrifice more, try harder, strive longer, and eventually get paid less than their white counterparts. Consequently, Black scholars and spokesmen have chosen to champion the cause of the Black masses as a more effective civil rights strategy rather than to cheer the accomplishments of the few Blacks who have made it against great odds.

Even Blacks who have succeeded in the larger white world and do not have to depend directly on support from the Black community continue to have a special obligation to improve conditions in the segregated Black community. This feeling stems primarily from the fact that Black mass pressure is largely responsible for whatever job breakthroughs the educated Blacks now enjoy. Successful Blacks cannot forget the decade of sacrifices in the 1960s—police brutality, imprisonment, and loss of life—which the Black masses made to get better jobs, voting rights, better education, and respect. They are well aware that their blackness sets them apart from the masses in American society. This blackness imposes upon them a common identity that prevails over all other identities and has inherent in it unique social pressures and role expectations.

The unique position of Blacks who have succeeded in the larger white society was vividly brought out by Richard Rogin in a case history of a Black executive in a wealthy white accounting firm in New York. This executive is justly proud that he fought his way out of poverty and inadequate public school training to become one of the 137 executives with this prestigious firm. While he realizes that it is unlikely that he could earn as much money in the Black community as he does in the white community, he would be delighted if he could somehow find a way to aid in the development of Black capitalism. Therefore, Rogin is convinced that this Black executive has "inside him, all around him, . . . the desperate clamor of the Black ghettos, crying out in the 'common cause' for true liberation," a cry successful "white American dreamers can never know."[29]

A close examination of the writings and oral expressions of Black scholars, leaders, and white liberals during the last decade strongly indicates that they underemphasized Black success and emphasized Black poverty as a well-calculated civil rights strategy. This was in response to the basic criticism of the civil rights movement of the late 1950s and early 1960s, which some said was too middle-class-oriented: they fought for middle-class privileges and the advancement of the educated Blacks and paid too little attention to the plight of the Black masses.

The overresponse to this pointed criticism was to denounce the Black middle class or ignore it altogether. It would seem that a more fruitful civil rights strategy would be to continue to fight for the improvement of conditions among the poor while presenting convincing evidence that the plight of the poor can be alleviated if both public and private institutions and agencies take the proper measures. Unless this more balanced view prevails, it will be relatively easy for anti-Black forces to convince the majority of American people that the plight of the Black masses is hopeless and that they must ever remain the "white man's burden."

There is already some evidence that the Black poverty stereotype is beginning to emerge as a barrier to Black progress. At present this problem seems to be most obvious in white colleges where a significant number of Black students are enrolled. Michael Meyers summarizes what has become a popular belief. He says that teachers and administrators in white colleges tend to look at Black people en masse.

> They particularly refuse to accept young black persons with middle class values. . . . Colleges, like the secondary and public school before them adopted key phrases to signal to white students that the new breed of minority students were, in effect, "different" and not to be taken seriously as incipient scholars.[30]

He contends that Black students are automatically typed as "high risk," "disadvantaged," "new directions," or "culturally deprived." Then he concludes:

> Colleges assumed *all* minority students were disadvantaged and, as students were admitted, they were automatically "tracked". In 1970, 62 percent of all black students enrolled in public colleges in New York State were put in so-called "Opportunity Programs".[31]

With a body of sound information about the socioeconomic and cultural backgrounds of middle-class Black children and youth in our schools and colleges, particularly in those institutions in the first stages of desegregation, teachers and counselors would be better prepared to understand Black students and to determine the type of guidance and instruction they need in order to properly develop their individual talents and potentials. Their guidance could more intelligently take into account the new Black opportunity structure in American society and how certain Blacks have managed to take advantage of it.

This need was emphasized by Thomas Sowell who did a comprehensive study of the high school and college counseling of Black students. He concluded that counseling is severely hampered by lack of information about the varied backgrounds of Black youth. He believes that current academic policies are often based on myths about the Black middle class.

> Many a brilliant black student is the first member of his family ever to go to college, so that he can expect no help at home, and the "guidance" at school is likely to be either non-existent or unbelievably bad . . . The "lack of informed and realistic guidance" available in the Southern Negro schools was paralleled by similar deficiencies in the integrated Southern schools, aggravated by a lesser concern for black students in such schools. At many Northern schools the situation is no better. A Ford Foundation report finds high school guidance counselling for minority students "markedly inadequate in both North and South".[32]

Consequently, precise, realistic information about Blacks "who have made it" or have succeeded in various areas of American life, and about the strategies and techniques they employed to overcome the handicaps inherent in race and poverty would be helpful to high school and college teachers and counselors who are expected to assist Black students in selecting academic programs and future careers.

Information about successful Blacks would also be helpful to top policy-makers and foundations concerned with improving the quality of education in American society and among minority groups specifically. This would be especially apropos for Blacks because they have always had great faith in the efficacy of education. They have assumed that by getting a "good" education, developing a salable occupational skill, and adhering to middle-class conduct, racial prejudice against them would eventually disappear. Just about all Black leaders have emphasized this approach to racial progress.[33] Therefore, Blacks have historically relied on schools as the most effective avenue of social mobility and of equality in American society.

The significant increase in Black secondary school and college enrollment during the last decade strongly indicates that Blacks have maintained their faith in the efficacy of education.

Although their efforts were often inadequate and only "token," over the years individual philanthropists, certain national foundations, segments of the corporate world, and government on all levels have supported the education of Blacks on the assumption that it would facilitate their progress. This basic assumption, which has been a constant, effective motivation for "self-improvement" among Blacks, has been seriously challenged by Christopher Jencks and his associates at Harvard University.[34] They conclude that, even if all children could be made to do equally well in equally good schools, economic inequality would still remain. In regards to school desegregation, they contend that:

> Our best guess, after reviewing all the evidence we could find, is that racial desegregation raises black elementary school students' test scores by a couple of points. But most of the test-score gaps between blacks and whites persist, even when they are in the same schools . . . neither the overall level of resources available to a school nor any other specific, easily identifiable school policy has a significant effect on students' cognitive skills or educational attainments.[35]

Then the authors theorized:

> Thus, even if we went beyond "equal opportunity" and allocated resources disportionately to schools whose students now do worst on tests . . . this would not improve these students' prospects very much.[36]

They conclude that:

> the evidence we have reviewed suggests (in terms of long-

term benefits for children) that the long-term effects of segregation on individual students are quite small . . . once the tradition of complete segregation is broken . . . mandatory busing makes less sense.''[37]

The Jencks' book is bound to have a far-reaching influence on educational policy in the United States. It was supported and launched by two of the most prestigious foundations in this country, the Guggenheim Memorial Foundation and the Carnegie Corporation, both of which have contributed much to the advancement of education. Also, the authors of this book represent one of the most prestigious universities in the world. Furthermore, the study was published at a time when there was an intense effort to reassess the educational policies and programs established during the last decade specifically to improve the condition of the poor in this nation, especially the Black poor. Therefore, the Jencks study, if taken seriously by top educational policy-makers, could make Daniel P. Moynihan's celebrated proposed policy of ''benign neglect'' of the race problem a national policy regarding the education of the disadvantaged minorities in this country.

This fear, that the Jencks study might discourage support of the education of Blacks, especially compensatory programs, was expressed by several educators in a recent edition of the *Harvard Educational Review*.[38] The entire issue was devoted to an analysis of Jencks' study. Though many criticisms were made of the methodology, data, and conclusions presented, for our particular purpose two basic premises should be challenged:

1. Essentially, Jencks and his associates elaborated upon and reinterpreted data gathered by James S. Coleman and his associates in 1966.[39] The actual research for the Coleman Report was begun during the early years of the 1960s. This was during a most critical period when schools and school systems throughout the United States were experiencing boycotts, teacher strikes, political pressure, and violence in efforts to meet even minimum compliance with the federal courts' deseg-

regation orders. As late as 1968, fourteen years after the Supreme Court's ruling in the *Brown Case*, and two years after the publication of the Coleman Report, 76.6 percent of Black children were still in predominantly Black schools in the nation, with 81.6 percent of Black children in the South in predominantly Black schools. Practically every major school system with a large number of Black children was finding ways to circumvent the courts' desegregation orders.[40] Most of the planning and actions by state and local governments, school boards, school administrators, and teachers were designed to prevent, or at least minimize, school desegregation. Strong antidesegregation forces in state governments were threatening to abolish the existing public school system and set up a "private school system" in which students' fees would be paid for by public taxes. (This was actually done in several communities throughout the South.) Local school boards became hopelessly enmeshed in antidesegregation politics, and there was a wave of white teachers applying for transfers out of desegregated schools.

During the early years of the 1960s, then, when Coleman was gathering data for his report, perhaps the most positive action engaged in by those interested in public education was to "Save our Schools" (SOS, as the movement was called in New Orleans). School officials were primarily concerned about how to get Black and white students in the same schools without completely destroying public education.[41] Apparently little or no thought and action were spent on improving the quality of public education per se or on making our schools more effective instruments in equalizing opportunity, which is the main concern of both the Coleman and Jencks reports.

In 1969, three years after publication of the Coleman Report, the Supreme Court found it necessary to change the "with all deliberate speed" stance of the 1954 decision to "at once." Since then, school desegregation in the South has proceeded much more orderly, so that, in 1971, just two years later, only 56.1 percent of Black children in the South were in predominantly Black schools. Since 1969, several promising programs to implement orderly desegregation and to provide expert educational assistance to disadvantaged children have been instituted.

2. With all other main avenues to social mobility unavailable or restricted (business, politics, government, the armed services, and the like), education has been the traditional, most reliable, and certainly the most available avenue to equality for a significant number of Black Americans.

The possible international impact of the Coleman and Jencks reports is indicated by an international survey of 250,000 students and 50,000 teachers from 9,700 schools in nineteen countries. According to some conclusions in this massive report:

> The study suggests even more strongly than the Coleman report that school factors do make a substantial difference . . . It challenges directly some claims made recently in the study headed by Christopher Jencks at Harvard that schools fail to reduce social inequality . . . it concluded that open access to public education is a key factor in allowing lower-class children to rise to the level of the academic elite. This increases their chances of greater economic success. [42]

More concrete information about the Black middle class may provide an important, necessary contradiction to Jencks' thesis that "education makes little difference" in equalizing opportunity in American society. If education is as important as it seems to be, then this fact should have some important value for top educational policy-makers and planners whose responsibility it is to develop policies and guidelines for improving our schools and colleges and for making education more relevant to our complex urban, industrial society.

In order to better understand the role of the Black middle class in American society, more information is needed about the racial policies and practices of key private and public institutions, agencies, organizations, and business enterprises that tend to hinder or, conversely, facilitate the socioeconomic advancement of the Black population. Of prime importance are labor unions, representative industries, professional societies (ABA, AMA, NEA, etc.), political parties, city governments, the courts, police departments, health services, the mass media, and some selected Black organizations, which may also significantly affect the social mobility of Blacks.

Extensive information, then, about the Black middle class could be very useful to policy-makers in various areas of city, state, and national life. For instance, with this body of information, public and private agencies in cities with a substantial middle class could more expeditiously recruit individuals from the Black community for service on commissions, committees, and boards charged with key areas of community planning and administration. If this were done in a forthright, systematic manner, based on extensive knowledge of the talents, interests, and resources of the Black middle class, this nation might better deal with the problems of many cities with increasingly large Black populations.[43] James Blackwell's and Marie Haug's study of Cleveland underscores the importance of such knowledge if large urban centers, with a steady influx of Blacks and with a white exodus, are to be able to survive and progress in the future as they have in the past. They contend that

> changing power relations between blacks and whites are taking place in the cities, but they are taking place in a time when cities are no longer viewed as meccas of sophistication, excitement, and potential wealth, but decaying, polluted, even obsolete places from which it is best to escape. Blacks who achieve political power in the urban setting may find themselves winning a bag of problems instead of a bag of gold.[44]

Then, after analyzing some difficult problems which Carl

Stokes, the former Black mayor of Cleveland, had to face, the authors conclude that inadequate knowledge about intragroup relations and differentiation within the Black community exacerbated these problems: "The tendency to stereotype minorities as undifferentiated wholes is undoubtedly responsible for some of the theoretical dilemmas which now haunt inter-group relations."[45]

Fred Cook's study of predominantly Black (61 percent) Newark is another convincing indication that cities with a large Black population must plan to make more extensive use of the leadership potentials in the Black middle class. He describes the knotty problem of leadership faced by the Black mayor, Kenneth Gibson, who asserts that " 'Wherever the Central Cities are going, Newark is going to get their first.' "[46] Cook describes Newark as—

> A study in the evils, tensions and frustrations that beset the central cities of America . . . In the Central Ward decent black families live as virtual prisoners in housing-authority projects, afraid to let their children outside even to play.
>
> There are at least two Newarks, separate and distinct . . . existing in an atmosphere of mutual suspicion and racial tension. There is the white-dominated, business-oriented Newark, and there are the densely populated sections where black and Puerto Ricans live.[47]

One of the mayor's most difficult problems is finding talented, racially acceptable citizens to serve on key committees, boards, commissions, and in administrative offices. The welfare of the city depends largely on the degree of success he will have in filling leadership vacancies left by the more affluent whites who have moved out of Newark to various suburbs.

Another urbanologist, James Boggs, criticizes cities with large Black populations for not using a larger number of skilled and talented Blacks in planning and administration. He would like to see qualified Blacks much more involved in improving programs in housing, health, education, and employment. As things now stand, he says:

> As blacks have grown in numbers within cities, we have witnessed the rapid exodus from cities and from the problems of the cities, of all those whites who could afford to leave . . . What blacks came to the cities hoping and expecting to find has been rapidly disappearing all around them . . . Thus instead of being in a position to benefit from city life and from being the largest minority in the cities, blacks have become the victims of cities.[48]

In short, planners and administrators in cities with an increasingly large Black population need more extensive information about the Black middle class in their efforts to effectively fill what might otherwise become a leadership vacuum left by white citizens who steadily move out of central cities to suburban areas. This need was underscored in an article written by Daniel P. Moynihan, who was a key presidential advisor on urban affairs. He pointed out that practically all of our metropolitan growth since 1960 has been in the suburbs that ring our cities. There has been a "continued exodus of wealthier whites out of the cities and the continued introduction of poorer blacks into the cities . . . yearly the net loss of white city dwellers averages 141,000; the net increase of Blacks is 370,000."[49] Looking at the urban crisis from the point of view of the federal government, Moynihan insisted that:

> One can hardly avoid the need for a national urban policy . . . The federal government must provide more and better information concerning urban affairs, and should sponsor extensive and sustained research into urban problems . . . Ways must be found to measure existing programs, plan new ones, and bring a sense of order and priorities into our attack on domestic ills.[50]

The kind of comprehensive planning both Moynihan and the Advisory Committee of the National Conference of Mayors recommend should be based on a sound knowledge of the differentiations and potentials in the Black community and should not assume, as even he suggested, that all of the Black population is "poorer" than the "whites who move out."

Again, extensive information about the Black middle class would be of special use to those who plan and participate in advertising and marketing, especially as it involves the mass media. Black leaders throughout the nation, particularly in southern cities, complain that Blacks are seriously underrepresented in the mass media. Concrete facts about the buying habits of the Black middle class would open the way for more enlightened employment policies than now exist. If a significant number of middle-class Blacks were employed in such visible occupations as sales, advertising, and the mass media, it would have a multiplier effect by helping to counter the negative image of Blacks as basically an economically and culturally deprived people. At the same time it would provide Blacks with the positions they deserve.[51]

While no reliable assessment has been made of the extent to which this negative, stereotyped image of Blacks hinders their progress (a basic question raised by Wattenberg and Scammon), there is evidence that it is considerable. Public responses as registered in local, state, and national polls and elections, legislative and congressional deliberations, and the avowed racial policies of some powerful organizations and institutions in American society too often indicate that the majority of whites tend to accept this old, traditional negative image of Blacks, and that even when given opportunities to succeed (as Daniel P. Moynihan so forcefully emphasized in his *The Negro Family: A Case for National Action*, 1965), they fail to take advantage of these opportunities.

More facts about the success patterns of the Black middle class would refute many of the Black stereotypes that impede Black progress. Therefore, Professor Kenneth B. Clark may be correct in thinking that successful Blacks could open paths of success for other Blacks. One thing is certain: since the vast majority, perhaps 85 percent, came from the Black masses and grew up in modest or even poverty conditions, they are likely to be a great deal more sensitive and responsive to the plight of the urban masses on the whole, and particularly the Black masses, than the white middle class has been.

NOTES

[1] U. S. Department of Commerce, Bureau of the Census, *The Social and Economic Characteristics of Negroes in the United States, 1970* (Washington, D. C.: U. S. Government Printing Office, 1971), p. 27.

[2] Everett C. Hughes, "Dilemmas and Contradictions of Status," *American Journal of Sociology*, No. 3 (1945): 353-359; C. Wright Mills, "The Middle Class in Middle-Sized Cities," *American Sociological Review* 11 (December 1946): 520-525; Gunnar Myrdal, *An American Dilemma* (New York: Harper and Brothers, Publishers, 1944), pp. 691-705; and E. Franklin Frazier, *The Negro in the United States* (New York: The Macmillan Co., 1957), pp. 291-292.

[3] The following statistical data on education and income are taken from *The Social and Economic Characteristics of Negroes in the United States, 1970*, p. 83, passim.

[4] Leonard Reissman, *Class in American Society* (Glencoe, Ill.: The Free Press, 1959), pp. 144-146. See also a classification of all occupations in terms of social-economic classes by Paul K. Hatt, "Stratification in the Mass Society," *American Sociological Review* 15 (April 1950): 219; National Opinion Research Center, "Jobs and Occupations: A Popular Evaluation," *Public Opinion News* 9 (1947): 3-13. Note also Donald R. Warren and Patrick C. Easto, "White Stratification Theory and Black Reality: A Neglected Problem of American Sociology," Paper presented at the 68th Annual Meeting, American Sociological Association, August 2, 1972. This paper by Warren and Easto deals at length with the problem of status inconsistency. They hold that Blacks experience double inconsistency—inconsistency due to ascribed ethnic rank relative to the white community and achievement inconsistency relative to education, income, and occupational

positions viewed from the standpoint of the Black community. They believe this problem can be solved by using a technique devised by Donald Ploch in 1968, according to which these three variables can be treated separately.

[5]Vernon E. Jordan, "The End of the Second Reconstruction?," *Contact* (1270 Sixth Avenue, New York, N. Y., July 1972), p. 15. See also "Whatever Happened to Black America?," *Newsweek* (February 19, 1973), p. 31.

[6]Joseph Scott, "The Black Bourgeoisie and Black Power," *The Black Scholar* 4, no. 4 (January 1973): 13.

[7]E. Franklin Frazier, *Black Bourgeoisie: The Rise of a New Middle Class in the United States* (New York: Collier Books, 1957 and 1962), pp. 162-175, passim.

[8]Sidney Kronus, *The Black Middle Class* (Columbus, Ohio: Charles E. Merrill, 1971).

[9]Oliver C. Cox, *Caste, Class and Race* (Garden City, New York: Doubleday, 1948); John Dollard, *Caste and Class in a Southern Town* (New York: Doubleday and Co., Inc., 1957); Allison Davis, Burleigh B. Gardner, and Mary R. Gardner, *Deep South* (Chicago: University of Chicago Press, 1941); St. Clair Drake and Horace R. Cayton, *Black Metropolis* (New York: Harper and Row, 1962); and John H. Rohrer, Munro S. Edmonson, Daniel C. Thompson, et al., *The Eighth Generation* (New York: Harper and Brothers, 1960).

[10]See Thomas Waters' "Review" in *Contemporary Sociology* 2, No. 1 (January 1973): 86-87.

[11]For a systematic analysis of the concept "social world" and how it was used in a study of the Black class structure in New Orleans, see Allison Davis and John Dollard, *Children of Bondage* (Washington, D. C.: American Council on Education, 1940), and a followup of that study, John H. Rohrer, Munro S. Edmonson, and Daniel C. Thompson, et al., *The Eighth Generation*, pp. 83-84, 298, passim.

[12]Gunnar Myrdal, *An American Dilemma*, pp. 694-695, 727-735. See also Daniel C. Thompson, *The Negro Leadership Class* (Englewood Cliffs, N. J.: Prentice-Hall, Inc., 1963), pp. 34-57.

[13]Horace Mann Bond, *Black American Scholars* (Detroit: Balamp Publishers, 1972), p. 22, passim.

[14]Kenneth B. Clark, *Dark Ghetto* (New York: Harper and Row, Publishers, 1965), pp. 190-191.

[15]For a full discussion of these organizations, see Charles H.

Wesley, *History of Sigma Pi Phi (Boule)* (The Association for the Study of Negro Life and History, Inc., 1954); also St. Clair Drake and Horace R. Cayton, *Black Metropolis* (New York: Harper and Row, 1945 and 1962), pp. 669-715.

[16]Eldridge Cleaver, "The Crisis of the Black Bourgeoisie," *The Black Scholar* 4, No. 4 (January 1973): 7-8.

[17]Ibid. See also Cleaver's "On Lumpen Ideology," *The Black Scholar* 4, No. 3 (November-December 1972): 2-10.

[18]August Meier and Elliott Rudwick, *Black Protest in the Sixties* (Chicago: Quadrangle Books, 1970), pp. 315-328.

[19]Trellie Jeffers, "The Black Black Woman and the Black Middle Class," *The Black Scholar* 4, Nos. 6-7 (March-April 1973): 37.

[20]E. Franklin Frazier, *Black Bourgeoisie*, pp. 192-195.

[21]Harold Cruse, *The Crisis of the Negro Intellectual* (New York: William Morrow and Co., Inc., 1967), pp. 178-179.

[22]Samuel D. Proctor, "Survival Techniques and the Black Middle Class," in Rhoda L. Goldstein, ed., *Black Life and Culture in the United States* (New York: Thomas Y. Crowell Co., 1971), pp. 280-284.

[23]Ibid., p. 288.

[24]Ibid.

[25]Kenneth B. Clark, *Dark Ghetto*, pp. 60-61.

[26]Some excellent examples of these are: Michael Harrington, *The Other America* (New York: Macmillan Co., 1962), see especially Chapter Four, "If You're Black, Stay Back," pp. 61-81; Elliot Liebow, *Tally's Corner: A Study of Negro Streetcorner Men* (Boston: Little, Brown, 1967); Paul Jacobs, et al., *Dialogue on Poverty* (New York: Bobbs-Merrill Co., Inc., 1966), see especially pp. 53-61 and 129-135; Whitney M. Young, Jr., *To Be Equal* (New York: McGraw-Hill, 1964), a comprehensive study of problems of the urban masses; William McCord, et al., *Life Styles in the Black Ghetto* (New York: W. W. Norton and Co., Inc., 1969), where several studies of the urban poor are presented; Jerry Cohen and William S. Murphy, *Burn, Baby Burn* (1966), which is an interpretation of the Los Angeles Race Riot in August 1965 (the basic cause cited is poverty); Andrew Billingsley, *Black Families in White America* (Englewood Cliffs, N. J.: Prentice-Hall, 1968), a systematic study of Black families from a welfare point of view, but only Chapter Five calls special attention to social class differences (pp. 122-146); Commission on Civil Disor-

ders (Otto Kerner, Chairman), *U. S. Riot Commission Report* (New York: Bantam Book, 1968), a much-publicized study which attributed urban riots to the basic problem of poverty in the Black ghetto; and Kenneth B. Clark, *Dark Ghetto*, 1965, a systematic study of Harlem, which is perhaps the most definitive study of the Black urban poor.

[27]Ben J. Wattenberg and Richard M. Scammon, "Black Progress and Liberal Rhetoric," *Commentary* (April 1973): 35-36.

[28]Gunnar Myrdal, *An American Dilemma*, p. 28.

[29]Richard Rogin, "Into the Middle Class: John Henry Howell Made It," *The New York Times Magazine*, June 24, 1973.

[30]Michael Meyers, "The New Black Apartheid," *Change* 4, No. 8 (October 1972): 8.

[31]Ibid., p. 9.

[32]Thomas Sowell, *Black Education Myths and Tragedies* (New York: David McKay Co., Inc., 1972), p. 143, passim.

[33]See Henry A. Bullock, *A History of Negro Education in the South* (Cambridge, Mass.: Harvard University Press, 1967), pp. 11, 194-224; Frederick Cooper, "Elevating the Race: The Social Thought of Black Leaders," *American Quarterly* 24, No. 5, pp. 605-624; and Whitney M. Young, Jr., *To Be Equal* (New York: McGraw-Hill Book Co., 1964), pp. 102-137.

[34]Christopher Jencks, et al., *Inequality: A Reassessment of the Effect of Family and Schooling in America* (New York: Basic Books, Inc., Publishers, 1972).

[35]Ibid., p. 149.

[36]Mary Jo Bane and Christopher Jencks, "The School and Equal Opportunity," *Saturday Review of Education* (September 16, 1972), lead article.

[37]Jencks et al., *Inequality*, p. 259.

[38]These well-known educators are: Ronald Edmonds, Harvard University; Andrew Billingsley, Howard University; James Comer, Yale Medical School; James M. Dyer, Carnegie Corporation of New York; William Hall, Princeton University; Robert Hill, National Urban League; Nan McGehee, University of Illinois at Chicago Circle; Lawrence Reddick, Temple University; Howard F. Taylor, Syracuse University; Stephen Wright, College Entrance Examination Board. Their statement is called "A Black Response to Christopher Jencks's Inequality and Certain Other Issues," *Harvard Education Review* 43, No. 1 (February 1973): 76-91.

[39]James S. Coleman, et al., *Equality of Educational Opportunity* (Washington, D. C.: U. S. Government Printing Office, 1966).

[40]For a full statistical analysis, see the U. S. Senate Committee on Equal Educational Opportunity, *Toward Equal Educational Opportunity* (Washington, D. C.: U. S. Government Printing Office, 1972), pp. 101-118.

[41]Herbert Wey and John Corey, *Action Patterns in School Desegregation* (Bloomington, Ind.: Phi Delta Kappa, 1959), pp. 23-31, passim, and Report of the Louisiana State Advisory Commission on Civil Rights, *The New Orleans School Crisis* (1961), pp. 31-37, passim.

[42]Reported in *The New York Times* (Sunday, May 27, 1973), Section E, p. 9. This is a review of a survey conducted by the International Association for the Evaluation of International Achievement in Education (IEA) in 1971-1972.

[43]For a full discussion, see National Advisory Commission on Civil Disorders (Otto Kerner, Chairman), *U. S. Riot Commission Report* (1968), pp. 389-409 and 417.

[44]James E. Blackwell and Marie Haug, "Relations Between Black Bosses and Black Unions," *The Black Scholar* 4, No. 4 (January 1973): 36.

[45]Ibid., p. 43.

[46]Fred J. Cook, "Newark," in Edgar G. Epps, *Race Relations: Current Perspectives* (Cambridge, Mass.: Winthrop Publishers, Inc., 1973), p. 368.

[47]Ibid., pp. 368-383.

[48]James Boggs, "Blacks in the Cities: Agenda for the 70s," *The Black Scholar* 4, No. 3 (November-December 1972): 52, passim.

[49]Daniel P. Moynihan, "Urban Crisis," *The New York Times Encyclopedic Almanac* (1970), p. 207.

[50]Ibid., p. 208.

[51]Nicholas Johnson, *How to Talk Back to Your Television Set* (New York: Bantam Books, 1970), pp. 90-105. Note also Chapter 15, "The News Media and the Disorders" in the Kerner Report (1968).

Selected Bibliography

Baldwin, James. *The Fire Next Time*. New York: The Dial Press, 1967.

Bane, Mary Jo, and Jencks, Christopher. "The School and Equal Opportunity," *Saturday Review of Education*, September 16, 1972, lead article.

Baran, Paul, and Sweezy, Paul. "Monopoly Capitalism and Race Relations," in Richard Frucht, *Black Society in the New World*. New York: Random House, 1971.

Benedict, Ruth. *Patterns of Culture*. New York: Houghton Mifflin Co., 1934.

Bennett, Lerone, Jr. *Confrontation: Black and White*. Baltimore: Penguin Books, Inc., 1965.

————. *What Manner of Man: A Biography of Martin Luther King, Jr*. Chicago: Johnson Publishing Co., Inc., 1968.

Berger, Monroe. *Equality by Statute*. New York: Doubleday and Co., Inc., 1968.

Billingsley, Andrew. *Black Families in White America*. Englewood Cliffs, N. J.: Prentice-Hall, Inc., 1968.

Blackwell, James E., and Janowitz, Morris. *Black Sociologist: Historical and Contemporary Perspectives*. Chicago: The University of Chicago Press, 1973.

————, and Haug, Maria. "Relations Between Black Bosses and Black Unions." *The Black Scholar* 4, No. 4 (January 1973): 36-43.

Boggs, James. "Blacks in the Cities: Agenda for the 70s." *The Black Scholar* 4 No. 3 (November-December 1972): 50-61.

Bond, Horace Mann. *Black American Scholars*. Detroit: Belamp Publishers, 1972.

Bontemps, Arna, ed. *American Negro Poetry*. New York: Hill and Wang, 1963.

Brink, William, and Harris, Louis. *Black and White: A Study of U. S. Racial Attitudes Today*. New York: Simon and Schuster, Publishers, 1967.

Bullock, Henry A. *A History of Negro Education in the South*. Cambridge, Mass.: Harvard University Press, 1967.

Carmichael, Stokely, and Hamilton, Charles V. *Black Power: The Politics of Liberation in America*. New York: A Vintage Book, 1967.

Chapman, Abraham, ed. *Black Voices*. New York: A Mentor Book, 1968.

————. "The Civil Rights Movement: Momentum and Organization," in Richard P. Young, ed., *Roots of Rebellion*. New York: Harper and Row, Publishers, 1970.

Clark, Kenneth B. *Dark Ghetto*. New York: Harper and Row, Publishers, 1965.

Cleaver, Eldridge. "On Lumpen Ideology." *The Black Scholar* 4, No. 3 (November-December 1972): 2-10.

————. "The Crisis of the Black Bourgeoisie." *The Black Scholar* 4, No. 4 (January 1973): 2-11.

————. "The White Race and Its Heroes," in Arthur C. Littleton and Mary W. Burger, eds., *Black Viewpoint*. New York: A Mentor Book, 1971.

Coleman, James S. *Equality of Educational Opportunity*. Washington, D. C.: U. S. Government Printing Office, 1966.

Cook, Fred J. "Newark," in Edgar G. Epps, *Race Relations: Current Perspectives*. Cambridge, Mass.: Winthrop Publishers, Inc., 1973.

Cooper, Frederick. "Elevating the Race: The Social Thought of Black Leaders." *American Quarterly* 24, No. 5 (December 1972): 605-625.

Cox, Oliver. *Caste, Class and Race: A Study in Social Dynamics*. New York: Doubleday and Co., 1948.

Crain, Robert L. *The Politics of Desegregation*. Chicago: Aldine Publishing Co., 1968.

Cronon, David E. *Black Moses: The Story of Marcus Garvey*. Madison: The University of Wisconsin Press, 1969.

Cruse, Harold. *The Crisis of the Negro Intellectual*. New York: William Morrow and Co., Inc., 1967.

David, Jay, ed. *Black Defiance*. New York: William Morrow and Co., Inc., 1972.

Davis, Allison, and Dollard, John. *Children of Bondage*. Washington, D. C.: American Council on Education, 1940.

―――. Gardner, Burleigh B., and Gardner, Mary R. *Deep South*. Chicago: University of Chicago Press, 1941.

Dollard, John. *Caste and Class in a Southern Town*. Garden City, N. Y.: Anchor Books, 1957.

―――. *Frustration and Aggression*. New Haven: Yale University Press, 1939.

Douglass, Frederick. "Lynch Law in the South." *The North American Review* 45, No. 428 (1892): 17-24.

Downs, Anthony. "The Nature of Racism in America, and How To Combat It," Unpublished manuscript written for the U. S. Civil Rights Commission, November 1968.

Drake, St. Clair, and Cayton, Horace R. *Black Metropolis*. New York: Harper and Row, Publishers, 1945 and 1962, Vol. II.

―――. "Social and Economic Status of the Negro in The United States." *Daedalus* 94, No. 4 (Fall 1965): 771-814.

DuBois, W. E. B. *The Philadelphia Negro*. New York: Schocken Books, 1967.

―――. *The Souls of Black Folk*. New York: Washington Square Press, 1930.

Durkheim, Emile. *Elementary Forms of Religious Life*. London: Allen and Unwin, 1915.

Edwards, Harry. *Black Students*. New York: The Free Press, 1970.

Essien-Udom, E. V. *Black Nationalism*. New York: Dell Publishing Co., Inc., 1962.

Farley, Reynolds. *Growth of the Black Population*. Chicago: Markham Publishing Co., 1970.

Fisher, Sethard, ed. *Power and the Black Community*. New York: Random House, Inc., 1970.

Fogelson, Robert M. *Violence As Protest*. New York: Anchor Books, 1971.

Foley, James A., and Foley, Robert K. *The College Scene*. New York: McGraw-Hill Book Co., 1969.

Forman, Robert E. *Black Ghettos, White Ghettos, and Slums*. Englewood Cliffs, N. J.: Prentice-Hall, Inc., 1971.

Franklin, John Hope. *From Slavery to Freedom*. New York: Vintage Books, 1969.

Frazier, E. Franklin. *Black Bourgeoisie: The Rise of a New Middle Class in the United States*. New York: Collier Books, 1957.

———. *The Negro in the United States*. New York: The Macmillan Co., 1957.

———. *The Negro Church in America*. New York: Schocken Books, 1966.

Genovese, Eugene. "Origins of The Folk Religion," An unpublished manuscript, now in publication.

———. *In Red and Black*. New York: Vintage Books, 1971.

Ginzberg, Eli, and Eichner, Alfred S. *The Troublesome Presence*. New York: A Mentor Book, 1966.

Ginzberg, Ralph. *100 Years of Lynchings*. New York: Lancer Books, 1962.

Grady, Henry W. *The New South*. New York: Robert Bonner's Sons, Inc., 1890.

Hamilton, Charles V. "Riots, Revolts and Relevant Response," in Floyd B. Barbour, ed., *The Black Power Revolt*. Boston: Porter Sargent Publishers, 1968.

———. *The Black Preacher in America*. New York: William Morrow and Co., Inc., 1972.

Hammond, James H. "The Mudsill Theory," in Leslie H. Fishel and Benjamin Quarles, *The Negro American: A Documentary History*. New York: Scott, Foresman and Co., 1967.

Harding, Vincent. "Toward The Black University," *Ebony Magazine* 25, No. 10 (August 1970): 156-159.

Harrington, Michael. *The Other America*. New York: Macmillan and Co., 1962.

Hatt, Paul K. "Stratification in the Mass Society," *American Sociological Review* 15 (April 1950): 216-222.

Herskovits, Melville J. *The Myth of the Negro Past*. New York: Harper and Brothers, 1941.

Hill, Herbert. "Black Labor in the American Economy," in Pat

Romero, *In Black America*. Washington, D. C.: United Publishing Corp., 1969.

Hooker, Robert W. "Displacement of Black Teachers in the Eleven Southern States," *Race Relations Information Center Special Report*, December 1970.

Hughes, Everett C. "Dilemmas and Contradictions of Status." *American Journal of Sociology*, No. 3 (1945): 353-359.

Hughes, Langston. *Fight for Freedom: The Story of the NAACP*. New York: Norton, 1962.

Hunt, Elgin F. *Social Science*. New York: The Macmillan Co., 1966.

Javits, Jacob K. *Discrimination U. S. A.* New York: A Washington Square Press Book, 1962.

Jeffers, Trellie. "The Black Woman and the Black Middle Class." *The Black Scholar* 4, Nos. 6-7 (March-April 1973): 37-41.

Jencks, Christopher, et al. *Inequality: A Reassessment of the Effect of Family and Schooling in America*. New York: Basic Books, Inc., Publishers, 1972.

Johnson, Nicholas. *How to Talk Back to Your Television Set*. New York: Bantam Books, 1970.

Jones, Major J. *Black Awareness: A Theology of Hope*. Nashville: Abingdon Press, 1971.

Jordan, Vernon E. "The End of the Second Reconstruction?" *Contact* (1270 Sixth Avenue, New York, New York) July 1972.

Key, V. O., Jr. *Southern Politics*. New York: Vintage Books, 1949.

Killian, Lewis, and Grigg, Charles. *Racial Crisis in America*. Englewood Cliffs, N. J.: Prentice-Hall Publishers, 1964.

————. *The Impossible Revolution?* New York: Random House, 1968.

Kissinger, Henry A. "The Policymaker and the Intellectual." *The Reporter*, March 5, 1959.

Kronus, Sidney. *The Black Middle Class*. Columbus, Ohio: Charles E. Merrill, 1971.

Ladner, Joyce A. *Tomorrow's Tomorrow*. Garden City, N. Y.: Doubleday and Co., Inc., 1971.

Lester, Julius. "The Necessity For Separation." *Ebony Magazine* 25, No. 10 (August 1970): 167-169.

Liebow, Elliot. *Tally's Corner*. New York: Little, Brown and Co., 1967.

Lincoln, C. Eric. "Preface" to James H. Cone, *Liberation*. New York: J. B. Lippincott Co., 1970.

————. *The Black Muslims in America*. Boston: Beacon Press, 1961.

Lipset, Seymour Martin. *Rebellion in the University*. Boston: Little Brown and Co., 1971.

————. and Rabb, Earl. *The Politics of Unreason*. New York: Harper Torchbook, 1970.

Littleton, Arthur C., and Burger, Mary W. *Black Viewpoints*. New York: A Mentor Book, 1964.

Logan, Rayford W. *The Betrayal of the Negro*. New York: Collier Books, 1968.

————. *The Negro in the United States*. New York: D. Van Nostrand, 1957.

Matthews, Donald R., and Prothro, James W. "Social and Economic Factors and Negro Voter Registration in the South," in Harry A. Bailey, Jr., *Negro Politics in America*. Columbus, Ohio: Charles E. Merrill Publishing Co., 1967.

Mays, Benjamin E. *Born to Rebel*. New York: Charles Scribner's Sons, 1971.

————. *The Negro's God*. New York: Atheneum Press, 1968.

————, and Nicholson, Joseph W. *The Negro's Church*. New York: Negro University Press, 1933.

Meier, August, and Rudwick, Elliot. *Black Protest in the Sixties*. Chicago: Quadrangle Books, 1970.

Merton, Robert K. *Social Theory and Social Structure*. New York: The Free Press, 1968.

Meyers, Michael. "The New Black Apartheid." *Change* 4, No. 8 (October 1972): 8-13.

Mills, C. Wright. "The Middle Class in Middle-Sized Cities." *American Sociological Review* 1 (December 1946): 520-525.

Mondale, William F. (Chairman, Select Committee, United States Senate). *Toward Equal Educational Opportunities*. Washington, D. C. U.: S. Government Printing Office, 1972.

Moon, Henry Lee. *The Emerging Thought of W. E. B. DuBois*. New York: Simon and Schuster, 1972.

Moynihan, Daniel P. "Urban Crisis." *The New York Times Encyclopedic Almanac*, 1970.

National Opinion Research Center. "Jobs and Occupation: A Popular Evaluation," *Public Opinion News* 9 (1947): 3-13.

Nelsen, Hart M. *The Black Church in America*. New York: Basic Books, Inc., 1971.

The New Orleans School Crisis. Report of the Louisiana State Advisory Commission on Civil Rights: 1961.

Page, Thomas N. *The Negro: The Southerner's Problem*. New York: Charles Scribner's Sons, 1904.

Parsons, Talcott, ed. *Theories of Society*. Glencoe, Ill.: The Free Press, 1961.

Phillips, W. W., Jr., "Survival Techniques of Black Americans," in Rhoda L. Goldstein, ed., *Black Life and Culture in the United States*. New York: Thomas Y. Crowell Co., 1971.

The President's Commission on Income Maintenance Programs. *Poverty Amid Plenty: The American Paradox*. Washington, D. C.: U. S. Government Printing Office, 1969.

Proctor, Samuel D. "Survival Techniques and the Black Middle Class," in Rhoda L. Goldstein, ed., *Black Life and Culture in the United States*. New York: Thomas Y. Crowell Co., 1971.

Quarles, Benjamin A. *Black Abolitionists*. New York: Oxford University Press, 1969.

————. *The Negro in the Making of America*. New York: Collier Books, 1964.

Record, Wilson. "White Sociologists and Black Studies," Presented at the American Sociological Association meeting in New Orleans, August 1972.

Reddick, L. D. *Crusader Without Violence: A Biography of Martin Luther King, Jr*. New York: Harper and Brothers, Publishers, 1959.

Reissman, Leonard. *Class in American Society*. Glencoe, Ill.: The Free Press, 1959.

Report of the Louisiana State Advisory Commission on Civil Rights. *The New Orleans School Crisis*. 1961.

Robinson, Armstead L., Foster, Craig C., and Ogiluie, Donald H., eds. *Black Studies in the University*. New York: Bantam Books, 1969.

Rogin, Richard. "Into the Middle Class: John Henry Howell Made It." *The New York Times Magazine*, June 24, 1973.

Rohrer, John H., Edmonson, Munro S., Thompson, Daniel C., et al. *The Eighth Generation*. New York: Harper and Brothers, Publishers, 1960.

Sanford, Nevitt, and Comstock, Craig. *Sanctions for Evil*. San Francisco: Jossey-Bass, Inc., Publishers, 1971.

Scheer, Robert, ed. "Eldridge Cleaver: Post-Prison Writings and Speeches," in Jay David, ed., *Black Defiance*. New York: William Morrow and Co., 1972.

Schulz, David A. *Coming Up Black*. Englewood Cliffs, N. J.: Prentice-Hall, Inc., 1969.

Scott, Joseph. "The Black Bourgeoisie and Black Power," *The Black Scholar* 4, No. 4 (January 1973): 12-18.

Sizemore, Barbara A. "Social Science and Education for a Black Identity," in James A. Banks and Jean D. Grambs, eds., *Black Self-Concept*. New York: McGraw-Hill Book Co., 1972.

Sowell, Thomas. *Black Education Myths and Tragedies*. New York: David McKay Co., Inc., 1972.

Stampp, Kenneth M. "The Negro in American History Textbooks, 1968," in David D. Anderson and Robert L. Wright, eds., *The Dark and Tangled Path: Race in America*. New York: Houghton Mifflin Co., 1971.

Staples, Robert E. "The Black Scholar in Academe." *Change Magazine* 4, No. 9 (November 1972): 42-48.

Stewart, Elbert W. *The Troubled Land*. New York: McGraw-Hill Book Co., 1972.

Thompson, Daniel C. "The History of Black Americans." *Faculty Forum*, No. 46 (October 1968): 1-6.

————. *The Negro Leadership Class*. Englewood Cliffs, N. J.: Prentice-Hall, Inc., 1963.

————. "New Orleans and the Riot Report." *New Orleans Magazine*, Official Publication of the New Orleans Chamber of Commerce, June 1968.

————. "The Rise of the Negro Protest." *The Annals of the American Academy of Political and Social Science*, Vol. 357, January 1965.

————. "The Role of the Federal Courts in the Changing Status of Negroes Since World War II." *Journal of Negro Education* (Spring 1961): 94-101.

————. "Social Class Factors in Public School Education as Related to Desegregation." *American Journal of Orthopsychiatry* 26, No. 3 (July 1956): 449-452.

————. "Teaching the Culturally Disadvantaged." *Speaking About*

Teaching. New York: College Entrance Examination Board, 1967.

————, and Guillory, Barbara M. "Socialization of Black Teenagers in an Upward Bound Program." Dillard University, an unpublished study, 1970.

Turner, James. "The Sociology of Black Nationalism," in Joyce A. Ladner, ed., *The Death of White Sociology*. New York: Vintage Books, 1973.

U. S. Department of Commerce, *Statistical Abstract of the United States*, 1972, Bureau of the Census.

———— and Bureau of the Census. *The Social and Economic Status of Negroes in the United States*. Bureau of Labor Statistics, Report No. 394, 1970.

U. S. Department of Labor. *The Negro: A Case for National Action*. Office of Planning and Research, Washington, D. C., March 1965.

U. S. Office of Education, Department of Health, Education and Welfare. "General Statement of Policies under Title VI of the Civil Rights Act of 1964 Respecting Desegregation of Elementary and Secondary Schools." April 1965.

U. S. Riot Commission Report. New York: The New York Times Co., 1968.

U. S. Riot Commission, Report of the National Advisory Commission on Civil Disorders. New York: A Bantam Book, 1968.

U. S. Senate Committee on Equal Educational Opportunity. *Toward Equal Educational Opportunity*. Washington, D. C.: U. S. Government Printing Office, 1972.

Wallace, Walter L. "Sociological Theories and Studies of Black Americans." A Chicago University Black Caucus Conference paper, 1972.

Warren, Donald R., and Easto, Patrick C., eds. "White Stratification Theory and Black Reality: A Neglected Problem of American Sociology." Paper presented at the 68th Annual meeting of the American Sociological Association, August 2, 1972.

Waters, Thomas. "Review" in *Contemporary Sociology* 2, No. 1 (January 1973): 86-87.

Wattenberg, Ben J., and Scammon, Richard M. "Black Progress and Liberal Rhetoric." *Commentary* (April 1973): 34-45.

Wesley, Charles H. *History of Sigma Pi Phi (Boule)*. The Association for the Study of Negro Life and History, Inc., 1954.

Wey, Herbert, and Corey, John. *Action Patterns in School Desegregation*. Bloomington, Ind.: Phi Delta Kappa, 1959.

Wilmore, Gayraud S. *Black Religion and Black Radicalism*. New York: Anchor Books, 1972.

Wish, Harvey. *The Negro Since Emancipation*. New York: Farrar, Strauss and Co., 1964.

Woodson, Carter G. *The History of the Negro Church*. Washington, D. C.: The Associated Publishers, 1921.

Woodward, C. Vann. *The Strange Career of Jim Crow*. New York: Oxford University Press, 1961.

X, Malcolm. "Message to the Grass Roots," in Richard P. Young, ed., *Roots of Rebellion*. New York: Harper and Row, Publishers, 1970.

Young, Whitney M., Jr. *Beyond Racism: Building an Open Society*. New York: McGraw Hill Book Co., 1969.

————. *To Be Equal*. New York: McGraw-Hill Book Co., 1964.

Index